City, Street and Citize

How can we learn from a multicultural society if we don't know how to recognise it? The contemporary city is more than ever a space for the intense convergence of diverse individuals who shift in and out of its urban terrains. The city street is perhaps the most prosaic of the city's public parts, allowing us a view of the very ordinary practices of life and livelihoods. By attending to the expressions of conviviality and contestation, *City, Street and Citizen* offers an alternative notion of 'multiculturalism' away from the ideological frame of nation, and away from the moral imperative of community. This book offers to the reader an account of the lived realities of allegiance, participation and belonging from the base of a multi-ethnic street in south London.

City, Street and Citizen focuses on the question of whether local life is significant for how individuals develop skills to live with urban change and cultural and ethnic diversity. To animate this question, Hall has turned to a city street and its dimensions of regularity and propinquity to explore interactions in the small shop spaces along the Walworth Road. The city street constitutes exchange, and as such it provides us with a useful space to consider the broader social and political significance of contact in the day-to-day life of multicultural cities.

Grounded in an ethnographic approach, this book will be of interest to academics and students in the fields of sociology, global urbanisation, migration and ethnicity as well as being relevant to politicians, policy makers, urban designers and architects involved in cultural diversity, public space and street-based economies.

Suzanne Hall is an urban ethnographer, and Lecturer and Researcher at LSE Cities (London School of Economics and Political Science, UK). Her research and teaching interests are foregrounded in local expressions of global urbanisation, particularly social and spatial forms of inclusion and exclusion, urban multiculture, the design of the city, and ethnography and visual methods. She is a recipient of the Rome Scholarship in Architecture (1998–1999) and the LSE's Robert McKenzie Prize for outstanding PhD research (2010).

Routledge advances in ethnography

Edited by Dick Hobbs, University of Essex and
Geoffrey Pearson, Goldsmiths College, University of London

Ethnography is a celebrated, if contested, research methodology that offers unprecedented access to people's intimate lives, their often hidden social worlds and the meanings they attach to these. The intensity of ethnographic fieldwork often makes considerable personal and emotional demands on the researcher, while the final product is a vivid human document with personal resonance impossible to recreate by the application of any other social science methodology. This series aims to highlight the best, most innovative ethnographic work available from both new and established scholars.

City, Street and Citizen
The measure of the ordinary

Suzanne Hall

Routledge
Taylor & Francis Group

LONDON AND NEW YORK

First published 2012 by Routledge
2 Park Square, Milton Park, Abingdon, Oxon, OX14 4RN

Simultaneously published in the USA and Canada
by Routledge
711 Third Avenue, New York, NY 10017

Routledge is an imprint of the Taylor & Francis Group, an informa business

First issued in paperback 2013

© 2012 Suzanne Hall

All rights reserved. No part of this book may be reprinted or reproduced or
utilised in any form or by any electronic, mechanical, or other means, now
known or hereafter invented, including photocopying and recording, or in any
information storage or retrieval system, without permission in writing from
the publishers.

British Library Cataloguing in Publication Data
A catalogue record for this book is available from the British Library

Library of Congress Cataloging in Publication Data
A catalog record for this book has been requested

Typeset in Times New Roman by
Swales & Willis Ltd, Exeter, Devon

ISBN: 978-0-415-68865-9 hbk
ISBN: 978-0-203-11859-7 ebk
ISBN: 978-0-415-52817-7 pbk

To Tony, Pip and Nicky Hall

Contents

Figures

Acknowledgements

'Odd that you should come all the way from South Africa to study the Walworth Road,' a friend remarked, not without raised eyebrow. I have relished this unexpected journey along a street that I have lived above and continue to travel along. This being a first book, there are many teachers, colleagues and friends I would like to acknowledge, both 'here' and 'there'. Let me start with the street, where 'Nick', 'Dorah' and 'Reyd' gave me a base, in the fullest sense of the word, to carry out my fieldwork. Numerous individuals who live or work off this street were generous enough to share their views, without which the substance of this book would not have accrued. Thank you to my neighbour and friend Jean La Fontaine for reading parts of this project as it emerged from its early observations.

In the early years of fieldwork, I made frequent use of the Southwark Local History Library, an invaluable public resource staffed by an astute group of librarians with a local knowledge not retrievable via the catalogue, Stephen Humphries amongst them. I hope the quality of this wonderful archive will not be severely affected by the austerity measures that currently abound in the UK.

LSE Cities and the Department of Sociology at the London School of Economics and Political Science has been the very best home from which to pursue a combination of spatial and social research. My thanks extend to my doctoral supervisors Janet Foster and Robert Taverner, and to Fran Tonkiss, Juliet Davis, Ricky Burdett, Claire Alexander, David Frisby and Paul Rock. Savitri Lopez-Negrete, Thiresh Govender, Maria Sisternas and David Church were not only talented students but infinitely more adept at computer-aided graphics than I, and I thank them for their contributions. I developed much of the thinking for this book through participating in the NYLON and Writing Cities Research Groups, and I am particularly grateful to Craig Calhoun, Jerry Frug, Vic Seidler and Richard Sennett and to the graduate students in these groups for their comments on work in progress. Richard Sennett and Les Back examined my Ph D. thesis, and their comments and writings have been invaluable in shaping this book. Equally, my early intellectual joy at exploring the city was sustained by teachers and colleagues at the University of the Witwatersrand and the University of Cape Town, and I would like to especially thank Jo Noero, Roelof Uytenbogaardt, Iain Low, David Dewar, Fabio Todeschini and Lindsay Bremner.

Dick Hobbs has been in this book from the start, and I am immensely pleased that he called me up during the fragile months post Ph.D. to ask if I would participate in an 'Advances in Ethnography' series he was putting together with Geoff Pearson. No one is able to write an email with the brevity and pertinence of Dick and it was in this form that I received his valued comments on the drafts of *City, Street and Citizen*. My thanks also to the teams at Routledge and Swales & Willis for editorial support and guidance.

My family has made it possible for this academic exploration to be integral to life, none more so than John Riddy, my in-house photographer, editor and unstinting support. Tony and Pip, Sam and Gusta, thank you for your wonderful company along the route.

Suzi Hall, October 2011

Permissions

Figure 4.1 in Chapter 4 is reprinted with the kind permission of Peggy Towesey.

Parts of Chapter 2 first appeared in a different form in Suzanne M. Hall and Ayona Datta (2010) 'The Translocal Street: Shop Signs and Local Multiculture along the Walworth Road, South London', in Robert Tavernor (guest editor), Theme Issue on 'London 2000–2010', in *City, Culture and Society*, 1: 69–77.

Parts of Chapter 3 first appeared in an earlier form in (2011) 'Being at Home: Space for Belonging in a London Caff', *Open House International* 34: 81–7.

Parts of Chapter 6 first appeared in (2012) 'High Street Adaptations: Ethnicity, Independent Retail Practices and Localism in London's Urban Margins', in *Environment and Planning A*, 43: 2571–88.

All reproduced with permission.

Introduction

Urban multiculture: an ordinary orientation

The sign above the shop-front read, 'Mixed Blessings Bakery. West Indian and English Bread'. The bakery was on my twenty-minute bus route from south London into the centre of the city, and from the top of the red double-decker 68 or 171 buses I could see the stack of oblong loaves that on cold days steamed up half of the shop-front. On holidays a haphazard queue would form along the pavement outside Mixed Blessings Bakery, while people waited to buy a warm, sweet piece of the Caribbean to take back to their south London homes. The bakery is one of many small shops along the mile length of the Walworth Road, and from the top of the bus I could see the dense, linear assemblage of these small shop spaces, and an array of people going about their everyday routines.

As a newcomer to London from South Africa, what struck me first about the Walworth Road was the unfamiliar collage of surfaces and expressions displayed by spaces, activities and cultures. The visible convergence of diversity that I first observed on this street may be of little surprise to the more accustomed Londoner's eye, and in a city populated through perpetual histories of immigration, scenes like those on the Walworth Road may well appear much like those on many other high streets across the city. What came to matter as a local resident in using the Walworth Road was the ordinariness of its differences: the basic value of social contact on the street refined through regular, face-to-face meetings.

My bus route to the London School of Economics ran past the tight alignment of shop-fronts on the Walworth Road, where the rhythm of spaces briefly paused on the east side of the street, providing a view of the shoppers at the East Street Market whose perennial allegiance, despite the changes in traders and goods, remains the pursuit of a bargain. At the northern end of the Walworth Road, the intensity of entrepreneurial life was abruptly truncated by the monolithic, prefabricated forms of the Elephant and Castle Shopping Centre and Heygate social housing estate. Built in the 1960s and 1970s respectively, these dreary monoliths follow the Modernist predilection for functional separation and are detached from the street. At the Elephant and Castle, buses and cars wound into two centrifugal roundabouts, which distributed the traffic over the Westminster, Waterloo, Blackfriars and London Bridges, crossing the River Thames as the great watery divide.

The presence of a number of cranes and sites under construction, and a billboard renaming the area 'South Central', indicated that the Elephant and Castle, a comparatively cheap but well-located area, was targeted for strategic redevelopment. A little further to the north, the script engraved on the obelisk at St George's Circus signalled that I was only one mile from the symbolic centres of London represented by Westminster, Fleet Street and St Paul's Cathedral. From here it took mere minutes on the bus to reach the bridges and to cross the River Thames, entering into a city proximate to, but entirely distinctive from, the Walworth Road. All in all, only twenty minutes to travel from one kind of urban experience to another: emerging from the eclectic array of small shops and large concrete housing estates along the Walworth Road, to the picturesque arrangements of world famous landmarks, Portland stone and plate glass that lend prestige to the city. This bus journey was to repeatedly remind me that traversing London and crossing the river was about experiencing the miscellaneous proximity of local worlds highly differentiated by income, culture and built fabric.

My time spent on the Walworth Road, both as a resident and a researcher, revealed the social and cultural formations of a diversifying city within the shared terrain of the street. Along its linear aggregation of a multitude of shop spaces and sub-worlds are the intersections of class, race, ethnicity, inequality and opportunity. In its ordinary dimensions a city street like the Walworth Road provides a palpable presence to our milieu, to the global process of social change in which societies are urbanising and diversifying. If the contemporary reconfigurations of 'community' and 'family' and of 'class', 'race', and 'ethnicity' have both a locus and a pace in our milieu, it is that of the accelerated city. *City, Street and Citizen* focuses on the impact of the unprecedented scale, speed and flows of global urbanisation on local forms of participation and allegiance. It is a fine-grained, ethnographic

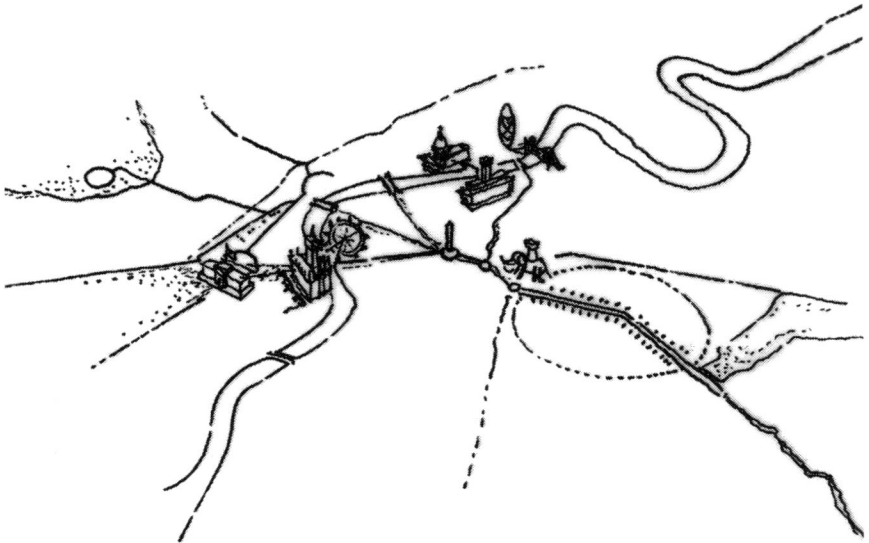

Figure 0.1 The proximity of the Walworth Road to the River Thames and to London's prestigious landscape.

exploration of how historic understandings and individual practices of belonging reconcile with or reject the ethnic and cultural diversity that manifests on the street.

At the heart of the book is the question of why it is imperative that everyday practices of urban multicultures are made visible. Why is it crucial to the dominant political and media framings of 'multiculturalism' in Britain and further afield that an alternative approach, based on empirical observation, needs articulation? During 2010, election campaigns in Britain and Europe were pointedly oriented around the issues of diversity coupled with citizenship[1]. In Britain a core focus, indeed the opening question for the first televised election debates, was the subject of diversity as encapsulated by immigration[2]. The fervent consensus across the Labour, Liberal Democrat and Conservative spectrum advocated tighter visa and border controls, conceptualising the idea of citizenship in a highly fluid, global world as one still predetermined at the national border point. And it is a discriminatory frontier, as recent immigration legislation in Britain suggests, where highly skilled workers are afforded greater entitlement to belong[3]. In Germany in 2010, Chancellor Angela Merkel asserted with resolute conviction that the 'multi-kulti' project had 'utterly failed'[4]. Mulitikulti's perceived demise was collectively synonymised by Germany's 2.5 million Turkish migrants (revealingly categorised as 'guest workers') who since the 1960s had contributed to the country through work, but whose perceived failure to integrate in Germany is flagged by the retention of the Turkish language as well the religious solidarity of Islam.

It is not only the interpretation of integration through homogenisation but the fear of influence of 'the foreigner' that has permeated recent European political legislation. President Sarkozy's ban on the burqa, promulgated in 2011[5], is a total restriction on wearing a full veil in the public realm, and is echoed in the ban on the construction of new minarets in Switzerland in 2009[6]. These siege-like strategies that embargo the religious differentiation of bodies and spaces seek to control diversity through the political frame of secular nationalism. The nationalist imperative underscores singular prescriptions for allegiance[7] despite deep economic dependencies on migrant workers in all their guises and the exchange of ideas and goods, never more apparent than in this global era. It is the provocation of migration exacerbated by the increasing flows of people since the 1990s that is the contemporary litmus of national tolerance or lack thereof to engage in the realities of a fluid and disparate global world.

The primacy of nation has also permeated the management of multiculturalism at the level of neighbourhoods, evidenced in Britain by the commitment to, 'a clear primary loyalty to this Nation' in the *Community Cohesion Report* (Home Office 2001: 20). The underlying prerequisite of consensus achieved via community under the auspices of nation and rendered through the political predilection for targets has shaped 'multiculturalism' as a project for organised intervention. The significant political oversight is the inadequate recognition of the multiple allegiances and visceral forms of mixing that spontaneously occur in urban life. Further, the contemporary city as an arrival point in a world-wide web of flows grounds an entirely different reality to the political dogma, as if nation and city are in a tug of war, with the ideology of containment heaving against the reality of movement.

I resort here to statistics to evidence in purely numeric terms, the scale and pace of the diversifying populace in London. *A Profile of Londoners by Country of Birth* (GLA 2008) reveals the velocity of change: 40 per cent of the UK's migrant population is concentrated in London; more than half of London's current migrant population arrived after 1990 and a quarter after 2000; and the variety of its migrant group is such that 42 per cent is comprised of ten primary groups. These include: India, Bangladesh, Ireland, Jamaica, Nigeria, Poland, Kenya, Sri Lanka, South Africa and Ghana. The figures render the combined impacts of contemporary and historic global endeavours of Empire and colonisation, as well as UK's membership within the European Union.

What then are the conceptual and pragmatic alternatives that allow us to understand ethnic and cultural diversity in the contemporary city? An essential start is the recognition that global economic forces have not only propelled the migrations of skilled and unskilled workforces into cities but have also resulted, as is evidenced in the aptly entitled research on *Divided Cities* (Fainstein, Gordon and Harloe 1992) and *Unequal City* (Hamnett 2003), in increasingly polarised urban landscapes. In Alexander's south London housing estate (2000) or Wacquant's *banlieue* on the outskirts of Paris (2007) the overlap of historic urban areas of deprivation and increased immigrant occupation over the past two decades is more than apparent. GIS mappings of London since 1990 render a spatial articulation of the urban margins, evidenced in historic areas of poverty within the city correlating with contemporary and increasing ethnic diversity in these locales. Deep and advanced marginalisation in such parts of the city therefore needs to be integral to understanding the constraints on and achievements of the varied forms of social integration that occur in these locales.

In this sense the Walworth Road provides a good empirical beginning: as a street located within the urban margins of London, it offers a contextual lens with which to view local expressions of social adaptation in the face of global change. While it is a street from which one can hear the chimes of Big Ben, it remains culturally and economically distinct from the prestigious Southbank landscape only a mile and a half to its north. Historic ward area surveys reveal that Walworth is a comparatively poor neighbourhood, ranking in 2001 as amongst the 10th percentile of the most deprived boroughs in England (Office for National Statistics 2001). The spatially concentrated patterns of deprivation are represented on the 2007 Indices of Multiple Deprivation maps at borough level that incorporate three of London's largest housing estates – the Heygate, Aylesbury and Brandon Estates – directly adjacent to the Walworth Road (Greater London Authority 2008a). Southwark, the south London borough in which Walworth is located, has an ethnically diverse populace with 48 per cent of its residents classified – to use the somewhat coarse 2001 census terminology – as other than 'White British'[8].

But beneath the statistics that signify Walworth as a diversifying urban margin is the need to explore how individuals and groups adapt to accelerated change, and in particular how they invest in their local worlds in social, cultural and economic ways. It is not simply that official census data and demographic percentages do little to render a complex or fine-grained explanation of the experiences of difference and change. In their authorised depictions of diversifying urban societies, the modes of categorisation and stratification camouflage the crucial nuances of cultural exchange and social interaction. While I acknowledge at the outset that conviviality and conflict are part of plural and uneven societies, the focus of *City, Street and Citizen* is the practices of probing and working out between diverse individuals and groups within the small shops along the street. A core question is whether physical contact matters for these practices: do the proximities and crossovers of bodies and spaces on a city street have a bearing on how we test and learn with respect to one another?

To address this question conceptually and methodologically, the ordinary orientations of space, time and practice come to the fore. My ethnographic exploration of the life and livelihoods of a multi-ethnic street is constituted by the organisation of distance and nearness, of regularity and duration, and of participation and retreat. Raymond Williams' (1958) enduring insistence that 'culture is ordinary' is premised on human contact: everyday interactions are the primary conduit for sharing and learning, and making and building. Equally essential to Williams' notion of contact is the respective influences of work and culture on one another. But Williams' reflection of the integral relationship between working-class life and labour within vernacular landscapes is of a different milieu. A question for our urban age is what the forms of work and associated modes of public contact are that permit learning within cities that are highly varied and rapidly changing.

The question encourages a different conceptualisation of the urban margin from those that have shaped valuable ethnographic studies of inequality, discrimination, work and the city. It requires a shift away from, rather than a dismissal of, the explicit categorisations of race, ethnicity and class evidenced in the spatial segregation of American cities, as is so pertinently captured in the lineage of street-based ethnographies including Anderson's *Code of the Street* (1999), Duneier's *Sidewalk* (1999), Liebow's *Tally's Corner* (1967) and Whyte's *Street Corner Society* (1943). The shift is necessary for contextual and analytic reasons: the patterns of segregation within London are spatially less explicit, which is not to say that the divisions are absent, but that the formations of boundaries that limit contact and the meeting points that permit it require more hybrid categories of analysis.

London's urban margins, then, are locales that are physically proximate to but culturally distant from its symbolically dominant and prestigious landscapes on which the narrative of a 'world-class' city is conferred. Contemporary urban margins are shaped by complex interplays of pasts and presents or what Sarah Nuttall (2009) has so acutely conceptualised as the formative and informative 'entanglements' of history, people and place. In Walworth these entanglements are merged by processes of industrialisation and urbanisation; colonisation and immigration; Second World War devastation and clearance; Welfarism and large-scale social housing delivery; and de-industrialisation and globalisation. But it is a mistake to frame or relegate these territories simply as marginal. Rather, London's urban margins are places where the cultures and divisions of class, race and ethnicity are densely inscribed, as are the aspirations and innovations practised within its emerging urban multicultures.

The analytic alignment of these layered histories with the everyday individual processes of probing and working out is revealed within the ordinary and shared spaces of human contact, or what Ash Amin (2002) refers to as 'micro-publics' – the social spaces in which individuals regularly come into contact. Convenience and purpose permit less self-conscious interactions that are potentially eased by the more explicit processes of working, playing or learning. Crucially, Amin argues that these prosaic publics are not simply spaces of encounter, but of participation, and they require a level of individual investment to sustain membership. Local worlds within the urban margins are therefore also spaces where much is at stake, since these are the places in which the less mobile – the elderly, the young, the poor and the newcomer – are often highly invested. The regular participation in less official public spaces where more informal memberships are able to develop is therefore primary to the formation of alternative publics.

What the street offers us is a space that is central to the life of an area, but it also extends past the area, linking places and people. An urban street situates and connects, both focusing and expanding the possibilities for contact between different individuals and groups. The Walworth Road is supported by a large number of residents living within a convenient walking distance of the street as well as a broader group of people who reach the street by way of other journeys. Some of these journeys are part of the daily or weekly routines of commute common to Londoners. Other journeys to the Walworth Road involve a distinctive break with the regularity and comfort of a familiar world; these are the migratory journeys made between one country and another by many of its proprietors and patrons, and require traversing great physical and cultural distances.

To travel these actual and perceptual distances, crossing the boundaries between the familiar and unfamiliar, demands particular social and cultural skills. The capacity to engage in difference and change requires an ability to live with more than one spatial and temporal sense of a local place – a 'here' as well as a 'there', and a 'then' as well as a 'now' – the ability to live with combinations of what is familiar or what is 'local'. But in today's cities, shaped by accelerated change, it is not only the migrant or émigré who needs to learn the multifarious skills of how to preserve custom and to learn anew. This adaptation is also required of the urban local who has seldom or never travelled, and whose fixed position in a rapidly transforming local landscape does not provide an antidote to the enormity of change.

The street is space within the urban margin shared by newcomers and established residents that allows us to explore practices of adaptation. Sociologists would ask the question: 'Who is it that is most able to adapt?', while a geographer or architect might ask, 'In which spaces is adaptation most like to occur?'. These are questions that should not be separated. When Dench, Gavron and Young (2006) tested the capacities of immigrants and long-standing residents to adapt to change in *The New East End*, their interviews focused on sites in which access to and entitlement of public resources is highly contested, in particular social housing. Social housing is not only a domestic realm where long-established forms of belonging are revealed in kinship patterns of family and class. In Britain it is also an allocated public resource and the questions of who gets housing and who gets it first is inevitably conflictual. But is racism or disdain of 'the foreigner' at the core of the conflict, or is contestation reproduced by the system in which public resources are organised and distributed? Similarly, is social housing – a domestic and state-owned space – a comparatively brittle urban territory, in which definitions of turf, privacy and what is public are less adaptable to rapid change?

In contrast to the social housing estates that comprise a large proportion of residences in walking distance from the Walworth Road, the independent shop spaces off the street appeared as a cheek-by-jowl series of sub-worlds that were neither overtly public nor private. The shops were adjacent to and distinct from the street, and interactions and memberships within the shops were regulated differently from those on the pavement to their fronts. I was interested in the forms of adaptation in these small interiors off the street in which things were both made and sold, and the extent to which the provision of goods and services fostered etiquette and exchange across cultures.

The street is ordinary in this sense – a space for stopping as much as for moving, a place to pause, to meet friends post a letter, to buy goods. It is an amalgam of interior rooms and sub-worlds off its edges in which forms of belonging are sustained through everyday conveniences. My research focus came to be the small independent shops along the mile length of the Walworth Road, and the social interactions between the proprietors and customers within them. These shops initially appeared to me as a dense aggregation of lives and livelihoods and I became intrigued by the overlap of work practices and social practices within the shop interiors. Questions emerged as to whether the acumen of the proprietors and the regular needs of customers would have bearing on the social possibilities and cultural improvisations within these shop spaces.

This is however, neither an ethnography of shopping nor of consumerism as a pleasurable and readily purchasable mode of cultural exchange. It is a scrutiny of multilingual forms of communication on a multi-ethnic street, and of the modes of expression afforded within local spaces of work, convenience and leisure. The focus on the shops has led me to larger questions of belonging, participation and allegiance in a diverse and unequal urban society. In particular, I explore whether capacities to engage in urban change and difference are connected to forms of inclusion integral to daily life including skill and meaningful work that, in the case of the street, are made publicly visible and are refined through social contact.

While the Walworth Road is a local street, its small-scale retail make-up has meant it is a route to a wider world, in which migration and mobility are central. Although its feudal beginnings were as a village high street subsequently structured by the parish, the manor and agricultural production, the small-scale patterns of land ownership along its edges readily adapted to the combined forces of industrialisation and urbanisation at the turn of the eighteenth century. The Post Office directory of London streets (Post Office 1881–1950) reveals a street that by the late 1800s was not only predominantly retail, but one where its proprietors included immigrants from Ireland, Italy and Eastern Europe. Tracing the Post Office records from 1881 to 1950, the pattern of immigrant proprietors persisted, including waves of immigrants from Turkey, Greece and Cyprus. The variegated pattern of immigrant occupations along the street is more than significant for my exploration of cultural adaptation and social mixing. As there is no predominant occupation by any particular ethnic group, the question that follows is: Do more variegated cultural expressions emerge within this heterogeneous context?

The persistence of an ethnic array was confirmed by my street survey conducted in 2006 (Hall 2009) where, amongst the 93 proprietors in the survey, their respective countries of origin included Afghanistan, China, Cyprus and Northern Cyprus, England, Ghana, Iran, Ireland, India, Italy, Jamaica, Malawi, Malaysia, Nigeria, Pakistan, Sierre Leone, Sudan, Trinidad, Turkey and Vietnam. The Walworth Road is ordinary then in this sense too: the variety of its ethnic and cultural diversity is not unremarkable in a city of immigrants, but its prolific diversity escapes an ethnic branding on the basis of a particular group and associated activity. It is neither the discernible Chinatown of London, New York or Toronto, nor the hip enclave of Brick Lane. What then are the variegated forms of allegiance, participation and belonging in such a varied urban landscape? And what are the differences that trigger conflict?

I therefore started my research with a place – the street – rather than an explicit category of people. This starting point links not only my two careers as architect and ethnographer, but also allows a tactile beginning to a process of finding out. It is essential for an architect to have a site to regularly visit in order to see and imagine the possibilities for space and design. But architects tend to spend far more time in their studios than on their sites, and as a resident of the Walworth Road for six years, two of which were dedicated to fieldwork, I was afforded a much slower process of looking. My initial visual reading of the street as a messy stretch of space was gradually supplemented by understandings attained from sitting, talking and observing. During this time-protracted process I listened, wrote and drew, retreating periodically to the Southwark Local History Library archives and official online survey sources to connect, as per C. Wright Mills' (1959) charge, 'histories and biographies'.

I found ethnography a useful way of navigating theory together with the larger questions of accelerated change and urban multiculture that have underscored my exploration of the Walworth Road. This is not simply because theory is given a vivid format through contact with individuals and spaces on the street, but because people's lives and livelihoods were inevitably more complex and far more differentiated than the less cluttered logic of the theoretical frame. The value of ethnography in understanding difference is that it renders a situated and multi-vocal sense of people and places as they live in, respond to and shape their social worlds. As an architect I have also questioned whether our understanding of interaction in space could be enhanced by a visual notation, and whether visual research or visualisation, as both an analytic and illustrative process, could provide explanatory layers to ethnographic exploration. I use visualisation or 'picturing' in my research as a process of both finding out and revealing. Typically the graphic is a process of compressing rather than reducing information and I have explored how analytic pictures can combine core relationships such as time and space, or mutualisms such as the global and local.

Figure 0.2 The linear assemblage of shops on the Walworth Road.

Ethnographic observation helps to render a social and cultural reading of how the impacts of urban change are experienced and how diversity is manifested in the life of a local place. But how do we extract from it political consequence? This introduction to *City, Street and Citizen* has stressed that the speed of change in the contemporary city has never been more accelerated, nor have its populations been more variegated. Stuart Hall's (1993: 361) clarification that 'the capacity to live with difference is, in my view, the coming question of the twenty-first century', directs us, I argue, to recognise and interpret contact between and amongst diverse individuals and groups across intimate, local, national and global scales. Out of the heightened flows between people and places across the globe over the past two decades his assertion demands that we pay attention to the ordinary or small politics that emerge within everyday life, and consider whether it reconfigures our understandings of class, community and kin. If we imagine the changing demography of Britain's national landscape as an uneven terrain of plains and peaks, its heights would propel sharply upwards at the points of greatest diversity – over our cities. We need then to further imagine how immigration, ethnicity and race reconfigure the singular idea of nation as an ideology applied flatly across territory, irrespective of its heightening urban peaks and expanding global routes.

Much like the spaces along a street, the chapters of *City, Street and Citizen* are structured as a composition of related but different parts. My intention is to reveal near and far views of a local world, and the varied experiences of how individuals engage in diversity and change in the context of their everyday lives. There are several links that provide continuity to these parts, a primary focus being to connect the organisation of social life on a multi-ethnic street to the space and time of accelerated urbanisation. My analysis is essentially ethnographic in its substance and method, and as we move across the chapters, the reader will see how explorations of local worlds are cognisant of the particularity and of the might of global forces. Similarly, I aim to merge the pasts and presents of the street, its city and its world relations, to fully acknowledge history's presence in the formations of a local urban landscape.

City, Street and Citizen is largely organised through three core explorations, the first of which is the histories and futures of the urban margin. The questions of who belongs in the urban margin, what forms of citizenship are conferred upon it by the structures of power, and what expressions of mixing or containment emerge within it, is developed in Chapters 1 and 2. In Chapter 1, 'Making practice visible', I specifically explore the question of how to reveal a qualitative understanding of urban multiculture in ways that have theoretical and practical pertinence to the wider debates about immigration, citizenship and multiculturalism. The work of this chapter is to probe at the methods and forms of urban ethnography, and to highlight its contribution in surfacing the variable, fluid and fallible dimensions of human life. I argue that it is precisely through the expressions of ambiguity and inconsistency that we become better attuned to understanding the mixings and overlaps integral to how we learn to live with difference. In Chapter 2, 'The boundaries of belonging', I focus on the historic structuring of the Walworth landscape, and analyse the ways in which boundaries are officially authorised and regulated. The chapter shifts between the symbolic persistence of social and spatial boundaries, and the extent to which historic forms of containment can be resisted or altered through practice.

In Chapters 3 and 4, I explore the lived dimensions of alternative publics and take the reader to two particular interiors off the street: Nick's Caff and Reyd's Bespoke Tailor Shop. Within these two distinctive spaces in which things are both made and sold and where the proprietor–customer relations are both social and cultural, I expand on Amin's notion of micro-publics. By observing the minutiae of these sub-worlds of skill and social space I explore the larger question of what constitutes alternative modes and spaces of *being public* in a city where its populace is diverse and fragmented and its local allegiances are distanced from larger orders of power and authority. Within these two different spaces I explore how conviviality is created out of shared gestures such as language and humour, shared interests like football and music, and shared social symbols like food and clothing. Both chapters centre on the work practices of the respective proprietors, and consider whether the attainment of a work skill has a correlation with the development of social skills.

The third key exploration is the political significance of everyday contact within ordinary social spaces and asks to what extent local forms of allegiance and participation contribute to ideas of belonging in a mixed and fluid urban society. In Chapter 5, 'The politics of nearness', I focus on the regular, face-to-face forms of contact in small shop spaces, and explore why 'the local' both inhibits and enhances the possibilities for different individuals to meet and to share. In 'Street measures', I turn more explicitly to how ordinary spaces are recognised and valued in policy and design terms. I contrast the values of the ordinary as described by various shop proprietors with those defined in policy and planning reports on the development of urban high streets and urban centres in London and the UK. This allows for an analysis of social, spatial and economic practices of adaptation on the part of diverse independent proprietors, and the alternative measures of value therein. Here I seek to challenge the notions of the village high street and the upmarket high street, which encapsulate dominant cultural notations of vitality and viability that frame much of the literature and policy around the value of high streets in the UK.

The concluding chapter asks the question of what kind of a city and citizen a street makes. In defining the street as a global-local space, I outline considerations for the analysis of everyday life in diverse and fluid cities, and the recognition of urban multicultures in ordinary spaces like the Walworth Road. I argue that everyday mixing and learning is necessarily located in local worlds, and that because these are realms in which much is at stake for individuals and groups, social contact in prosaic publics accommodates conviviality, contestation and contradiction. By expanding on the question of what it means to be local in a global world, I highlight that social contact sustained through regular practices and familiar spaces ultimately constitutes crucial, but often unrecognised, forms of belonging. I return to questions of what choices people have to participate in urban change and expand not only on the role of skill as the ability to adapt and communicate, but on the need for policy and planning to recognise the social, cultural and economic significance of the ordinary and the local.

The approach of this book is sociological and ethnographic: it focuses on the forces and experiences of profound global urbanisation and on how individuals navigate the consequences of accelerated urban change. By attending to the ordinary dimensions of everyday life in the city, the aim of this book is to offer an alternative notion of 'multiculturalism' away from the ideological frame of the nation, and away from the moral imperative of community. *City, Street and Citizen* offers to the reader an account of the lived realities of allegiance, participation and belonging from the base of a multi-ethnic street in south London.

Notes

1   See for example the UK General Election 2010 (http://www.general-election-2010. co.uk); and the Dutch General Election 2010 (http://www.rnw.nl).
2   The First Election Debate televised live on 15 April 2010 focused on domestic affairs. The first question from the studio audience was: 'What key elements for a fair and workable immigration policy need to be put in place to make it work effectively?'
3   The point-based immigration system for the United Kingdom commenced in 2008 and regulates immigration on the basis of five tiers of skills. Since their election in 2010, the Conservative Party promise to 'ensure a steady downward trend on every route to long-term immigration.' (http://www.conservative.com/news-stories/2010/09).
4   'There has been intense debate about multiculturalism in Germany in recent months. Correspondents say Mrs Merkel faces pressure from within her CDU and its allies to

take a tougher stance and require immigrants to do more to adapt to German society.'
Reported on 17 October 2010 (http://www/bbc.co.uk/news/world-europe-11559451).

5   In 2009 President Sarkozy's disdain for the burqa was expressed in an address to
parliament. The ban came into force in April 2011.

6   In November 2009, 22 out of 26 cantons in Switzerland voted in a referendum in favour
of banning the building of minarets.

7   Charles Taylor (2009) offers a threefold alternative approach to political secularism:
maximum freedom of expression as the right 'to state deep convictions'; respect between
diverse groups; and representation as 'a politics for managing how diverse views
coexist'. See his public lecture: 'The Future of the Secular' at The New School,
2009/03/05, [http://fora.tv/2009/03/05/Charles_Taylor] accessed 23 December 2010.

8   We know for example that in 2001, 53 per cent of all ethnic minority groups living in
the UK resided in London (Hamnett 2003), indicating that demographic heterogeneity
in the UK is primarily an urban phenomenon, moreover, one explicitly concentrated in
London (Office for National Statistics 2001).

1 Making practice visible

Is the language of power quantitative? And if so, how do we reveal a qualitative understanding of urban multiculture not only for those who operate in the echelons of power, but in ways that have theoretical and pragmatic pertinence to the wider debates about immigration, citizenship and multiculturalism? The aggregation and classification of individuals by way of ethnicity, income and religion through survey techniques is a primary official mode – one scientifically validated, politically authorised and readily accessible – of representing the variety of individuals who live in the city. But the tools of the survey short-circuit our understanding of how diverse individuals and groups establish meeting points and assert divisions in a context of accelerated urban change. The challenge for fine-grained research is how to reveal individual experiences alongside the histories of migration, racism and class that are saturated in London's local landscapes. The task extends to how urban ethnography might contribute to the contemporary debates and policy formations about social, cultural and economic forms of belonging. What ideas and representational forms could ethnography develop to speak to popular culture, to theory and to power?

I know of no better description of the fine-grained observation of social life than Les Back's (1996) articulation of 'serious true fiction'. What Back and other skilled ethnographers point us to is an analysis of how people do things or say things in ways that *ring true* as opposed to objective or factual renderings of 'a' or 'the' truth. Ethnography offers us explicitly subjective accounts of reality, and it is precisely because it reveals the variable, fallible and ingenious dimensions of human life that it has validity. However, while ethnography's pertinence depends on conveying meanings that capture relationships between people and their circumstances, its content is not fully achieved in the form of a story. The skilled contemporary writers of 'serious true fiction' show us that the intellectual and imaginative task of validating ethnographic findings – of connecting individual experiences of local worlds with how urban societies are shaped – is paramount.

Simultaneity, ambiguity and contradiction

The achievement of ethnography is to compel and to claim through writing 'how culture lives in practice' (Calhoun and Sennett 2007: 2). When Hobbs for example, writes in *Doing the Business* (1988) about the cultural proximities between thieving and policing in London he reveals the making of East London through the mutually reinforcing practices of power and those of contravention. Hobbs' art is the interplay of involved and invested research together with a Mailer-like prose in which the writer is ever present, yielding for the reader not simply a work of criminology, but an acute account of the subaltern city revealed through the intricacies of cultural and institutional underworlds. But it is precisely because Hobbs' work is not limited to the subaltern that it has broader significance. Hobbs' ethnography subverts and so reveals the visible or apparent city as Suketu Mehta's journalism does in *Maximum City* (2004): the distortions of rule and order are charged through human voices and actions, and it is in the untidy overlaps between regulation and life, that we as reader could in no way anticipate, that the ethnographic fieldwork and writing is vitalised.

This chapter explores the role of ethnography in articulating the relationship between human experience and the parallel shapes of global urbanisation. It focuses on the question: To what extent is local life significant to cosmopolitan formations? The question poses for contemporary urban ethnography a very different consideration of what is 'local' through a rethinking of how to link C. Wright Mills' 'biographies and histories' to the velocity of global change. Burawoy *et al.*'s (2002) exploration of a 'global ethnography' recognises the fluidity of cultures (Hannerz 1997) shaped by the perpetual shifting of ideas, goods and people across the planet, and the multi-sited relationships (Marcus 1995) that constitute social, cultural and economic expressions. The local is conceived not only as a space in a state of flux, but as one of a number of interconnected sub-worlds.

But there is another underlying research capacity from which ethnography has yielded its critical substance and which I argue is key to understanding how ethnic and cultural differences are negotiated in ever-changing local worlds. Acute urban ethnography is the process of revealing not only the global–local or dominant–subaltern relationships, but the unanticipated (and often inconsistent) expressions of human frailty and ingenuity, and how these intersect with the economic forces and political frameworks of our time. It is the qualitative dimensions of the unanticipated to which I now turn and in particular to the analytic value of simultaneity and ambiguity in understanding what Les Back (2009a) has highlighted as Britain's 'metropolitan paradox', where both dialogue and racism are evoked within its diversifying cities.

Because this paradox of being open and closed to differences is concurrent not only in cities but also in individual lives, this chapter seeks to connect the practice of *being local* to two dispositions that are more entangled than a purer (but arguably more distanced) notion of tolerance: the cosmopolitan imagination and the provincial one. The peculiar practices of being open and adaptable to the unfamiliar alongside parochial ways of preserving what one is already accustomed to are therefore explored. I do this in response to fieldwork and the important inconsistencies that are central to ethnographic inquiry: ideas that are theoretically clear and distinct are often experienced in more variegated ways within the complex lives and spaces of the city. In chapters that follow for example, individuals reveal themselves as both spontaneously open to differences and simultaneously able to verbalise prejudiced views. Spaces are revealed as micro worlds of social improvisation and cultural innovation, and at the same time occupied in peculiarly insular ways. The contradictions that often surface in the different acts of saying and doing are of consequence for understanding the social ways of figuring out and mixing in the diverse city. How then do we deal conceptually and methodologically with these enigmatic simultaneities? In what way does the practice of ethnography and the ethnography of practice provide an empirical beginning and interpretive directions for revealing the significant paradoxes integral to the everyday dynamics of the city?

Back (2009a) proposes 'a cosmopolitan method' for exploring the complexities of contradiction in Britain's diverse cities where multiple forms of communication and overlap are paralleled with avid expressions of racial and ethnic segregation. Back's approach (2009a, 2009b) is vested explicitly in the methods of paying attention, and emphasises how sensory understandings drawn from sounds, tastes and smells might complement or even unsettle that which is said. It advocates, as does Johannes Fabian (1983) in his seminal anthropological text *Time and the Other*, a much closer methodological and substantive relationship between the subject and 'object' of ethnography. For ethnographers like Fabian and Back, fieldwork is practice, and the acquirement of understanding (as opposed to the excavation of 'data') is best developed though the processes of lived engagement. Fabian directs us to a greater interrogation of the acts of being (1983: 164) and away from prevalent taxonomies in sociology and anthropology that have ranked subjects by type and time ('primitive' for example is a temporal distancing and hierarchical categorisation of the Other): 'As I see it now, the anthropologist and his interlocutors only "know" when they meet each other in one and the same contemporality' (1983: 164).

Back's 'cosmopolitan method' and Fabian's 'contemporality' provoke a different notion of 'the local' for the fieldworker, where the field includes exposure to a highly subjective collection of lived territories evoked through talk, walk, touch and sight, in which the ethnographer has an explicit presence. And it is precisely within the local acts of being that individual, group and national identities are unsettled and reshaped by experience. In the remains of this chapter I'd like to pursue the idea that the local is a practised territory and that, by virtue of the diversity of its respective occupants and shapers, it has multiple boundaries, layers of time and accumulations of culture. But aside from the hardly unsurprising notion that the local is an aggregation of experiences or a palimpsest of pasts and presents, is the need to further explore the social significance of simultaneity.

Both the purposeful and unconscious practices of paradox and ambiguity are, I suggest, at the core of an ethnographic exploration of how individuals and groups belong with respect to one another. I'd like to start by placing the city at the foreground of the ethnographic exploration of *City, Street and Citizen*. In the integral relationships between the spaces, speeds and rhythms of the city, ethnography pursues the lived relationships between structure and agency or how individuals address circumstance. By observing how socially intimate and collective spaces are occupied across hours, days and years, ethnography reveals how accelerated urbanisation affects social contact and urban culture.

Pace and space

Speed is a quality of dramatic time, and exemplifies the thrust and shape of twenty-first century urbanisation evident in the radical growth of mega cities across the globe. Ananya Roy (2011) refers to our time and place as 'a sudden century', one where the human condition is increasingly integral to the urban one. Roy explores speed through the steroid-induced growth of Asian cities injected by the global pursuit of 'world class' status. While Shanghai is the default measure of Asian success, its pinnacle forms and securitised zones are perpetuated in the remaking of the everywhere and nowhere spaces of Dubai, Mumbai and Abu Dhabi. What is most compelling about Roy's exploration is that it pursues the physical and cultural shapes and textures induced by speed, to ask what kind of urban politics is possible within a pace of change exaggerated by emerging economies. Roy's method is to contrast: to set suicide rates amongst the 500,000 migrant workers in the world's largest factory compound, Foxcon, side-by-side with the iPad and iPhone gadgets made by the Foxcon workers that proliferate affluent western lives. Roy sets urban spaces of production alongside global imperatives for consumption, and shows how ideas about the forms and objects of the 'world-class' city circulate, as does the exploitation of migrant labour to build these prolific urban landscapes.

The pervasive temporal and spatial language of urban extremes – 'speed', 'mega' – is undoubtedly useful for understanding the unprecedented global impacts on the eruption of cities. World maps of urbanisation acutely register Africa and Asia as zones of the urban extreme and urban studies have rightly focused on the radical inequalities produced in the stark contrasts between high-rise prestige and low-rise 'squatter' settlements. However, speed is a measure of time that propels forward, implying that the present is merely fleeting and that the past is a bygone place. Speed imposes a tabula rasa urban condition, one that omits how the 'ordinary' parts of cities are mutually transformed by history and by global urbanisation.

Sukhdev Sandhu (2004) evokes a far more jumbled sense of the emerging city by describing London as 'this higgledy-piggledy commotion of a metropolis' (2004: 259), and it follows that London's space-time configurations of accelerated urban change have acquired different qualities. London is essentially an amalgam city that grew steadily until its unsurpassed growth in the nineteenth century, jointly heralded by industrialisation and the colonial expansion of the British Empire. Over its industrial century the city swelled from one million to eight million inhabitants and acquired a metropolitan status and size that remains today. However, while the city's population growth appears as static, London's population is in constant flux, and work, tertiary education and tourism enrol daily, weekly and annual migrations in significant numbers.

Understanding London's pace and space today requires a mutual analysis of its emergence over time with its contemporary reshaping by global forces. The notion of London's urban amalgamations opens up opportunities for exploring its space-time simultaneities: the overlaps of pasts and presents; the connections of its microcosms to the city and beyond; and the relationships between its floating and entrenched populations. These urban amalgamations are therefore crucial for understanding London's waves of immigration and settlement: for analysing in social terms that ever-paradoxical description of the 'second-generation immigrant'; and for exploring how ideas of belonging differ for the post-Second World War phase of immigration from the later phase of immigration from the 1990s onwards. This leads to questions of: what kinds of spaces provide meeting points for a far more variegated, dislocated public? and: how does social or cultural contact emerge within the space-time attuned to accelerated cities? Let's start with the notion of small space and rooted time, and explore how the interconnected idea of physical proximity and social propinquity has evolved as one direction for thinking about cultural difference and social connection in the changing city.

The effect of heterogeneity defined by Louis Wirth (1938) in his seminal essay 'Urbanism as a way of life', is drawn out of the dramatic process of urbanisation at the turn of the twentieth century in American cities. Wirth pursued the social consequences of flux, and outlined a deep scepticism for the capacity of interaction as a footing for social harmony between the different groups migrating into American cities. Wirth's urban analysis of the large-scale, dense concentration of different groups emphasised an aggregation of segmented parts and the negative prospects for human associations therein:

> a motley of people and cultures, of highly differentiated modes of life between which there is only the faintest communication, the greatest indifference and the broadest tolerance, occasionally bitter strife, but always the sharpest contrast.
>
> (1938: 20)

Wirth's theory of urban heterogeneity was deeply vested in the spatial and social proximities afforded by rural societies where neighbourliness and kinship pre-empted forms of 'folk solidarity'. Moreover the rooted notion of these vernacular solidarities – tied to place, gradually refined over time (and presumably ethnically homogenous) – stood in oppositional contrast to what he perceived as the transitory and therefore amorphous nature of urban societies.

For Wirth the growing scale of the city increased variation and weakened aggregation. But his analysis of the 'cosmopolitan urbanite' focused on *lifestyle* to which he attributed a footloose and detached urban predilection, mirroring Durkheim's (1893) *anomie* and Simmel's (1903) *blasé flâneur*. While Wirth privileged the small space and slow pace of rural locales as precursors to solidarity, he similarly predicted the impossibility of urban social intimacy across different groups. Seminal ethnographic studies of race and ethnicity in American cities over the twentieth century (Whyte 1943; Gans 1962; Liebow 1967; Suttles 1968; Duneier 1992; Anderson 1999) point to the practices of kinship and neighbourliness within urban local areas that Wirth's theory had emphatically denied. However, these ethnographies also articulate the external ordering and containment of segments of the city and its respective inhabitants on the basis of income, race and ethnicity. Through human voices and experiences the stratifying effects of American urbanisation and industrialisation are revealed, as are the intensified dependencies on locality and kinship on the part of the urban poor.

The impact of profound urban segregation and its space-time qualities of detachment and stasis is rendered most acute when issues of work and mobility, rather than lifestyle, are introduced into the analytic frame. Liebow's account of unemployed and itinerant workers waiting for piecework in *Tally's Corner: A Study of Negro Streetcorner Men* (1967) is an account of adult lives confined to limited and degrading work prospects. While social solidarity amongst these adults is evident, it is a cohesion that is in significant part formed out of a racialised and polarised urban condition. Four decades on, Newman's (2006) ethnography of the contemporary low-wage labour market takes place in fast food franchises in Harlem and exposes the stunted trajectory of minimum wage work. But in Newman's account, the pervasive economic condition of limited choice is no longer confined to particular urban neighbourhoods. Rather it is cyclically carried across the city in migrant and black bodies, moving from franchise to franchise, and from low-wage employment to unemployment. In Liebow's contained urbanism there is solidarity but not participation whilst in Newman's there is work but not inclusion: these are forms of conscription rather than citizenship and the sense of public space in which to engage, mix or mobilise is therefore radically curtailed.

Within the urban context of polarisation and racism in Britain, and particularly in response to the violent confrontations in Oldham, Burnley and Bradford in 2001, Ash Amin (2002) offers us the idea of small and invested local spaces as alternative public terrains to prestigious tourist sites on the one hand, or publicly regulated social housing estates on the other. Amin pursues the value of repeated and regular time, hence his local emphasis. But Amin's spatial expression of the 'local' is not invested in territorial belonging or residence as the basis of community; it extends to the idea of active participations in the form of shared projects that are integral to everyday life. Amin's 'micro-publics' include workplaces, schools, youth clubs and community centres as the basis for engagement between ethnic and cultural groups. An important point here is not simply the value of these 'local' spaces themselves, but also how the accumulation of a number of micro-publics allow individuals to navigate *within and across* the territories of the city.

Because of the prevalence of urban boundaries circumscribed by class and ethnicity for example, as well as those habitually reinforced by comfort and familiarity, individuals need to socially acquire repertoires to traverse and participate in different spaces of the city. This is the real time social politics of overlap as opposed to the state regulation of assimilation, acutely articulated by Paul Gilroy's notion of a convivial multiculture:

> Conviviality is a social pattern in which different metropolitan groups dwell in close proximity, but where their racial, linguistic and religious particularities do not [. . .] add up to discontinuities of experience or insurmountable problems

of communication. In these conditions, a degree of differentiation can be combined with large amounts of overlapping.

(2006: 40)

Gilroy turns to the ordinary spaces and modes of everyday interactions that shape and express affinity: the Arsenal football ground during a game; the two-tone worlds of funk, reggae and ska; and perhaps most illustratively, to the National Health Service (NHS) where the administering of skill and care in the context of individual need and stress involves and indeed is sustained by Britain's 'heterocultural' populace.

How can ethnography reveal and expand on the compelling but broad ideas of micro-publics and conviviality? Would we gain a different and possibly more multifarious sense of public meeting points or overlaps through a closer scrutiny of how public space is occupied in space *and* time? What representations would challenge the unintended proliferation of stereotypes sometimes advanced in fieldwork by a 'liberal complacency' (Armstrong 1998) or 'romantic fascination' (Burawoy *et al*. 2000) of the urban margins? The study of London's urban margins is historically embedded in a rich but moral anthropologic-philanthropic tradition, exemplified for example, in the seminal nineteenth-century studies of Charles Booth and Henry Mayhew. And while it is a tradition that has yielded powerful and evocative portrayals of urban poverty, it has tended to segregate the urban poor from the context of its making.

Improvisation and duration

In Craig Calhoun's (2003) exploration of ways of being cosmopolitan within a world that is as much about movement and change as it is about settlement and traditions, Calhoun highlights two directions for thinking about living with difference and change. He refers to Sennett's tactile analysis of urban life and the public realm, where meeting grounds are sustained by the physical and sensory dimensions of interaction and secular ritual. Sennett himself (2008) aligns to the 'performative' or 'dramaturgical' school that includes Erving Goffman and Clifford Geertz, and argues for the cultural expressions of *being public*, and more particularly for the 'bodily signals' between strangers in space that constitute meeting. For Sennett, 'the public realm can simply be defined as a place where strangers meet' (2008a:1), thereby proposing a deviation from his teacher Hannah Arendt, whose public realm was conceived of as a collective and political terrain for vocalisation between free and equal citizens.

Sennett's work on the social embodiment of the urban milieu, in particular *The Fall of Public Man* (1977) and *Flesh and Stone* (1996) forefronts the integral relationship between urban bodies and public space, where performance in public space is a bodily form of refining who we are with respect to self and other. The expression permitted within secular rituals allows Sennett to draw on the interconnections between culture and politics. But in Sennett's historic analysis (1977) public performance is configured within a context of explicit political structures and commonly understood codes of participation. How do these codes of public performance alter in heterogeneous cities where public life is not only more plural, but where political structure is more opaque? When Sennett takes us away from the Athenian agora to contemporary Greenwich Village (1996) he presents us with a further dilemma: when we focus on individuals in the context of everyday life, how much contact is enough to sustain a sense of public culture? He describes a context of physical proximity without social propinquity – a dense aggregation of different ethnic and cultural groups where contact is largely reduced to the gaze.

The second direction that Calhoun refers to is one explicitly focused on active modes of cultural exchange, as distinctive from a more 'ethical' and therefore distanced form of universal tolerance of and respect for difference. Carol Breckenridge, Sheldon Pollock, Homi Bhabha and Dipesh Chakrabarty's (2002) edition on *Cosmopolitanism* provides the steer for this important avenue of the practice of social mixing and cultural crossings as a human, and therefore incomplete and imperfect process. While transition provides fertile analytic ground for understanding cosmopolitan practice, these writers identify the fracturing powers of nationalism, the polarising forces of globalisation and the discriminatory governance of multiculturalism as central to the analysis of both cultural uprooting and cultural adaptation. But it is Sheldon Pollock's (2000) notion of a 'cosmopolitan vernacular' that allows us to think through how local worlds transform 'across space and through time' without forgoing cultural particularity. Pollock offers to the ethnographer of local worlds three considerations: in what ways do vernacular practices connect locals 'to a larger world rather than a smaller place'? (2000: 591); to what extent can local practices resist political or cultural domination? and: what choices are available to individuals to participate in change?

The social and cultural capacities to respond to transition, both in Sennett's proposition of a sensuous process of testing in public space, and in Breckenridge *et al.*'s focus on the inquisitive processes of transformation, are animate and deeply dependent on communication. But they are also reliant on the structure of opportunity and choice. In *City, Street and Citizen*, these adaptive capacities are explored through the two space-time frames of *improvisation and duration.* Improvisation is explored as an *in situ*, quick-footed practice of 'making do and getting by' that is not only a means of survival but often also a precursor for innovation. Duration is analysed as a longer-term practice with the purpose of building enduring prospects and relationships across time. Both practices are apparent within the shops along the Walworth Road, but as the reader will learn, improvisation and duration acquire distinctive social modes and spatial forms, and have differing consequences for interaction and exchange.

Improvisation is the immigrant's prerogative. The adaptations that are taken up as a matter of imposition – for example the change of work status that often accompanies change of national residence – is one aspect of improvisation well chronicled in historic and contemporary accounts of how immigrant workers 'land' in London. Ruth Glass (1960) recorded the unequivocal downgrading of work status of newcomers from the Caribbean to London in the 1950s, which reflected not only the dismal state of the post-war economy, but also the racialised prohibitions on access to skilled work. In a not dissimilar vein, Godley (2000) traced the occupational structure for Eastern European Jewish immigrants to the UK between 1880 and 1914, revealing that during this period two-thirds of these immigrants in London were employed in the tailoring trades. While it follows that clothing was during that period, the largest manufacturing trade in London in terms of numbers employed (Hall 1960), what is of interest in the paradigm of immigrant improvisation is that tailoring was not a prominent trade that these immigrants had brought with them from Eastern Europe (Kahan 1978; Godley 2000). Immigration, rather than tradition, had turned these first-generation immigrants into the tailors and seamstresses that filled the sweatshops of London's East End.

Ethnic minority self-employment is another avenue of adaptation, one forged by limited access to work opportunities in the formal employment sectors, and one which since the 1980s is recognised as an expanding feature of advanced urban economies (see for example Barrett, Jones and McEvoy 1996). In street-based retail, 'ethnic minority capitalism' has survived in the context of unsupportive regulation and oversaturated markets, and these adaptations are therefore viewed as curtailed responses to unequal structural conditions. Although these constraints will be raised in my scrutiny of the economic life of the Walworth Road, I turn with greater emphasis to the modes of improvisation that are readily yielded through cultural expression rather than economic limitation. Further, the modes of innovation and experiment on the Walworth Road may well emerge out of an entrepreneurial imperative, but they are paralleled with human contact and expression. Improvisations on the street are essentially about reciprocal modes of communication – spontaneous and considered – between proprietors and customers, and between 'newcomers' and established residents.

To observe the variegated forms of these improvisations, the ethnographer must pursue slithers of space and increments of time. Within the shops along the Walworth Road I have learnt that one and the same space can be occupied entirely differently through both the arrangements of space, as well as divisions of the hourly time slots across the day. There is simply a density to the occupation of 'space-time' that belies the clarity of first glance observations. To start with, there is a social thickness to the shop façade formed by the display of goods and services referred to by one proprietor on the Walworth Road as the 'silent salesman'. But in multi-ethnic streets like the Walworth Road, the silent salesman has had to acquire multilingual communication skills, including on the one hand the choice of language, humour and imagery to reach a varied clientele, and on the other a sequence of items to address cultural needs and aspirations. There are the spatial distinctions from front to back of shops that are not simply mercantile pursuits of organisation, but intricate arrangements of public and private territories, secular and spiritual domains and singular and variegated cultural references.

The significance of these spatial divisions are also played out in the social organisation of time. In a local eating establishment and meeting place on the Walworth Road, for example, there is a cyclical orchestration of micro-publics across the working day, in which workers, pensioners, families and habitués all select, with regular precision, their respective tables and times of occupation. While these fluctuating patterns of use in the city seem obvious, it was only through sitting day after day in these interiors off the street that I began to appreciate how rhythms of time offer, within one space, a choice for a variety of participants; not only of where to go but also of when to participate. Had I only ventured into a Caff off the Walworth Road during mid-morning, I might surmise that the space was a very male affair; an eating-place for men engaged in physical work around the area. If I had visited the same space mostly in the evening, I might characterise the Caff as home to the born-and-bred remnants of Walworth's white working class who tended to gather at a few tables at the front of the shop around five on most evenings. And if I missed that brief half hour on Wednesday mornings, I wouldn't see Mustafa roll in in his wheelchair and order in his stroke-infected accent his usual 'lemon tart and 'cinno'. Increments of time are crucial for understanding how these commonplace publics are shaped by the occupation of space-time across the day.

The ethnographic eye and ear is generally attentive to the microcosmic dimensions of human expression and improvisation, and skilled ethnographers recognise and interpret the value of social nuances and tacit gestures (although not always with sufficient attention to the role of space and time). But it is perhaps more difficult, given the intense investment required for ethnographic observation, to trace larger time frames and to consider what implications these have on how individuals develop their opportunities and choices across their life spans. For the ethnographers of prospect – how social mobility is advanced or limited by class, race or gender – extended time is a crucial but often overlooked factor. In Paul Willis' *Learning to Labour* (1977) the reader is given ample insight into the relegation of working-class kids to working-class jobs in a Britain on the last legs of its industrial endeavour. Willis follows the same group of boys from school to shop floor and expands on how abilities are formed by working-class culture and social order; how 'practical ability', 'physical humour', 'unofficial bartering' and violence shape a passage of underperformance that endures from school to factory. But how fixed is this trajectory of curtailed expectation? In what ways would Willis' important account be reviewed if we were to see the young boys as men, some years on from the fieldwork period?

The idea of duration allows the ethnographer to explore what endures over an extended time frame and to understand the extent to which individuals acquire skills and adopt strategies to challenge imposed trajectories. In this book I pursue two routes to understanding how power and disposition affect prospect and mobility within the confines of class, race and ethnicity. The first is one developed in Claire Alexander's ethnography, *The Asian Gang* (2000). Alexander's account of a group of Asian adolescents in a south London neighbourhood was developed over a five-year fieldwork period, and we come to know the boys from the base of their youth centre and the range of places where they develop their private and public persona, including school, home, college and work. Alexander's account yields the social codes of solidarity amongst the boys, in part attributed to how they are labelled (immigrant children) and the local world they are residents of (a marginal social housing estate). But Alexander's ethnography also reveals the testing that occurs within individual and group formations, and importantly shows that the trajectories of these diverse boys are varied and not entirely predictable. Alexander's ethnography occurs over a lengthy transitional period and is therefore as much multi-temporal as it is multi-sited.

The second route to exploring duration is the ethnography of skill and, as Richard Sennett portrays in *The Craftsman* (2008b), the acquisition of a work skill and the time it takes to acquire it and refine it is a social and cultural practice. The significance of Sennett's exploration is not solely that individuals learn an art or a craft or a form of work gradually, but that in a time-protracted internship they learn a language of sensibility and in so doing they find and assert their individual and societal value. In conversation with Sennett, he suggests that skill permits 'autonomy and address': a relative independence of thought and action; and the dexterity to communicate to a broader audience. Is the empowerment afforded by skill, then, one that allows for any individual to transcend the limited work or life trajectories that have historically been imposed on the basis of colour of skin, accent or gender? Further, does the acquisition of skill potentially enhance the forms of communication across race, class or ethnicity? These are core questions for understanding the overlap of life and livelihoods on a multi-ethnic street, and the idea of duration will be developed through work trajectories and skills acquired and practised by the proprietors on the Walworth Road.

To the field

I started my fieldwork in the spring of 2006 from the base of Nick's Caff, the space on the Walworth Road that I was most familiar with. I put on clothes that were smart enough to look serious but casual enough not to appear too out of place, and walked a few blocks from my home to reach the Caff. Although I was researching my own back yard I was a stranger to the field in professional and personal ways. I had practised as an architect, not ethnographer, and moreover had only recently arrived from South Africa. I had grown up in the height of South Africa's heinous apartheid years in privileged, white suburbia, and although my work as an architect had taken me into townships on the edges of Johannesburg and Cape Town, I had never lived in a remotely mixed, let alone urban environment. I had entered London on a holiday visa and joined John in his studio flat three floors up above the Walworth Road. I was the newcomer, moving about with an *A-to-Z* of London perpetually in my backpack, and while subconsciously engaging with questions of my own belonging, I began to explore how the diverse individuals on the Walworth Road experienced and expressed their ties to people and place.

I had used Nick's Caff prior to my research project; it was a place I frequented for its traditional English breakfasts and lunchtime roasts, as well as for passing conversations with Nick, its proprietor. The Caff had an interesting mix of people in it, and this, coupled with Nick's agreement for me to start my research in his Caff, provided me with a base for my fieldwork. Nick's say-so provided me with my first points of access to regulars in his Caff: 'It's fine darlin'. Once I'd vouched for you it's fine. Because you don't have the same accent as here, you're a bit of an outsider. You got a posher accent . . . and you don't have any tattoos!' Initially, many of the regulars in the Caff that I spoke to were introduced to me through Nick. These regulars had varied occupational backgrounds, employment statuses and places of origin. Significantly, their ages ranged between approximately thirty and seventy years, and this allowed for conversations about how the Walworth Road was remembered, how it had changed, as well as a sense of individual trajectories within the span of adult lives.

After a couple of months of sitting in the Caff on most week days, I was able to more readily approach customers in the Caff as well as proprietors along the street. One Caff regular suggested I should go and 'have a chat' with Reyd, whose bespoke tailor shop I had regularly passed by. I began my first meeting with Reyd antici-pating a fairly brief, introductory conversation of approximately an hour, much like those I had had with other proprietors along the Walworth Road. But in Reyd's case, my more usual period of about an hour of conversation expanded into four hours, with an open invitation to return. After many conversations with Nick and Reyd, it became apparent that the practices and interactions in their respective shop spaces provided an important variety of sociabilities and cultural expression. By being in Nick's Caff a couple of days of the week over the course of a year, and of numerous but more intermittent visits to Reyd's shop over a two-year period, I was able to juxtapose these two proximate but distinctive local interiors.

In both spaces I could align the work practices of Nick and Reyd with the social practices associated within their particular workspaces. Nick's Caff and Reyd's Bespoke Tailor Shop were both work places associated with immigrant com-munities who had established work positions in London at different points in history. Nick's parents had emigrated to London from Cyprus in the 1950s before Nick was born, while Reyd's parents had made their journey from Jamaica during that same decade when Reyd was a small child. Further, both the Caff and the tailor shop sustained particular cultural links with the urban working class, and both tailoring and running a caff were occupations undergoing substantial adaptations in line with changes in contemporary urban production and consumption. Moreover, Nick had grown up in Walworth and Reyd in Peckham (a neighbouring area), and both described themselves as 'South Londoners'. But their respective under-standings of *being local* were also strongly shaped by their particular connections to other places. The justification for focusing on these two shops therefore rests on a mixture of circumstantial and intuitive validation.

During my two-year period of fieldwork I altered the pace and focus of my observation. There were periods when I simply returned to the Caff day after day, and other times when I walked the Walworth Road to explore other per-spectives of the street. In September 2006, I conducted both a verbal and visual survey along the east and west lengths of the street, to capture a broader and more systematic overview of the range of shops and proprietors across the spectrum of the Walworth Road. I conducted a face-to-face survey of each of the independent shops along the street (see the Appendix). After the two-week survey period, I had a basic introduction to 128 independent proprietors and their respective shop spaces.

However, the depth and substance of social interactions within these spaces escaped the survey format, and was only partially suggested in the informal or semi-structured interviews that I held with eight of the independent shop proprietors. These eight proprietors, all male and mostly between forty and fifty years old, were selected on the basis that they had shops on the Walworth Road for over ten years. Three had occupied their retail spaces for over forty years as family businesses. These interviews generally lasted an hour, and the proprietors' respective measures of their shops' longevity emerged as a common narrative. Endurance on the street was most strongly associated with relationships forged between proprietors and customers, some of which spanned generations.

Ethnographic research inevitably requires a certain closeness between the researcher and those researched, and the management of these relationships formed an important part of my research process. Both Nick and Reyd became friends and were individuals with whom I enjoyed talking. This investment of time and, to an extent, of emotion opened up opportunities for different sets of questions and answers in fieldwork conversations. I learnt, particularly in the Caff, that some of my best conversations with individuals followed after a few initial meetings – extended time in the field became a valuable research asset. Similarly inconsistencies in individuals' formal, verbal presentations of self, versus their informal, spontaneous interactions with others, only became apparent after a number of conversations and observations had accumulated. These ambiguities included, for example, a sharp disjuncture between bigoted views on race and ethnicity expressed in the Caff, contrasted with far more generous and open individual relationships sustained amongst the variety of the Caff regulars.

The incongruity between words and actions was an important cue for understanding some of the collisions between real-time social experiences and the broader societal portrayals of difference and stigma perpetuated, for example, via the media. Moreover, these ambiguities are the ethnographer's privilege, since they are accessed through the process of spending time and gaining trust. However the risk for ethnography, as Wacquant (2002) acerbically points out in his essay on street-based ethnographies of poverty and race in America, is that these incongruities are potentially smoothed out by characterising individuals in the field by type or persona. I would add that characterisations or stereotypical portrayals of people and of places reduces the opportunity for revealing a more situated theory of mixing, where public space is understood as a day-to-day realm for openly expressing fears and affinities, and a place for regularly confronting capacities to engage with change. I therefore aim to avoid a simplistic articulation of the 'white-working-class racist' just as much as a moral description of the 'hard-working, family-oriented public character' that could be used to portray many of the people I met.

What Wacquant's analysis of the potential pitfalls of ethnographic research leaves out is the recognition of the explanatory value of expression itself. There were moments in my fieldwork where I felt disturbed, particularly in the instances of the matter-of-fact delivery of bigotry. Undoubtedly, these bigotries required causal explanation, but in the research process it is equally crucial to recognise what delivery of expression elicits on the spot – a simultaneous capacity to feel and to think when we are confronted by powerful communication. There is also the relationship between poignancy and sociological meaning – the moment when the guard slips and when things are said or done that are both infinitely revealing and impossible to forget. Much like Simmel's idea of the 'snapshot', these momentary fragments – a pause, a slip, a stutter – have crucial explanatory value since they reveal the overlap of thought, sentiment and emotion, 'The paradox of the snapshot is that although it is literally like a fleeting image, it is also one that can be made to endure' (Frisby 1981: 103). By separating emotional explanation from rational explanation, the researcher undermines the value of expression as fundamental to the constitution of meaning.

Ethnography demands that voices from the field are edited without sanitising them, a task made difficult by the trust gained while in the field. The methodological consequence of granting anonymity and gaining consent, as a customary ethnographic practice, is not simply an ethical matter but also a substantive one. Anonymity directly relates to the researcher's capacity to reveal the full range of dimensions of a character, without exposing the researched to the risks of formal identification. By creating anonymity, the researcher can more easily expose illicit or unpleasant realities; anonymity protects the integrity of the research findings. Constructing anonymity relates to the extent of disguise created, and in my research the degrees of disguise required were not clear-cut. I adopted different approaches for the street than for the individuals and small spaces within the street. As far as possible, all participants have remained anonymous, and in most cases individuals selected their pseudonyms with appropriate concern or humour. In spite of the veneer of this disguise, it is likely that people who know this street well would recognise themselves or others. Although I have renamed the shops, I have resisted subjecting the street and area to an alternative naming. This is because the actual location of the Walworth Road in relation to the space of the city, and in relation to the structures of time, power and inhabitation, is of key explanatory substance.

Homi Bhabha (2004 [1994], preface) explores the emergence of cultural meaning in diverse urban contexts through 'personhood' as individual practice. Bhabha directs the reader to the analytic value of individual expression and how individuals communicate their sense of self with others. He flips Sheldon Pollock's frame of the 'cosmopolitan vernacular', and in exploring 'vernacular cosmopolitanism' Bhabha connects the city as a postcolonial meeting ground shaped by inter-cultural relationships that are vitalised by everyday interactions and expressions of personhood. The ethnographer can extract from Bhabha the significance of the act of recognition as both a cultural and political concern: the crucial importance of listening to and recognising 'the unheard' or what Suketu Mehta describes as the surfacing of 'unofficial stories' that are invisible to the lens of power. Bert Weir, a pensioner from a south London housing estate close to the Walworth Road, illustrates:

> I'm seventy this week, and in all my life so far no one's ever asked me my thoughts on anything. No one's ever thought I had anything to say that was

worth hearing. I don't think anyone ever thought I had anything meaningful to say, I suppose.

(Cited in Parker 1983: 255)

Bert's words capture the poignant omission of people and places rendered invisible by broader overviews of society. Prior to what I regarded as my formal period of fieldwork, I undertook preliminary research on the history of Walworth at the Southwark Local History Library. I was struck by the comparatively diminutive shelf space occupied by the section on 'Walworth', and I turned to the variety of official surveys of south London in the form of maps, census data and *Post Office London Directories* that recorded how the Walworth area had measurably grown and changed over time. True to my architectural sensibility I started at the front of the library in the map section, where I could engage with the familiarity of a visual language. At that stage, it seemed appropriate to start with the conventions of a chronological representation of change over time. However, when I started my ethnographic fieldwork, a disjuncture surfaced between the diverse histories of Walworth as told by people on the street, and the singularity of the official records on the history of the area.

For a start, there was only limited official information on Black histories, what Stephen Bourne's book, *Speak of Me as I Am: The Black Presence in Southwark since 1600* (2005), reveals as the omission of the significant contribution of Black people to the area over a period of five centuries: 'Black historical figures from the past had been made invisible, and there was a wall of silence around Britain's Black History' (2005: 5). There was similarly very little first-hand accounts from the working class. Michael Collins' *The Likes of Us: A Biography of the White Working Class* (2004) attributes to the class-based organisation of power and knowledge the vetting of an account of history on the part of the professional class, and the stereotypical portrayal of Walworth's working class on the part of 'outsiders' (although his problematic portrayal of the white working class focuses on this group as the victims of change, without any recognition of other modes of adaptation in contemporary life).

These gaps between official representations and individual understandings of Walworth's past presented me with the methodological and substantive concern of how to work with the significance of the past, and more specifically how to make connections between past and present. The exclusion of voice in the historic representation of Walworth's and Southwark's pasts remained a key concern for my ethnography of everyday life on the Walworth Road. By following practices across place and time – what people do and the spaces they do things in – the researcher traces the cultural and social formations that are vested in individual experiences of the changing city. In the chapters that follow, voices, gestures and sentiments are therefore interspersed with maps, census data and street surveys.

Picturing difference and change

Research is a process of exploration and communication: both a finding out and a revealing. In his book *Telling about Society,* Becker (2007) raises the key issue of the interpretive space created between the writer and the reader, and in the process of representing society he considers the form and purpose of different modes of telling. What, for example, is the meaning of the quantitative regularity of the census table and how might this differ from the way a reader interprets an untitled photograph? Becker introduces questions for the researcher about the interpretive space between the writer and the reader in which there is sufficient room for the complexity of social meanings to surface. But at what point is it appropriate to limit or to expand this interpretive space when representing society, and more particularly, how do selected modes of analysis and representation capture the variegated expressions on the Walworth Road?

For the architect, these questions are as much to do with writing as picturing and in the case of the Walworth Road both writing and picturing need to articulate the hybrid communications evident in the surfaces, spaces and social life of the street. Sandhu's (2004) analysis of how Black and Asian writers have imagined London makes valuable connections between the authors' experiences of their own difference in the city, and their composite representations of life told through collecting, combining, mixing and layering. I found Sandhu's reference to juxtaposition and collage useful for both reading and representing the street. Collage contains the idea of combinations of different things that compose a differentiated whole, useful for thinking about and capturing the organisation of space and people within the shop spaces on the Walworth Road. The economic imperatives of staying in business, for example, demanded combinations of entrepreneurial acumen and social skill: the Nigerian barber shop had carved out space from its male territory to include a nail bar run by Asian women; convenience stores and laundrettes let small areas within their shops fronts to offer telephone and mending services respectively; the bakery aimed to sell bread to West Indian and English tastes; the regulars at Nick's Caff included a wide array of ages and ethnicities; and boxers, actors and assorted mod enthusiasts made their way across London to Reyd's for a sharp suit.

But while the idea of a collage suggests a differentiated whole, everyday mixing was not always understood or felt by individuals on the Walworth Road as productive. When for example Mustafa, a local pensioner, positively claims that 'Walworth Road is one of the best streets in Southwark – it's got all nationalities', Mike, also a local pensioner, gives a contrary perspective of the street, 'used to be our sort on the street, cockneys, most of them in the graveyard now'. To pursue an understanding of difference through the collage, it is not enough to explore the overlaps in the organisation of people and places. It is also necessary to pursue and picture the unequal impacts of history on individuals and groups on the Walworth Road.

I worked with visual photographic collages – both those found on the street as well as my own combinations – and layered drawings to explore ways of capturing these important social and cultural combinations. Through drawing, I explored how to evoke the appropriations of spaces as tiered or aggregated arrangements of people, time and space. The process of making these drawings during fieldwork prompted me to question the validity of separating the public realm from the private as a way of understanding how cities are occupied. The layered drawings of both Nick's Caff and Reyd's Bespoke Tailor Shop reveal the combinations of public, semi-public and private spaces as a symbiotic arrangement of social life and work practices, where borders between public and private life were less overt.

To understand the peculiar combinations of places evoked in individual narratives and shop displays, I began to work with a series of drawings that juxtaposed different places in order to explore their connections or contrasts. These drawings worked by paralleling different scales of place. I could visually trace, for example, something as simple as the proprietor's place of origin in the world to the proprietor's shop on the Walworth Road. The effect of combining these two entirely different worlds yielded the immediate visual impact of the plethora of connections between the local and wider world. These visualisations, both processes and effects, revealed textures of spatial order over time, and generated questions around what forms of space are resistant or adaptive to change, as well as the kinds of institutions and urban fabrics that come to constitute the symbolic order of place.

Conclusions

What do the practices of doing, testing and expressing give to our understanding of mixing in the city of accelerated change? I have approached this question from the ethnographic vantage point yielded by the stories, voices, bodies and spaces on the Walworth Road. The multi-ethnic street I have come to know is a social amalgamation of patches of space and increments of time in which varied interactions emerge. In observing these differentiations, individuals expressions and interactions permit the ethnographer to re-examine our sense of what is public, alongside understandings of who belongs and how. However, in exploring local worlds as layerings of space, time and experience, I have emphasised the imperative of connecting microcosms of small spaces and intimate interactions to urbanisation as a global process of change in which cities are both diversifying and polarising. My unit of analysis is 'the everyday street', a phrase intended to combine individual expressions of difference with historic aggregations of people and spaces along the Walworth Road.

The primary avenues of ethnographic enquiry and articulation proposed in this chapter are vested in a basic regard for the dimensions of human experience that are inaccessible to quantitative analysis: human frailty and human ingenuity being central. The regard for these human dimensions has opened up a discussion of the validity and essence of ethnography: a time-protracted practice of observation where simultaneity rather than singular clarity provides the substance for the analysis of everyday life. To this end I have highlighted why ambiguities and incongruities are the stuff of human interactions, and why these contingent expressions of uncertainty and probing are crucial for our understanding of how individuals and groups live with difference and change. The sociological and political project of 'making practice visible' is, I argue, made explicit through a fine-grained and historic analysis of space and time, and although the speed and flux of global change is more than palpable in London's cityscapes, I have clarified why it is valuable to begin with a space-time understanding of London as a perpetually amalgamated city.

In the context of a multi-ethnic street within an increasingly diverse city, the dimensions of space and time yield crucial substance for more nuanced understandings of participation, allegiance and belonging. Spatial qualities themselves need to be understood as simultaneous: as this chapter suggests, notions of alternative or prosaic publics are potentially advanced by more entangled expressions of public and private, secular and spiritual and microcosmic and worldly. Similarly, temporal dimensions allow for diverse citizens to make choices not only about where to participate, but when to do so. Thirty minutes might well make a difference in the daily organisation of how individuals and groups coordinate their participation with respect to one another. And within the course of one day, a single space or shop interior is host to a variety of participants. We need to learn when and how these space-time layers overlap and remain distinct, and what forms of meeting these layers and intersections accommodate.

Finally, I turn to adaptation or the lived capacities to respond to change, and consider how our understanding of mixing and participation would benefit from exploring the quick-footed practices of 'making do and getting by' adjacent to the longer-term practices of building enduring prospects and relationships. I position the strategies of improvisation and duration adopted by proprietors along the Walworth Road alongside the choices individuals have to develop or alter their trajectories. I therefore focus on the practice of skill as a gradual acquisition of both cultural and technical sensibility. I explore how skill, together with the inheritance of class, race and ethnicity, potentially allows for an expansion of affinities and affiliations that are cognisant of but broader than kith or kin.

2 The boundaries of belonging

Cab driver:	Oh yeah, so what are you studying?
Suzi:	How different people meet and mix on the Walworth Road.
Cab driver:	The Walworth Road?
	(Pause)
	I'm stumped, I am.
	(Pause)
	If you'd said Brick Lane, I'd understand.

(London cab driver: fieldnotes 2007)

The Walworth Road is at once a global and a local street, shaped by an intersection of world-wide migrations and displacements, and *in situ* resolutions. Its own combination of multicultural and parochial terrains is perhaps easily overlooked against more overt, acceptable or pleasing urban mixings. How do we conceptualise these concurrent processes of moving and remaining, of global and local, in the context of an ordinary street? I'd like to address this question by turning to a theme frequently evoked during my fieldwork conversations – that of the boundary. A boundary is a form of ordering that denotes a physical and perceptual moment of differentiation. Whether historic or contemporary it is a marking that commands a political and cultural attitude to crossing: a zone from which one is compelled to venture beyond; and a limit set to establish containment. The emblematic notion of a boundary as linear is therefore misleadingly sparse. Boundaries are saturated spaces in which legal and experiential markings are densely accumulated. In this sense a boundary is closer to a labyrinth than to a line and an exploration of the historic layers, dead-ends and escape routes within it would therefore lead to a similarly complex view of who belongs, where, and under what conditions.

A boundary is also an atmospheric and historic space of both transition and stasis. In this chapter I focus on the overlapping practices of staying within or moving beyond the boundaries asserted in south London over time, and draw on territorial narratives, cadastral demarcations, and the symbols of stature or denigration that come to describe a place. These mixed sources abstracted from everyday observations and local history archives serve to highlight two points of exploration. First, is the notion that past and present urban landscapes are palpably interwoven. The transgression or persistence of boundaries in Walworth today is threaded to the divisive extent of the River Thames, the organisation of poverty rooted in the eighteenth-century heightening of industrial and philanthropic zeal; and in the post-war aftermath of Empire and Commonwealth. History has merged the grey, concrete mass of Walworth's social housing estates and the tightly terraced rows of mortar and multiculture along the Walworth Road. From here stems the second notion: that to understand the intersections not only of people and places, but of pasts and presents, as so eloquently purported in Avta Brah's *Cartographies of Diaspora* (1996), the processes of containment and crossing need to be understood together. And it is in the urban margin, where land and rents are still comparatively cheap and where housing estates are plentiful, that the social and spatial boundaries of class are most likely to intersect with the on-going waves of global migration.

Movement and containment, crossing and demarcating: these are the entwined vitalities of Walworth's boundaries. The methods used to pursue the experiences of boundaries on the Walworth Road are bifocal, and are necessary to see a wider view of global space and historic time, as well as an intimate view of local settlement. The lens for distant viewing focuses on the kind of street that emerges out of global patterns of mobility, displacement and connectivity. The lens for close viewing focuses on the Walworth neighbourhood to observe what it means to pause, settle or remain in a local place. I introduce the Walworth Road through exploring what it means for diverse individuals to share street space, when some would have travelled distances across origins and nations to arrive at the Walworth Road, while others already living in proximity to the street may have seldom or never travelled.

Are the qualities of a boundary pre-determined by the rigours of power and law, or by evolving cultural and social practices? This chapter will explore two qualities of boundary closely tied to time: resistant as those firmly contained by the past, and malleable as those reshaping to accommodate a sense of the future. A frontier is a crossing that contains a sense of the imminent, a place about to be, a space of arrival and discovery, as well as uncertainty. One dimension of a frontier is transition, and I trace Walworth Road's history as a retail space continually occupied and transformed by successive waves of immigrant entrepreneurs since the 1800s. In researching the perpetual presence of migratory histories in shaping the street, I ask how ethnic and cultural differences are rendered visible or invisible. I contrast the urban frontier with the spatial and social delineations that are historically pervasive and difficult to penetrate, despite the scale and pace of change. Here I turn to the immensity of symbolic boundaries that have emerged over time and that continue to profoundly impact contemporary interactions.

The urban frontier

> I like the Walworth Road very much. One of the best roads in Southwark, got all nationalities . . . and everyone's doing what they want to do.
>
> (Mustafa, who is in his seventies and
> who grew up in Brixton: fieldnotes 2006)

A frontier exemplifies a state of change or the paradox of perpetual impermanence, and is as much a space as it is a practice of transition. Transient boundaries offer one way of conceptualising urban, as opposed to national, boundaries in the context of a dynamic and disparate global world. In her essay '*The Global City: Strategic Site/New Frontier*', Sassen (2001) emphasises the relationship between place, production and practice in the global economy. She identifies 'a new geography of centres and margins' (2001: 4), highlighting the centrality of global cities in the process of economic globalisation. Sassen also points to juxtapositions within global cities: of prestigious, service-oriented spaces of international finance; and marginal spaces occupied by those who have difficulty in accessing the formal sector. While the stratifications of urban economies, people and places are concentrated in global cities, Sassen argues for an understanding of the localisation of practices of production, moving away from the conceptualisation of 'otherness' (as immigration or ethnicity, for example) to 'newness'. Here the urban frontier and its work environments potentially represent not only a diverse collection of entrepreneurial and cultural skills, but also the possibility for urban cultures to emerge through new work practices and forms of production.

But how do we begin to observe or understand 'newness', and what methods of analysis and representation are able to capture the seemingly ephemeral experiences of arrival, discovery and transformation? During the course of my fieldwork I came to think of the Walworth Road as a deeply saturated social and spatial labyrinth. The density of networks and connections, legitimate and illicit ways of being, entrepreneurial pursuits and the on-going maintenance of a plethora of daily routines all happened behind the layer of what was apparent at first glance. While these vital invisibilities are often obscure in any social space, they seemed increasingly significant for reaching an understanding of the Walworth Road, since its visual presentation is of a somewhat messy, everyday street, without the dominant repertoire of flagship stores or easily recognisable public spaces. On the basis of visual recognition or lack thereof, it is possible to overlook or dismiss the underlying value of apparently ordinary streets like the Walworth Road.

Early on in my fieldwork in September 2006 I set out to discover, through a visual and verbal survey, where the proprietors of the independent shops along the street had come from. By tracing the respective journeys of the proprietors between the mile length of the Walworth Road and places across the world, it became possible to picture the truly world-wide criss-crossings of multiple origins, cultures and ethnicities that congregated on this street (Figure 2.1). My colleague Thiresh and I spent two weeks walking the Walworth Road, I took the east side, Thiresh took the west, and we recorded every unit along the street. We stepped into each independent shop to ask three short questions of the respective proprietors: 'How long has this shop been on the Walworth Road?'; 'Is the shop owned or rented?'; and 'What is the country that you were born in?'. Of the three questions, the one least readily answered related to ownership. To my surprise, there were only a few occasions when an interviewee was reluctant to answer any of the questions – either the proprietor was away or the proprietor or shop attendant was too busy or ill at ease to answer. In most instances, the proprietor, a family member or an associate

Figure 2.1 A map of the Walworth Road is aligned with a map of the world.

was available, and we generally had a five-minute period of grace in which to interrupt the entrepreneurial rhythm.

From this initial survey we learnt that there were 227 units along the mile length of the street. Although these units were predominantly retail, they included a small scattering of public buildings and services, such as the Newington Public Library, the Cummings Museum and the Walworth Clinic. Most shop-fronts ranged from approximately 4.5 metres for a single unit to approximately 9 metres for a double unit, indicating the density and comparatively small scale of the units that make up this retail strip. Over 60 per cent of the retail units were independent shops, neither belonging to a chain nor a franchise, and in most cases during our survey the proprietor was directly engaged in the shop activities. In the 128 independent shops we recorded on the street, we carried out 93 interviews, and discovered that there were over 20 different countries of origin amongst the proprietors, with no single place of origin predominating. England remained the relatively highest amongst the countries of origin (26 per cent), followed by Turkey (11 per cent), India (7.5 per cent), Pakistan (7.5 per cent), Ghana (5 per cent), Jamaica (5 per cent), Nigeria (5 per cent) and Vietnam (5 per cent). Afghanistan, China, Cyprus and Northern Cyprus, Iran, Ireland, Italy, Malawi, Malaysia, Sudan, Sierra Leone and Trinidad were amongst the remaining countries of origin (see the Appendix for details).

Looking back on the Walworth Road–World drawing after the fieldwork period, it is worth reflecting what kind of boundary or space of crossing is evoked by this representation. A map of the former British Empire is partly evident, reflected in the high proportion of the proprietors' countries of origin being former colonies of Britain. The juxtaposed maps of street and world also connect the 'third world' or 'developing world' to the Walworth Road, by linking places in Africa, the Middle East and the East to microcosms on this London street. While South America would have featured prominently on this drawing had I incorporated the Elephant and Castle proprietors in my survey. North America and Western Europe are largely absent from the pinpoint origins marked on the map. This provokes questions of not only why certain individuals and groups end up in or go to certain places in the city, but also why they might remain there over long periods of time.

Indeed, the process, if not the exact pattern, of immigration by entrepreneurs to the Walworth Road is historic, as confirmed by the *Post Office London Directory: Streets and Commercial Directory* (Post Office 1881–1950), an annual survey of every proprietor and his or her respective trade on London streets from the late industrial to the post-war period. Tracing the Walworth Road records across this period, there is evidence of a densely occupied retail street activated by numerous small, independent shops. Records of tailors, cheesemongers and jellied-eel caterers are tabulated alongside proprietors who had emigrated from different places including Greece, Turkey, Italy, Ireland and Eastern Europe. Of broader significance is that with increased industrialisation and urbanisation, the quantity and diversity of cultures participating in the retail life of the Walworth Road increased.

The confluence of origins, colonial pasts and disparate global development are some of the historic and contemporary themes of migration and diaspora that are evident when focusing on the Walworth Road as a form of urban frontier. However, pinpointing fulfils only one convention of map reading, and involves locating and orienting oneself by finding markers on a map. If we were to read the map like a traveller, then our attention would shift to the distances between places, and the journey needed to undertake a particular route. By shifting focus to the plethora of orthogonal lines that criss-cross between the map of the Walworth Road and the world, questions emerge as to how these multiple crossings and connections of people are experienced. How do people manage their journeys between familiar and unfamiliar worlds. and develop their lives and aspirations across these global and local 'scapes'? To focus on what kind of place and what kind of sociability emerges from these dense intersections of difference on the Walworth Road is to explore an interstitial urban landscape: the process of crossing; the shared spaces of intersection; and the effort and imagination required to travel across geographic distance and personal familiarity.

Because this drawing has flattened out different time periods to equate to the present, it shows a singular moment, and questions around the speed and scale of change, and what impetus this has on experiences of transformation are not directly prompted. While the survey had its uses of overview, I turned to ethnography to probe at the work and social practices of the diverse proprietors and their efforts to engage with their equally diverse customers within this zone of crossing. What are the modes of communication in this zone? Do they take the form of *mélange* or a density of discrete dialects? Regularity is at the core of social interactions on the Walworth Road, inculcated through the habitual practices of largely local customers whose trips to the street are closely tied to day-to-day routines and the attendance to perfunctory needs. But so too are the multilingual modes of communication required to reach a diverse populace, where proprietors artfully maintain a balance between the entrepreneurial imperative for profit, and their social and cultural connections with their customers.

In the two chapters that follow, I take the reader past the line of shop-fronts and into the interiors of Nick's Caff and Reyd's Bespoke Tailor shop. Here we will observe the up-close expressions of regularity and mixing. But for a start, I'd like to introduce the reader to a range of the small shops along the Walworth Road, and focus on the choreography of visual displays and spatial arrangements. In the texture, language and sequencing of surfaces we can observe one primary dimension of how proprietors hone their communication skills not only to entice their customers, but also to secure their return. These sequences of display are used by proprietors on the Walworth Road to combine the apparent banality of product with a density of cultural associations to attract a variegated customer base. The ways in which individual, ethnic and cultural differences are purposefully arranged serve to distinguish not only the shop products, but also the identity of the proprietor and how he or she anticipates the needs and preferences of prospective customers. The experiential particularity of each shop is therefore defined by the careful composition of a visual form of communication from shop signage, to shop-front, to the mercantile and personal items within each interior.

At this point, the reader might be inclined to question whether visual contact or material forms of display are limited forms of social exchange, which while permitting self-expression, are momentary. Simmel (1949) explored a 'light' mode of interaction through his concept of 'sociability', and emphasised its inherent social and even playful aspect by positioning the role of form over that of content. However, Simmel's sociability depends on the idea of reciprocal exchange or a basic level of social recognition, for form is empty of meaning without someone to deliver it, and someone else to respond accordingly. The proprietors on the Walworth Road use the public–private interface along the street as a space for communication, in which both personal expression and cultural translations are offered. This thick interface is therefore an available form of social legibility to be read in the presence of many cultures, and is an important first point of interaction and expression.

In many of the independent shops the displays were shaped by a combination of cultural and personal affinities. In one halal convenience shop, for example, the space was divided into two areas. The first, closest to the street, had a range of food products, including the meat counter, while the second space, further from the street, stocked food goods more oriented to North African and Muslim customers. In this second space there were pictures of Mecca and a small prayer area. The proprietor, who had recently arrived from Sudan, promoted his primary public display or his street frontage through signage in both Arabic and English, using a selection of words aimed at including a wide customer base: 'Absar Food Store. Camberwell Halal Butchers and Grocery. Afro Caribbean and Mediterranean Fresh Fruit & Veg'.

Other shop signage along the Walworth Road also represented a desire to reach a diverse customer base, sometimes with humour such as, 'Mixed Blessings Bakery. West Indian and English Bread'. Cultural amalgamation was not the only mode of hybridity represented, and signage such as 'Roze and Lawanson Nigerian Market. Money Transfer. Wedding Garments' and 'Afroworld Food Store. Cosmetics, wigs and fruit and veg' alluded to the curious combinations of merchandise and services offered within these independent shops (Figure 2.2). These tactical expressions of

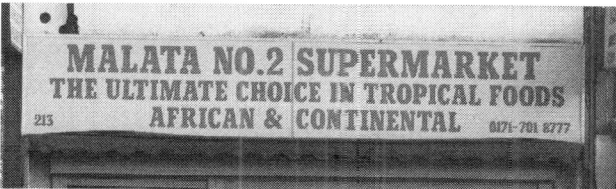

Figure 2.2
The hybrid shop signs on the Walworth Road.

combining goods and services, and culture and ethnicity, are embedded in the particularities of the Walworth Road as an aggregation of a multitude of near and far local worlds.

Sometimes spaces within shops were divided into small areas to be used or rented out separately. It was not uncommon to see small spaces of approximately 1 metre by 2 metres within the shop-front area, used for purposes such as clothes mending or phone card sales (Figure 2.3). The availability of small rental spaces within these shops was particularly apparent in barbers and salons, where chairs were rented out individually to cutters and stylists, as well as nail beauticians, on a week-by-week basis. This meant that the head lessee was exposed to less risk, while entrepreneurial access was simultaneously provided to the very small-scale operator. While these spatial subdivisions grow out of the imperative of business, they accrue a collage-like rendition of an urban high street that to the outsider may appear as messy and inchoate, but which is a carefully considered arrangement of entrepreneurial and cultural intersections. What remained consistent is the spatial pattern of a high street largely lined with small-scale increments of retail space, generally of narrow frontage, always limited to the ground floor, and with a visual and spatial identity revealed in the items and sequence of display. The spatial rhythm of small spaces could be understood as an urban framework for subjectivity, or a collective collage of global migrations made manifest in a porous urban boundary.

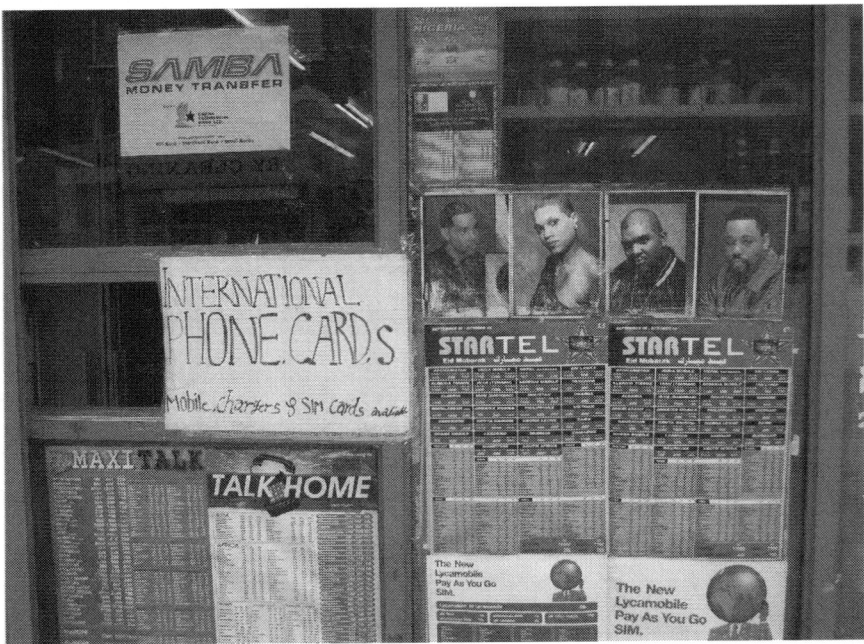

Figure 2.3 A small phone shop attached to a larger convenience shop.

However, just as the urban frontier is a space of exploration full of the potential of 'newness', so too is it an uncertain terrain. In contrast to the hybrid visual displays on the Walworth Road, narratives of place reflected a different sense of how some established residents made sense of this transient street space. The range of individuals that I spoke with used very different markers of change to encapsulate a sense of the street as shaped by the past and the present. Many of the memories of the Walworth Road were caught between fairly recent markers of a 'white' and 'working-class' street and its present associations with a far more diverse one. Mike, who was in his seventies and who moved to Walworth from the East End in the late 1980s, remembered the Walworth Road as 'ordinary, cockney-type society', despite the alternative historic account provided by the *Post Office London Directories* (1881–1950). Contrary to Mike's perception, the directory records for the Walworth Road indicate that this shop-lined street was occupied and trans-formed by both English residents and a host of 'newcomers'.

Two factors may partly explain Mike's perceptions, the first being that although the record of street proprietors reflects a level of ethnic diversity, comparable records like the census data render a far more homogeneous representation of who was occupying space in Walworth at that same time. This is important not only for an understanding of how and where local areas change and diversify during periods of economic and social restructuring. The census records are based on place of residence and represent, up until the late 1980s, a population that resided in Walworth who were largely white and born in the UK. In the 1861 census, for example, only 468 residents named as 'foreigners' (or born outside of the UK) were registered out of a total of 44,463 persons in the district of Newington (in which Walworth is incorporated). It was only in the 1991 census that a category of ethnicity was added to the census data. In contrast, a mixture of proprietors on the Walworth Road is historically captured in the stretch of this retail street. The second explana-tion refers to the differing waves of immigrants, and while the post-war wave on the Walworth Road reflects proprietors from Cyprus, Northern Cyprus, Greece, Ireland and Italy, subsequent waves from the 1980s have tended to be more variegated in both racial and ethnic terms, as confirmed by my survey. This begs the question, to be pursued in further chapters, as to what perceptions lead to a ranking of certain immigrants by Walworth residents as more acceptable than others.

Unlike Mike, Gary, who grew up in post-war Walworth and who was in his fifties, highlighted the significance of special places and related activities off the Walworth Road: 'East Street market was the main thing, people came for miles, that's the only thing that's really changed There used to be a flea market, with medals and bullets and anything from the army. And everybody knew one another. Just like a village.' Gary moved out to the suburbs as an adult and returned to the Walworth Road each weekday for work, where a microcosm of the village he remembered was sustained by the daily meeting of his close network of friends in their local caff. He talked about a slow process of transformation driven by economic change, 'Change happened slowly. I suppose 80s, 90s it changed, when the prices of the houses started going up . . . My friends are all over the world now. You can't change things, it's like a river, you just go and go.' Jack, who was not much older than Gary and who lived in Camberwell, a few bus stops to the south of Walworth, referred to the process of change as one marked by a lack of interpersonal familiarity on the street: 'I can walk up the Walworth Road today and I might not see a single person I know. When I was young, I'd walk up and know everybody. Your mates, their friends, our friends, relatives.'

What Mike, Gary and Jack's descriptions broadly chart is a perceived shift from a familiar to an unfamiliar world, one in which, according to their narratives, escalated change was more palpable from the late 1980s. The rapid dismantling and disappearance of manufacturing and industry that had been nurtured by London's river landscape had, by that stage, heralded the entry of a service-based, global economy, and with it new waves of migration. The urban frontier as a space of change, encapsulated by the Walworth Road as an entry point for the small retail and immigrant entrepreneur, continues to be a place of newness and uncertainty. The imaginative and agile entrepreneurial practices represented in the visual displays of the independent shops are as much a part of this newness as are the hesitant or resistant expressions of those for whom change is synonymous with insecurity. For the remainder of this chapter I turn to the formation and endurance of rigid boundaries within Walworth, to question in what ways official mechanisms such as social classification and spatial ranking affect capacities to cross boundaries.

Symbolic spatial order

In its way, Dragon Castle's presence in so dispiritingly hideous a centre of urban deprivation is just as incongruous as finding Jim's sitcom crumpet on the bridge of the USS Enterprise. Certainly, it's a shock to walk through a door on such a gruesome main road and be greeted by a gently splashing fountain, and to find an ocular feast of red paper dragons, tassel-strewn lanterns and golden chandeliers so luminescently vulgar, they'd be asked to leave a Las Vegas casino on the grounds of taste. Myself, I liked this retro gaudiness, and loved how it was framed, through smeary windows, by dirty red buses trundling down a filthy road on a dank, drizzly day.

(Norman 2008: Restaurant review of
Dragon Castle on the Walworth Road)

On crossing the river and reaching the Walworth Road, the reviewer of the unsuspecting Dragon's Castle is unable to restrain his caricature. Through an overcrowding of adjectives and adverbs he elicits a kind of place caught between Dickensian London and Disneyland. The review subscribes to a long-established sense of south London on the other side of the river away from dominant cultural values; a place saturated with the symbols and stigma of urban poverty. Boundaries reflect physical and perceptual patterns of distinguishing between things such as a 'here and there' and a 'them and us'. But the endurance of boundaries, as the reviewer's caustic words suggests, has much to do with ranking and relegating:

words like "vulgar" and "filthy" denote a vivid classification of the Walworth Road. To explore the *symbolic spatial order* of Walworth in its south London setting, I contrast the official mechanisms by which places and people are historically ordered with how people in Walworth see themselves. Similarly, Lamont and Molnar (2002) define boundaries as 'relational processes' between prescriptive structures and lived experiences, and emphasise how 'widely available schemas shape the drawing of boundaries within face-to-face communities' (2002: 183).

If the symbolic spatial order of a place is mutually enforced by official systems of division and cultural codes of ranking, how does the Walworth Road 'fit' in the symbolic spatial order of London? Suttles (1972) ascribed individual readings of the city to a collectively assigned 'cognitive map' or a classification of people and places accumulated through the historic and social ranking of city space. The connection between seeing places and grading the worth of people who live in these differentiated parts of the city is more recently explored by Sampson (2009). But Sampson focuses on the 'signs of disorder', referring to the 'visual clues' prompted by social signs such as 'verbal harassment' or 'public intoxication' and physical signs such as 'graffiti on buildings' and 'garbage on the streets'.

However, Sampson's analysis of visual disorder is understood through the individual agency of those who perceive disorder, without reference to the systems of power that designate order, in part constructed and regulated in the physical landscape over time. The analytic value of a symbolic spatial order is the understanding of the reciprocal processes by which boundaries are officially inculcated and regulated, their subsequent animation in the stature and texture of the physical environment, and the gradual accrual of commonly held perceptions of what a place is like and who is deemed to belong in such a locale. I would like to expand on the symbolic spatial order of Walworth through three prominent constructions of the boundary: the physical division of the River Thames; the organisation of poverty and relief made manifest in the institutions of place; and the homogenisation of the working class in the *en masse* resolution of post-war social housing estates.

The River Thames is a physical fact, a sufficiently broad and fast-moving current of water to make the ease of crossing it difficult without bridges. Even today, with the numerous bridges spanning between north and south, the physical and mental process of crossing the river features prominently in descriptions that combine the effects of division and distance. In *Soft City*, Jonathan Raban articulates the perceptual distance asserted by the river between a London to the north and south of the watery divide: 'I have friends who live in Clapham, only three miles away, but to visit them is a definite journey, for it involves crossing the river' (1974: 163). Similarly, in my conversations with local Walworth residents, the Thames was often used to position local ways of life as distinctive from the north of the river, and describing oneself as a 'South Londoner' was a popular construction. The impetus of the boundary effect of the Thames is culturally cumulative, incorporating both physical and imagined divisions (Figure 2.4).

In Gary Robson's research (2000) on south-east London, he too makes explicit reference to a cultural disposition that has historically emerged out of a way of

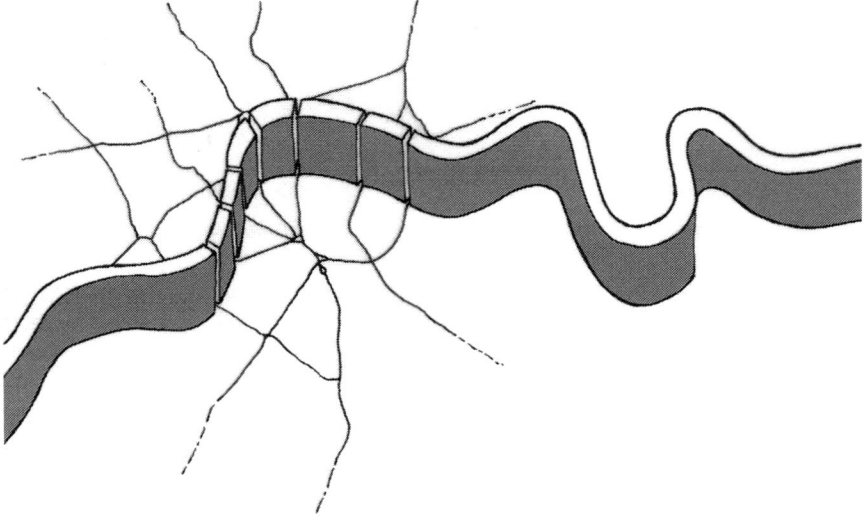

Figure 2.4 The physical and perceptual boundary effect of the River Thames.

characterising what he refers to as the 'unruly' south, one which in part relates to the location of South London on the *other side* of the River Thames. Robson's analysis of a 'South-East London habitus', points to the mutually reinforcing portrayal of, and tendency towards, representations and enactments of local culture: 'They express ways of thinking about the area which I suggest informs both external attributive representations of it by the symbolic repertoire of cultural identifications subscribed to and utilised by sections of its population' (2000: 40–3).

The Thames as a symbolic urban boundary, narrated as division, distance and differentiation, is historically emphasised by the divergent form and pace of urban development across London over time. The morphological and economic disparities between the two areas north and south of the River Thames is acutely described by Peter Ackroyd as an enduring 'urban discrimination' (2001: 692). In my time at the Southwark Local History Library, I worked my way through their collection of historic maps, and was struck by the persistence of the north–south urban distinction particularly evident in various maps of London commissioned up to the industrial period. I have selected three maps – Hogenberg's map of London (1553), Roque's map of London (1769) and Greenwood's map of London (1824) – to illustrate not only the chronological persistence of London's north–south divide, but also its morphological disparities that suggest connections between political, spatial and social forms of order. In working with these historic maps the challenge was therefore not only to trace the changing form of urban development over time, but also to search for the cartographic clues and cultural symbols that pointed to ways of life. I began by relating patterns of urban form including territorial demarcations, extents of land ownership and the distribution of public and social institutions, to the emergence of ways of life and associated cultural references within a local place.

While it may seem incongruous in an ethnography of contemporary life to refer back almost five centuries to Hogenburg's map of London (1553), this early representation emphasises a London formed of two distinct sides. To the north of the River Thames is a city of impressive walls, great streets and prominent public spaces and institutions. Only one bridge extends southwards; where London Bridge touches the South Bank, a comparatively diminutive cluster of urban development is shown. Routes appear as a primary feature of the pattern of development in the south, and the relationship of London to the hinterland in the south was established via connections that had not only practical but also spiritual significance. Two Roman roads, later referred to as Kennington Park Road and Newington Causeway that border the area of Walworth today, connected 'Londinium' with Canterbury and its cathedral in the south. While very little built form is shown south of the Thames, there are large tracts of land, including gardens and fields. Of enduring urban significance are two persistent qualities: of a subsidiary area south of the river; and of an area connected to the city and to hinterland via critical through routes, spatial qualities that continue to define the relationship of the Walworth area and the Walworth Road to London today.

At this point, I'd like to focus explicitly on the historic organisation of poverty in Walworth, made apparent in the institutional forms of power that crucially regulated not only poverty, but also relief. Zooming in on Roque's map of London (1769), an image of London prior to the full impetus of the industrial revolution, the small cluster of development adjacent to the Walworth Road is constituted by the territory of Walworth Manor and the manor house. Walworth village is surrounded by extensive portions of open land, predominantly held in church ownership or designated as public commonage. The domain of Walworth Manor designates a local boundary established through small patches of territory that were contained by the scale of the authority of the manor house and parish, or gentry and church. It is a sense of small territory that persists today, with some established Walworth residents still referring to 'my manor'. Evans too (2006) describes the experience of London as a city of villages in her ethnography based on a white working-class community in Bermondsey, which neighbours Walworth to the east. She points to the historic development of London through the constellation of local territories that were individually regulated and experienced, even today, as separate from one another:

> My assumption about white working class homogeneity quickly dissolved and I learned what anyone moving through working-class London ought to know: the city is historically divided into manors, which were, and sometimes continue to be, closely defined territories about which people are often fiercely proud and protective.

(2006: 19)

But how were the boundaries of these 'closely defined territories' regulated, and why does this scale of territory persist in how locals understand the extents of their local domains today? One crucial connection can be traced to how the parish administered its authority during the period of exponential population growth and increase in poverty associated with the industrial era. By following the strand of how poverty was historically regulated in Walworth during industrial urbanisation, it is possible to draw links to the endurance of high indices of deprivation in Walworth today. The 1801 census for Walworth, designated then as the 'Parish of St Mary Newington', indicates there was a population of 14,847 people. The near ten-fold pace of growth is reflected in the population figure for 1881 of 107,850. The urban poverty that expanded alongside this growth was officially recorded and managed, and from Himmelfarb's important thesis on *The Idea of Poverty: England in the Early Industrial Age* (1984), we are directed towards the crucial analytical connection between the way in which not only poverty but also relief was conceptualised and administered.

The entry for 1770 in the *Poor Rate Book* from the Parish of St Mary Newington (Walworth) described the Parish as being: 'burdened with numerous and expensive poor' (cited in Boast 2005: 6). The characterisation of the urban poor as burden reflects the patriarchal relationship between pauper and parish as defined by the *Old Poor Law* of 1601. The *Old Poor Law* established an institutional partnership between centralised authority and its decentralised local parishes, where charity was parish-centred and locally administered. Poor rates were raised from local taxes on property, and a classification system was developed to define whether the potential recipient would qualify for relief. The enduring identification of 'the worthy' versus 'the unworthy' poor, which continues to circulate in the current political arena, was defined through official terms of categorisation based on the ideology of social hierarchy and the dissemination of charity.

The purpose of briefly introducing the profound effect of the Poor Laws on the structure of English society is to highlight not only the way the poor were viewed and administered, but to consider the impact of the institutionalisation of poverty on spatial and social boundaries in Walworth today. Haylett (2001) draws on the enduring legacy of the categorisation of the poor through the discourse of 'welfare' that has politically circulated in the UK since the emergence of 'a post-World-War-2 welfare state' (2001: 354). Haylett focuses on the formulation of New Labour welfare policies since 1997, and the representations of the poor in the arena of politics, press and academy as the 'underclass', in particular the portrayal of the white working-class poor as 'socially excluded', 'welfare dependent', 'lowlife', 'losers' and 'yobs' (2001: 354). Since the Conservative-Liberal Democrat political alliance in 2010, the vocabulary is charged with a moral fervour, where the measure of acceptability is best exemplified by 'working families'. The political rhetoric of reform, as both Himmelfarb's and Haylett's theses reveal, is one in which the understanding of poverty itself is replaced by the regulation of relief. In the process of administering relief, the necessary focus on the underlying structural conditions of poverty is shifted to the ranking of the poor.

The cultural work of social ranking is in part achieved by caricature, and the caricature of decline attached to poor or working-class bodies is one firmly entrenched in the English cultural imagination, perhaps no more deftly crafted than by the writers of Victorian London such as Charles Dickens and Henry Mayhew.

The stigma attached to working-class physicality, attire, gesture and accent are equally evoked in the textures of underclass spaces, and spatial forms of political control can be seen as symbolic codes that influence ways that people and places are collectively viewed, as well as the ways individuals in these places come to view themselves. This is made evident in the types of institutions that emerged in Walworth to provide for and control the poor during periods of heightened economic change.

Although the area to the south of the Thames remained comparatively undeveloped until the early 1800s when contrasted with the north, Greenwood's map of London (1824) surfaces a pattern of urban development in the south that had begun to cluster around the intersections and edges of primary routes. A node of public facilities had developed at the Elephant and Castle, which Dickens referred to in *Bleak House* (1852) as 'a street of little shops lying somewhere in that ganglion of roads from Kent to Surrey [. . .] centring at the far-famed Elephant' (cited in Young 1930). With the Elephant and Castle acting as the nerve centre for the south it was increasingly encircled by successive waves of transport ushered in by technological innovations, from the horse-drawn buses (1829) and trams (1852), to the railway and station (1862) and tube stop (1890). As modes of transport assisting the north–south connection, streets like the Walworth Road transformed into urban high streets, pulsating with activity and central to the life and livelihoods of the diverse communities that formed adjacent to its edges. This quality of the urban street as a vibrant connector located within an area but also linking to other areas, served partially to expand the sense of the Walworth Manor boundary as a small and contained territory.

However, in contrast with the emergence of an active retail strip along the Walworth Road, Greenwood's map also reveals the new kinds of institutions that had emerged to cater for the rescaling of the city under the forces of urbanisation. On it Bedlam Hospital (1815), infamous for its incarceration of 'the insane', marks the current location of the Imperial War Museum and Walworth Manor has expanded into Walworth New Town. Only a few decades on, Collins' *Standard Map of London* (1870) shows a number of workhouses within or in proximity to Walworth New Town. The prisons and workhouses symbolise the new nineteenth-century systems of order and surveillance in place to regulate the burgeoning scale of poverty. Jeremy Bentham's published scheme for pauper management (1796) exemplifies the shift in sentiment from locally administered charity on the part of the parish to a centralised regime of management oriented around large-scale, privately operated institutions. Scrutiny (Bentham used the term 'inspection') was coupled with profitability, thereby rendering the poor as productive inmates.

The *New Poor Law* (1834) introduced the legal articulation of a new view of poverty and relief, one that reclassified the poor on the principle of 'less-eligibility' thereby limiting relief for 'the able-bodied' (Himmelfarb 1984). The governance of relief was reconceptualised on the basis of publicly administered (but often privately operated), centralised management. The *Consolidated General Order* (1847) established the rules for the organisation of the workhouse, and the procedure for defining the 'inmate' through systematic regulation dependent on social classification and spatial segregation: the *admission* of pauper, subject to examination in an examination room, cleansing and dressing in a uniform; the *classification* of the pauper into one of seven classes and the assignment of a corresponding ward within the workhouse; the *division* of the pauper's day into intervals for sleep, work and eating, signalled by the ringing of a bell; the *direction* of the diet of the pauper; and the *punishment* of the pauper on the qualification of 'disorderly' or 'refractory' conduct.

What was the impact of such a profound regime of surveillance, classification and control, and how did this affect the individual and collective sense of working-class identity in Walworth? Institutions like the workhouse served as spaces to exert authority over citizens within its walled interiors through the sense of pervasive observation as the ultimate form of control (Foucault 1977). But the symbolic effect of power transcended outside the walls of the institution too, imposing on the institutionalised individual the label of shame, and imposing on urban poor the all too visible threat of the workhouse. Institutions like the workhouse shaped the particularity of the working-class landscape at the turn of the nineteenth century, and although the physical presence of workhouses continued into the early twentieth century, their symbolic endurance is inscribed in the collective memories of place.

How boundaries persist

It is easy to overlook the inky workhouse institutions on historic maps, without regard for their impact on the collective memory of the working class today. The places and institutions that were central to how working-class life was lived are embedded in personal memories, as is etched in the tone and content of Collins' aforementioned book, *The Likes of Us: A Biography of the White Working Class* (2004). Amongst his descriptions of the cultural spaces claimed by the Walworth working class, such as the music halls, gin palaces and penny gaffs, are his descriptions of the spaces imposed on the working class, exemplified by the workhouse. Collins' story reveals the historic accumulation of the regulation and confinement of poverty and class. The symbolic impact of the institutions in which both poverty and relief were organised saturates the sense of an area over time and plays an enduring role in how people and places are viewed from both the inside and the outside.

Thus the symbolic spatial order of a place may serve to reinforce the boundaries that confine and relegate people to place. The emblematic strength of institutions serves not only to inculcate power, but to visually portray a social ranking of people and spaces through the cognitive maps that Suttles described, in which spatial symbols are key. The complexity of life in a local place is easily reduced to caricatures and stereotypes, to be sustained long past the existence of the actual institution. Bhabha (1994) contributes to our understanding of the work that the stereotype does in the context of colonial discourse, specifically through how otherness is constructed. His definition of a threefold process of how the stereotype is authorised can be applied to the organisation of poverty and relief in places like Walworth: the creation of a 'subject people' or the urban poor; the validation of their subjugation in this case through the imperative of relief; and the institution and maintenance of regimes of control as so explicitly exemplified in the workhouse.

In tracing the historic maps of Walworth culminating in the height of the industrial era, we have explored how social ranking or authorised systems of classification are made culturally visible. Differentiation (and in particular relegation) lies at the heart of the ranking process described, but in the section that follows I'd like to expand on the apparent antithesis of this approach, and explore the effects of the homogenisation of people and place. Both ways of producing the stereotype through caricature (based on exaggeration) and standardisation (based on simplification) rely on the power of an evocative image or characterisation shaped within an established system of order. Williams (1958) referred to the making of 'the "masses" formula' as the purposeful homogenisation of the working class, arguing that 'there are in fact no masses, but only ways of seeing people as masses' (1958: 18).

I would like to pursue the physical construction of 'the masses formula' by turning to the large-scale, post-war social housing estates in proximity to the Walworth Road. The largest of these are the Heygate Estate (1970–1974) comprising 1,194 units, and the Aylesbury Estate (1963) comprising 2,700 units, making it the largest estate in Europe within one contained area. For the outsider, the Aylesbury Estate is synonymous with social decline, and it was the place Tony Blair selected to underscore Labour's promise to defeat poverty and overcome social exclusion at the start of Labour's election victory in 1997.

Although the social housing projects were envisaged as a modern solution for replacing derelict and or war damaged housing, one of its significant consequences most evident in large-scale, inner city estates of 500 units or more (Power 1996) is extreme polarisation. Power's research (1987, 1996) and that of Power and Tunstall (1991) and Power and Wilson (2000) reveal the cumulative effects of scale together with spatial and social exclusion, or 'area-based poverty' within such housing estates in England and Wales. Power's valuable work shows how 'estate stigma' is attached to places and people as forms of social labelling that have enormous resilience and are extremely difficult to alter, particularly when they are constituted in large-scale territories. Stigmas operate simultaneously as reflective and predictive; that is they perpetuate a reputation gained over time, and they project that reputation into the present and future, as enduring symbols of people and place.

John, who described himself as 'a local council tenant', recalls the stigmatisation of living in a large social housing estate to the south of Walworth:

> We lived in Peckham, in a council house my family, big family. We had a garden, we had a dog, and then when I was five years old the council decided to regenerate Peckham and they tore all those houses down. I mean it was miles and miles of, of, council housing, and destroyed the communities that lived there and built the notorious North Peckham Estate, which was opened in the 70s. So what really happened was the tight-knit kind of community that I first lived in was just literally destroyed overnight. I mean it was a terrible, terrible

thing that happened to the area. I don't think the area ever recovered, because since then, as you know, they have regenerated Peckham again, by tearing down the North Peckham Estate. So what I say is, 'What Hitler failed to do during the Blitz, Southwark Council have done twice in my life-time.' (laughs) [. . .] My grandparents ended up in Wood Dene in Peckham, which is now about to be, at last, demolished. We called it 'The Kremlin', and in fact the bus conductor used to say, 'Anyone for the Kremlin?' and we used to jump off the bus. It was awful. A horror estate.

(Interview 2007)

John's powerful memory of fortification and imprisonment attached to the place in which his family lived echoes with other descriptions of other estates. One resident likened the isolation of her estate to, 'being on a desert island' (Power and Tunstall 1991), while Foster's (1995) residents in an east London housing estate associate the containment of their estate with 'Alcatraz', and go on to relate the concrete form with 'a *prison*'. In these cases the sense of stigma is strongly characterised by the combined effects of spatial segregation, large-scale monolithic forms, and concrete materiality.

John goes on to talk about the contemporary social implications of large-scale physical segregation:

Each council estate is territorial, we don't talk to each other, we don't mix with each other. It's not that we don't like each other. It's just that we're so overpopulated, so many tower blocks and concrete buildings, we become very insular on our estates and very protective. There is communication at some levels. We do have the local forum where the representatives from each estate are elected to talk about funding – you know, which estate needs new lifts, or whatever. But other than that we don't socialise or integrate. And then you've got the class division.

(Interview 2007)

John's narrative of territoriality coupled with insularity is more than simply an individual perception, and it raises the question of how to penetrate the symbolic and social boundaries around the monolithic housing estate structures that feature prominently in Walworth's urban landscape. It is a crucial consideration, pointing in part to the need for other kinds of spaces and meeting grounds, and in part to Southwark Council's contemporary legacy as 'the largest social landlord in London, with nearly 40,000 tenants and 14,000 leaseholders' (Thompson and Abery 2006: 5). During the years of inflated economic prosperity that led up to the global economic crisis in 2008, the regeneration of the Heygate and Aylesbury Estates was commissioned. The progress of both projects has been tempered by the recession. Both processes rely on piece-by-piece infill projects, which may assist in dismantling the perceptual scale of these worlds. Both processes also rely on the insertion of a number of private units to subsidise the regeneration projects, and the proximity of these estates to the centre of London underwrites the strategic market value of these estates. The profound risk, agitated by recent political propositions to reduce the subsidies on public housing rentals, is that well-located social housing estates, such as the Heygate and Aylesbury, will be subject to market speculation and gentrification, and with it a gradual eradication of the urban poor from the important prospects and conveniences of the inner London.

It is therefore, not only the effects of stigma that feature in narratives of post-war regeneration in working-class areas, but also the expression of loss. The impetus of marginalisation is revealed in the expressions of how ordinary people in Walworth have been separated from their past: 'I have been astonished at the extent to which things, once commonplace, have now vanished . . . Redevelopment struck the final blow at the pre-war communities so, in just a few decades, a way of life practically vanished' (Carter 1985: Preface). Carter's observation of profound change in Southwark is of redevelopment processes dismantling working-class communities and their associated ways of life. Regeneration can be indiscriminate in its eradication; places that are valued, rituals and events that are enacted, simply disappear.

Boast's (2005) and Bourne's (2005) books deal with the local history of Walworth and Southwark, respectively and in many ways they are descriptions of eradication and omission. Their historic accounts refer to the institutions and destinations within Southwark that belong to bygone eras: the Royal Surrey Zoological Gardens, which attracted a 8,000 visitors a day; the Royal Surrey Music Hall and its great glass construction predating the Crystal Palace; and the sturdy Metropolitan Tabernacle hosting acclaimed evangelical and musical performances. But the gardens, entertainment halls and movie houses are no longer evident on current cartography, and many of Southwark's historic institutions have disappeared from the map. In the Walworth area, however, this is the consequence not sub-stantially or solely of war damage suffered in the Blitz, but of a persistent cycle of regeneration programmes, named by one local historian as 'the dead hand of official intervention'.

The theme of large-scale regeneration in Southwark is ongoing and the Elephant and Castle, and the Heygate and Aylesbury Estates are a central part of Southwark's regeneration plans. But images of regeneration tend to re-assert the cultural value of the north over the south and emphasise the proximity of St Paul's Cathedral, Tate Modern and the London Eye as key to the area's potential regeneration. While the connection to the north is undoubtedly important, the limited recognition of existing, locally significant landmarks, suggests the propensity for regeneration initiatives to look towards the symbolic confidence captured by the image of London to the north of the Thames. It is still too early to evaluate whether the regeneration processes will be able to reconcile the diverse cultures along the Walworth Road with new urban forms that symbolise greater affluence and new ways of life in the local area. Boundaries are being redrawn, but will they take the expression of crossing or containment?

Conclusions

The city street is at once a line and a labyrinth: a link connecting people and places, and an alignment of urban rooms formed by an edge to the front and an aggregation of sub-worlds to the rear. The fronts are extroverted in their urban nature: they align to meet the foreground city, making themselves visible through their shop-front surfaces inscribed with entrepreneurial and cultural motives. On the Walworth Road their visual order is collage and their language multilingual, surfacing an urban frontier of migration and multiculture that is as contemporary as it is historic. To the rear are a series of social and spatial territories that have over the centuries been maintained by law and life; by the on-going conversation between power and culture. The order conferred by authority is symbolic, made visible in the spaces and memories of poverty and class. To come to basic terms with Walworth as an urban margin in the inner city, thinking through the urban boundary as simultaneously a place of crossing and of containment, allows for wide and near views of past and present, and global and local.

Urban frontiers like the Walworth Road are places of cultural vitality set within small territories encumbered with historic boundaries. Here the frontier is a space of inclusion and exclusion, and social life on the Walworth Road relates in part to the possibilities of 'newness', in part to the constraints of deprivation. Core to this chapter is how boundaries become legible; how the perceptual substance of their urban dimensions are read and interpreted. In exploring the intersections of new and established residents on the Walworth Road, I have contrasted two different forms of legibility. The first is exemplified by the hybrid shop-fronts of independent shops along the Walworth Road. Displays are generally temporary, and signs, products and spatial arrangements are regularly adapted to the aspirations of the proprietor and the anticipated needs of the client. These displays are eclectic and ephemeral, and evoke a messy and temporary streetscape to the passer-by.

The second is evident in the cumulative effects of different forms of authority. These include: the cultural dominance signified strongly by the division between north and south London marked by the Thames; the rigorous classification of the urban poor and the organisation of the provision of relief; and the homogenisation of the working-class population in the provision of large-scale social housing estates such as the Heygate and the Aylesbury. These historic containments made visible by patterns of dominance, standardisation and fragmentation are resilient over extensive time periods, reinforced by the combined schemas of landscape, territory, law and access to public resources. Classification and ranking appear as consistent mechanisms for supporting these schemas.

It is remarkably easy, on the basis of our visual perceptions, to overlook or dismiss the underlying complexities of life and livelihoods on the Walworth Road. But the intimacies by which different individuals meet and mix is barely perceivable in the visual displays or symbolic orders of the urban margin. To reach the nuanced dimensions of small spaces, to hear and watch the accumulation of gestures and intonations into interaction and exchange, requires other forms of sensory engagement. Moving off the street, away from scrutiny, ranking, 'cognitive mapping' or 'signs of disorder', we now retreat into the sub-worlds of the city, and into two interiors off the Walworth Road. For the presence of life on this multi-ethnic street further complicates the generalised rendition of the boundaries and symbols of the urban margin. Onwards then, to 'large matters in small kingdoms'. [1]

Notes

1   My thanks to Julian Barnes (2011) for the elegance of his description.

3   The art of sitting

Nick's Caff is a small meeting place in a large and rapidly changing city. Within the interior off the street, experiences of belonging span from the vast distance of global migrations into London, down to which table regular customers feel comfortable to sit at. Those who occupy the tables in Nick's Caff include the remnants of a white working-class neighbourhood alongside first, second and third generations of immigrants. Together they offer us a view of the impact of global change on local life. In Nick's Caff the 'foreigner' and 'local' sit literally and conceptually at the same table: both are migrants of a sort by the sheer force of profound change. The first migrant is one displaced from a familiar sense of place or culture by virtue of distance; the émigré who has travelled away from one place to another, usually in pursuit of better prospects. Nick's father emigrated from Cyprus to London in the 1950s. After working his way up in restaurant kitchens, Nick's father bought a caff off the Walworth Road, and named it *The Bosphorus* in homage to a cultural homeland elsewhere. Since the 1960s the Caff and flat above it has served as Nick's family home and workplace.

The second migrant at the table is one who has seldom or never travelled, but is dislodged from a familiar place because of radical alterations to ways of life and livelihoods in the city and neighbourhood. This migrant is the traveller of accelerated time, and includes the locals on the Walworth Road who have witnessed substantial transformations to the local landscape compressed over the past four decades. Crucial to this exploration of how 'newcomers' and 'established residents', or migrants of distance and of time, come to know one another, is the shared space of Nick's Caff. Across the regular occupation of the sixteen tables in the Caff, conversations and routines reveal how the remnants of a white, working-class community engage with urban change, how the composition of a Cypriot family has extended to include friends and regulars, and how three generations of Nick's and his wife Dorah's families have straddled 'being foreign' and 'being local'.

The occupation of the Caff is organised by socially acquired measures of space, time and etiquette, allowing individuals to claim a place to sit within the rhythm of the day, while participating in the performances that regulate conversation, eye contact, distance and intimacy. Interactions in the Caff were sustained through regular attendance – in some cases by individuals who have used the Caff most days of the week over decades. My own ritual of sitting in the Caff most mornings over a ten-month period yielded observations of how an array of regulars reconstitute their sense of being local. But narratives of displacement, fear and bigotry also prevailed. The sense of belonging fluctuates for both established residents and newcomers, all of whom, in the context of deep urban change, reconcile their parallel experiences of being in place and at home and being misplaced and alienated. From this ordinary space off an ordinary street, small and large questions emerge: how do day-to-day and face-to-face forms of contact influence a local sense of belonging?; and, what kinds of space provide meeting points for a far more variegated, dislocated public?

To relegate Nick's Caff solely to the status of an eating establishment would be to overlook its role as a local meeting place in the city. Its semi-public interior hosts a multitude of urban rituals, where people converse and others watch, some congregate in groups, while others exercise their preference to remain on their own. Nick's Caff provides a base to consider the complexities of belonging in a local place like the Walworth Road: it is long established; it is used regularly by born-and-bred locals and by a range of newcomers; and its sociability extends from the solidarity of an extended family of relatives and friends to the more singular practices of diverse individuals. The Caff is a contemporary urban venue in which to explore a located urban sociability, or an ordinary cosmopolitanism as advanced by Paul Gilroy (2006) – based on a congregation of difference where both conviviality and contestation are at hand.

The regularity and probing subliminally integral to everyday acts of belonging are expanded in this chapter through the three frames of *work, allegiances* and *divisions*. The space and practice of *work* is the essential starting point to unpacking how diverse individuals interact in the Caff. It is not simply that the Caff is a work place and social space in which life and livelihoods overlap. More acutely the Caff is a local space where the stakes are raised: for the proprietor there is the question of securing and maintaining the support of a varied clientele. For the customer there is the question of how to claim a piece of space to regularly occupy, while observing established codes of conduct. Importantly, the Caff is also an extension of home by virtue of the sustained regularity over months and years of many of its customers. Within this intimate territory, personal matters, updates on football and heated political discussions were all aired. Enactments of *allegiance* and assertions of *divisions* occurred within this combined establishment of home, work and leisure.

The public uses of work

The emergence of the London caff required the symbiosis of at least two cultures to forge its qualities for a particular kind of meeting and eating in the city. These included the initiation of a casual and affordable eating establishment brought largely by Italian immigrants to London in the 1950s, and the take-up of a local, sociable place by the urban working class to eat home-cooked food away from home (Heathcote 2004). The London caff emerged across the imaginations of cultures, and across the Formica tabletops and accompaniments of malt vinegar and brown sauce it has come to encompass other migrant and minority groups, including Greek, Turkish and Cypriot proprietors, and a range of customers, including those from a changing working class.

Nick's Caff emerged as a social space on the Walworth Road out of the initial efforts of Nick's parents, who emigrated to London from Cyprus in the 1950s. Since then, the demographics of the local Walworth population have diversified considerably. The demise of the Docks in the 1980s synonymised the erasure of industry and manufacturing from London's productive capacity and heralded the loss of working-class jobs. Ethnic diversity, a result of immigration, progressively increased in Walworth, as quantified in the 1991 and 2001 census. The trend evidenced toward the end of the twentieth century was a parallel increase in the economic and spatial disparity of London's landscape (Hamnett 2003). The loss of familiarity, and the impact of displacement through the economic forces of globalisation, begs the question of where people meet in the changing city to voice fears, to forge affiliations, and to participate in meeting spaces outside of the domestic or ethnic realm. Are the prospects for intercultural meeting as Sennett (1996) observed in the multicultural terrain of Greenwich Village, spaces where different individuals come together, but essentially remain apart; a form of courteous but distanced co-location?

Writers exploring the deep structural divisions within the multicultural city, and the ghettoisation of groups by ethnicity and income groups, question whether prestigious forms of public space, or what Gilroy (2006) refers to as 'emblematic public culture', have a role in accommodating productive meeting grounds between diverse individuals and groups. As previously highlighted, Ash Amin's (2002) acute analysis of the tumultuous frictions in Oldham, Burnley and Bradford in 2001 explicitly turns away from the set of established public spaces in the foreground of the city as a meeting ground. He argues that spaces of fleeting occupation do little by way of actively engaging different individuals in sustained interaction. Amin's alternative – 'micro-publics' – emphasises local meeting spaces of regular engagement where there is a shared stake, one in which, I will argue, involvement is heightened by face-to-face contact. Bhabha (2004 [1994]) adds to this sense of alternative publics by asserting that it is in the interstitial spaces of the city, neither overtly public nor domestic, that intercultural social life can be accommodated and experienced. I'd like to pursue the role of micro or interstitial publics by thinking through the idea of a 'prosaic public': a space of habitual, local and up-close forms of contact, the uses of which, at the very least, are to include diverse individuals in shared space.

Workplace

Nick's Caff exemplified a fairly old fashioned interior, and felt almost as if one was stepping into the 1960s, to the time when Nick's Dad first bought the cafe and named it *The Bosphorus*. In it were sixteen tables comprising four unequal rows, and a clear designation through routine and preference of who used which table. Family and regulars sat upfront closest to Nick at the counter. People who came to the Caff for a meal or for company, but preferred less engagement tended to sit at the sides. This is where I sat, with my back to the street so that I had a full view of the Caff but from where, behind my book or cup of coffee I felt less conspicuous. Nick was usually at the front counter adjacent to the steps leading up to his family's home above the shop. Dorah's presence in the Caff was more intermittent, as her time was divided between serving in the Caff, helping in the kitchen and being at home. Behind the counter was a hatch to the kitchen basement, and above it were the chalkboard menus of standard meals and daily specials. These included breakfast variations of egg and chips, and traditional English meals like steak and kidney pie, spotted dick and jam roly-poly. The cheapest item on the menu and one frequently ordered was a mug of tea, and for 50p a pensioner or those who popped in during the day had a local place to spend time.

Key to its appropriation by its customers, the Caff was a place to go to regularly, either spontaneously or as part of a routine. It was a place where one could do nothing much without being moved on; there was no institutional setting or formal membership required for being there. One may go through the formality of ordering a cup of tea, but more importantly the Caff was a place where one could spend time and take your time. Tables were solid-framed timber with easy-to-wipe Formica tops, set with the relatively standard collection of malt vinegar, brown sauce, tomato sauce, and salt and pepper (Figure 3.1). Chairs were the same solid timber and were robust and comfortable. A large TV commanded prime position on one sidewall where a poster of a Van Gogh painting had been demoted to make way for the flat screen. The TV played soaps and reality television, and on special occasions, football.

Figure 3.1 Formica tabletops and standard accompaniments.

Front doors to the shop were set back from the street, and once you had stepped in from the pavement you were in the throng of the place. Nick's Caff was unimposing from the outside and the fairly conventional sign above the shop suggested little other than an ordinary eating establishment off the street. The seclusion of the private home above the shop was evidenced from the street in the domestic paraphernalia of net curtains and wilted pot plants. The Caff's position between the public thoroughfare outside and the home above was significant to how individuals appropriated space in the semi-public interior off the street (Figure 3.2).

Daily rhythm

The daily rhythm of occupation of Nick's Caff was integral to its space, a central feature of which was the propinquity of work and home. The Caff opened between six thirty and seven in the morning and closed approximately twelve hours later. It remained open seven days a week, but closed on Sundays before lunch. Each year in August Nick and Dorah took two weeks leave to visit their second home in Cyprus, closing the Caff over that period. Beyond the limited reprieve of Sunday afternoons and their two-week period of annual holiday, Nick and Dorah's working

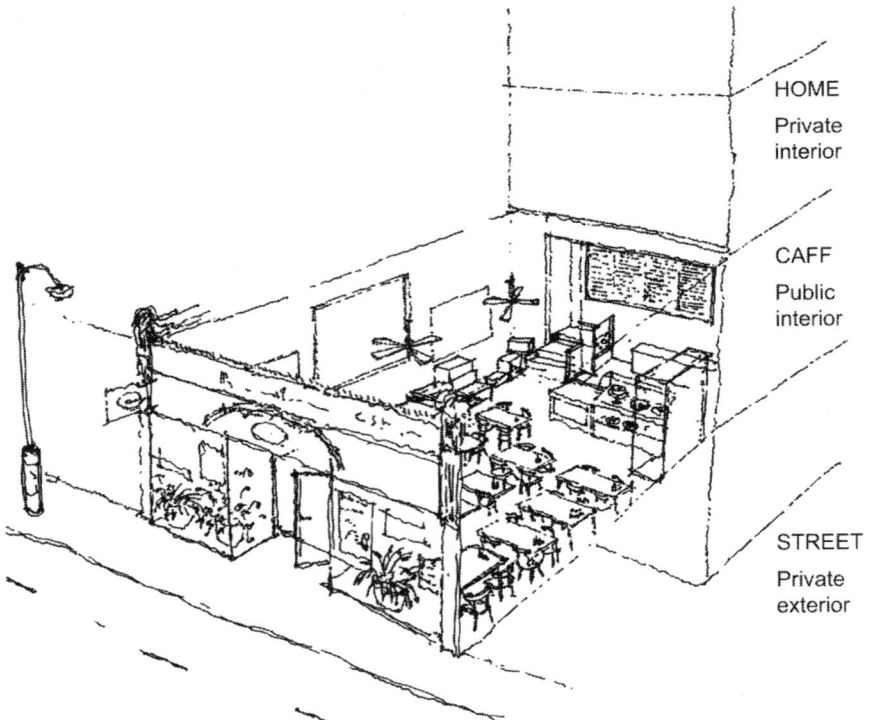

HOME
Private interior

CAFF
Public interior

STREET
Private exterior

Figure 3.2 Sketch of Nick's Caff, between the public street and the home above.

hours were long and demanding. Their working lives required sustained interaction on a daily basis with a range of personalities, each with their preferences and peculiarities.

Within the daily rhythm of work and occupation within the Caff, a spatial and temporal structure emerged that accommodated the routines, fluctuations and nuanced requirements of both Nick and Dorah's family and their varied customers. The rhythm of the Caff across the day brought moments of intensity and relative quiet, and the predictable variations of tempo allowed for different patterns of sociability across the day. The space of the Caff was therefore delineated not only by the physical separation of the tables, but also by the bands of time throughout the day, accommodating the waves of different kinds of clientele at particular intervals (Figure 3.3).

There were peak time periods when the Caff was fairly full. The first customers of the weekday were generally on their way to work, and either stopped in briefly for a takeaway or stayed for a quick breakfast. Around ten in the morning the Caff began to fill visibly and audibly, mostly with construction workers from sites in the area as well as people from local workshops and small industries. At lunchtime the third set of regulars came in and included workers from local offices, shops and institutions. This time period also incorporated once-a-week groups such as the young mentally handicapped adults from Cambridge House, who helped themselves to drinks from the fridge and engaged Nick in jokes and banter. Around five in the afternoon, the most persistent regulars settled in around the two family tables. They sat there until Nick and Dorah closed up at six thirty.

Aside from Nick and Dorah's family, this group included locals who had been coming to the Caff for years. Sonja, who was in her late sixties and was born in and grew up in Walworth, came to the Caff before the start of her working day, returning at the end of it. She had met her late partner in the Caff. Sonja was often joined by her daughter and her teenage grandson who occasionally did his homework at the Caff table, and it appeared as if the front table of Nick's Caff was an extension of her living room, her place where she socialised with family and friends. Mike, who was in his seventies and lived on his own, often strolled across from his flat in the sheltered housing for the elderly, accommodation that Nick had helped him to secure. He regularly joined this extended 'family', and dismissed the people at the sheltered housing with an irritated flick, asserting, 'This is where my friends are.'

Although local shop workers came in and out during the day, and the odd person popped in for tea and late lunch or early dinner, there were particular lulls in the rhythm of the Caff. The consistency and duration of these lulls were legible to customers, and it was often individuals on their own, and in particular pensioners, who would use the Caff during these interim periods. For the price of a cup of tea, the pensioner could comfortably occupy a table for the two hours between the mid morning and afternoon peaks, without overstaying their welcome.

Aside from the noticeable groups of regulars who used the Caff, there were individuals who frequented the Caff as part of their daily or weekly routines. People on shift work or piecework away from home, like Dave who was a forklift operator,

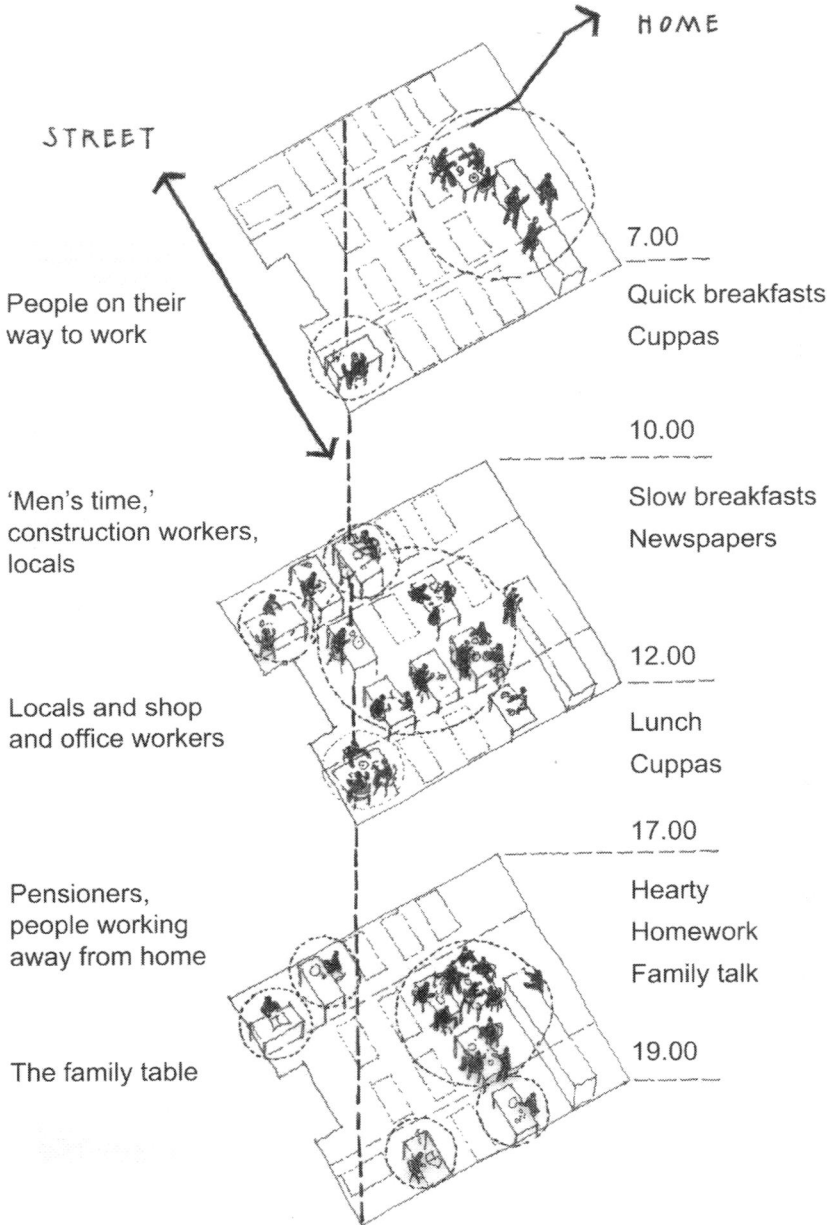

STREET

HOME

7.00

People on their
way to work

Quick breakfasts

Cuppas

10.00

'Men's time,'
construction workers,
locals

Slow breakfasts

Newspapers

12.00

Locals and shop
and office workers

Lunch

Cuppas

17.00

Pensioners,
people working
away from home

Hearty

Homework

Family talk

19.00

The family table

Figure 3.3 The fluctuating rhythms of the Caff during weekdays.

used the Caff periodically when they worked in London. They knew they could be assured of a fresh, home-cooked meal and the familiar comforts of a traditional caff menu and space. Mark, who was a self-employed computer programmer, generally came in around eleven in the morning, read a paper, opened his mail, and ordered his usual choice of cooked breakfast. He mostly sat on his own, at his side table facing the street. He told me that the Caff was the place, 'where I do my thinking'. Hinga, who left Sierra Leone twelve years ago during the height of the civil war, started coming to the Caff during my fieldwork. He quietly slipped in at the same time most mornings avoiding the morning rush, and sat upfront, close to Nick. He usually ordered tea and toast, and ate while glancing up at the television, never making eye contact. Hinga never partook in any of the general conversations, and did not conform to any particular groups in the Caff. But Nick's Caff was one of his local places and he reserved his space through the regular act of sitting.

In Nick's Caff sitting was a social process tied to a local place, where regularity was an important dimension of a basic mode of belonging. Many customers claimed this belonging through the repeated maintenance of time and place, sitting in the Caff more or less at the same time of day and mostly in the same space. Through acquiring an understanding of the predictable social routines in the Caff, individuals could exercise explicit choices about when to visit the Caff, whom to avoid, and whom to meet up with. Once inside the Caff, the size of the table provided a small but valuable measure of social distance without entirely separating anyone from the general activities around them. The positions of the tables, the defined area of the table as a personal space, and the fluctuating use of the space throughout the rhythm of the day all assisted the claiming of personal territories within the larger space of the Caff. These nuanced occupations of time and space, most explicitly assisted by the collective rhythm of the Caff, point to the value of analysing public space as a layered set of interactions. Each layer subtly influences the next, accruing a combination of small sociabilities, and allowing for an extremely diverse range of individual and groups to share a local space. The mediation for this sharing depends on the certainty of the rhythm and the legibility afforded largely by the regularity that is a product of a local setting.

Similarly, Cavan's ethnography of bar room behaviour (1966) described the sociability of sitting in the context of the public bar by explaining the seating choices that are exercised by position ('proximities and boundaries'), by posture ('display' and 'poise') and conduct ('characters' and 'behaviours'). In Cavan's bar room, social legibility is afforded by the performance of tacit gestures, and in Nick's Caff it is the subscription to secular rituals of regularity and repetition that affords inclusion. The use of iteration in cultural life is that it provides consistency: a predictable format on which to base judgement and acquire intuition about when and how to act. The rituals of work, eating and leisure in the Caff reveal the collective organisation of space and time within this public interior. But as Goffman (1967) has shown us, rituals are also face-to-face forms of sociability: they serve to enrol membership through gesture or legible entry points and common codes of conduct. In cities of accelerated change where there is great ethnic and cultural variety, everyday rituals are of intercultural use. They potentially provide recognisable rhythms, thereby offering diverse individuals a format of time, space and etiquette in which to engage with one another.

Proprietors and patrons

For Nick and Dorah, the Caff was a workplace entered into as young adults, and as a family workplace it was a place to invest in personally and socially. As interactive and responsible 'workers', their identities exemplify a synergy between who they are and what they do for a living. Within the rhythm of the Caff, Nick and Dorah were able to respond to the fluctuating pace of the day, using quieter moments to eat in the Caff at the family table, to attend to other matters not always central to the Caff, and to talk to customers. The Caff's significance as a distinctly personal place relates in part to the daily congregation of an extended family, to the propinquity of work and home and to the presence of Nick and Dorah's personalities in the Caff. Nick's particular form of engagement was a direct involvement with the diverse individuals in the Caff. Nick was a 'public character', the individual on the street whom Jane Jacobs (1961) described as the person who explicitly concerned himself with the people around him. This public role was epitomised by a conversation we had one morning. I spoke to Nick about a regular customer, who was a patient at a local psychiatric hospital. Nick said, 'He's doing better. He comes in, talks about the football World Cup. At first I could see he didn't want to talk. Slowly I started to include him. I could see it's important, right. He needs to be included.'

In my case, a particular circumstance shifted Nick's remit of concern. My relationship to the Caff and to Nick changed when, early in 2005, my son was born a month ahead of the expected date. Various factors compounded the potential stress of this situation; my partner was away working in Japan under the assurances that 'all first babies come late'. I was still a newcomer to London, confined to hospital with no nearby family or local network to call on apart from my mum who was fortuitously visiting at the opportune moment. She however, was in a part of London unfamiliar to her, and so we agreed that she should pop in to Nick's Caff, to find out about bus passes, the laundromat and general neighbourhood information. During the days that followed, my mum went on to Nick's Caff after hospital visits, for fags (or in her case 'cigarettes'), a chat and general contact and assurance. Nick gave us immeasurable support, and it was both his public character, as well as his local presence in a social space off the street, that afforded support in a difficult circumstance.

Nick's role as a local public character was acquired and refined through a combination of his work skills and social skills. Nick had become more than adept at watching and engaging people. He had grown up with a few of his customers and he had come to know his regulars. He could astutely describe a person and the current circumstances they were in. For instance, he would mention that one of the daily regulars, Gary, was 'very laid back' and 'not good with too much stress'. Or, with characteristic humour, he described another weekly regular's brother as being 'in the last chapter of his life, but he's so tight, he won't die – so he doesn't have to pay for the funeral, right!'. In the rhythm of the Caff, Nick and Dorah were able to be proprietor and person; they efficiently managed their responsibilities in the Caff, enacted daily habits and, in the quieter spells, engaged with clientele, friends and family. As this was a local establishment, the local scene combined work, space and time in a particular manner. Work was structured by the repetitive tasks of running the Caff and serving within it. But work was also vitalised by the regular and spontaneous engagements between the local proprietors and local customers.

Nick and Dorah's work identities were also established through the routes taken by their respective immigrant parents to secure their workplaces in London. This small shop provided a platform for Nick's parents to invest their entrepreneurial skills in their adopted city. Nick was five when his dad brought the shop: 'This place [the Caff] was owned by another Cypriot fella, one thing led to another. This one happened to fall in the right place probably because of it being a Cypriot fella.' Nick's Dad had come to London on his own, fifteen years before he had resources to buy the Caff. He was invited into the country on the basis of being granted a work permit:

> When he first came he was in north London. The restaurant he was working for was in the area. He had a job in the Trocadero. He worked up to sous-chef. Then he got lots of jobs for the other Cypriots. That's what our boys did. All the foreigners nowadays work in the kitchens . . . In about 1963 it [the restaurant] closed. It was after that when we came here. We lived locally, and he knew it [the Caff] was for sale.
>
> (Fieldwork conversation 2006)

From kitchen to Caff, Nick's family made progress through taking menial jobs, establishing access to small entrepreneurial activities, and by engaging in ethnic and local networks. A line of social mobility had been forged within three generations, from kitchen to Caff, to profession. Nick first went to college and then on to work in the Caff, together with his sister, whom I have never met, but whose voice I heard calling up orders from the kitchen, confirming the presence of an unseen person working below in the basement. Dorah was married at eighteen and had worked in the Caff since then. Although Nick and Dorah claimed working-class affinities and identities, social mobility across the generations of their family will shift what it means for them to be working class. The Caff was both work and a way of life that Nick and Dorah inherited, but it is an inheritance that they would not pass on to their children. Nick and Dorah placed great value on education and both of their daughters were awarded scholarships towards private education for their secondary schooling. Their children went on to pursue qualifications at tertiary institutions.

Allegiances

Nick's Caff was personified by the presence of Nick, Dorah, their teenage daughters and their extended family of relatives and local friends. It was difficult to separate the daily congregation and conversations of this extended family from the feel of the Caff interior. The front door to the Caff was off the street and was also the front door to Nick and Dorah's home above the shop. At the tables occupied each day by family and regulars, there was a mix of ages, of locals and of first, second and third generation immigrants. This daily gathering over the decades of friends and family around shared tables had permeated the sense of place and had permitted a certain accommodation of different people. Mark commented that his comfort in the Caff related to the presence of family in it: 'The mix of ages is really good – it's one of the reasons this place [Nick's Caff] feels good – the mix of ages, the associations with family . . . It's a family place. Nick's family are around.' Although Mark had children, they no longer lived with him. On occasions, I saw Mark's two children meet him at the Caff, a place they seem comfortable to regularly meet in together.

Habitués

The sense of Nick's Caff being *a place to be at home outside home* is underpinned by different modes of belonging in the city, by different experiences of home and different experiences of family. The potential for belonging in the Caff was reinforced by the constant presence of Nick and Dorah, and by the family-like relationships Nick and Dorah had developed with some of their regulars. The need to belong also related to those in the Caff who by choice, circumstance or age lived alone in the city. As I was leaving one evening, Dorah was chatting with the regulars at the family table about closing the Caff for the family's two-week annual holiday. Dorah mentioned her concern for one of the regulars, Freddie: 'He's the only one I worry about when we go away . . . when he walks out of this door every evening, there's no one to go to. That's it.' They carried on chatting and when Freddie walked in Sonja called out, 'You're late, where you been?' and Cathy, Sonja's daughter, added, 'You've got detention!'

There were many individuals who used the Caff who no longer had an immediate family to socialise with daily. The Caff provided an alternative 'family' for them by being a place to go to and by affording them contact with people with whom they had sustained a sense of belonging. Jack, who was in his sixties, and had grown up in Camberwell to the south of Walworth, had been coming regularly to Nick's Caff for 'Years, years. Since my divorce, I come here for supper on my way home. It's very much like a social club. What you'd call "caff society" – know what I mean. Once you've been coming long enough you almost become Nick's family.' Gary who was in his late forties, was also a long-time regular at the Caff. He was born in the area but no longer lived in Walworth. He commuted in from the suburbs everyday where he lived with his wife and children. He came in for business and popped in and out of the Caff often during the day. In the evening he was usually at the 'family' table, where he ate his dinner, away from his immediate family but with his brother and local friends. Gary said, 'I've always used the Caff. They treat me like family . . . if I don't come in he [Nick] phones me . . . All my friends come to eat here.' I asked Gary if his own family ate at the Caff and he replied,

'They have done', implying that they seldom do, and that Nick's table of regulars were 'family' outside of family and quite literally 'at home' outside home.

Locals

The people in the Caff who were born in the area and who had grown up there during the 1950s and 1960s, prior to what they described as a period of noticeable change, came to know Walworth as a local place, partly defined by the practices of a predominantly white working-class community. These locals in the Caff qualified a sense of community through the criteria of being born in and growing up in the area, thereby sharing common experiences, practices and rites of passage. Today the Walworth Road is epitomised by diverse ethnicities and transforming cultures; it is a place where old and new adapt to greater or lesser degree to substantial urban change. Part of how the different people within the Caff identified themselves and others reflected how they viewed and dealt with change. Many of the Caff's born-and-bred locals remembered the Walworth Road as a local place that was substantially reinforced by knowing one another. Sonja simply stated, 'If you walked down the street you knew people.'

While the Walworth Road may once have been a place where people knew each other, places like the Caff now represent the *small localities* in the city that Simmel (1903) had associated more specifically with life in villages and small towns. Simmel had related the social interaction within small localities as dependent on the individual being known, and thereby located. It is probable, in Simmel's conceptualisation of small town interaction, that this local scale of meeting occurred between fairly homogeneous groups, whose affinities were not only defined within the boundaries of a local territory, but also by the boundaries of origin, ethnicity and class. However, this enactment of small sociabilities extended to the city too, as is highlighted in Wilmott and Young's (1957) seminal account of local life in Bethnal Green in the East End in the late 1950s. They describe the pub and the shop as the two significant local meeting places: 'The pubs and shops in Bethnal Green serve so well as "neighbourhood centres" because there are so many of them: they provide the same small face-to-face groups with continual opportunities to meet' (1957: 153). The pub exemplifies an historic feature of local community life in working-class London, but few pubs remain on the Walworth Road today. Jack describes the changing role of the local pub:

> There's been subtle changes. Take the closing down of the pubs. Every street had a pub, and that was like a community centre. You could come home of an evening, take off your working-class clothes, get your newspaper, go down to the pub. That was before television . . . When I was young you could literally drink seven days a week and it wouldn't make a dent in your pocket (I'm talking about when I was single, of course). It wasn't just a question of drinking, it was a social club. The way I got to know people was the pub . . . a kind of drinking school developed.
>
> (Fieldwork conversation 2006)

Haine's (1992) social history of the role of the Parisian working-class café defines how these combined drinking establishments and meeting places provided a local base for social and political organisation. In describing the particular social role of small-scale meeting spaces, he emphasises both the repetition and the informal structure afforded by these local establishments. Haine articulates the 'casual closeness' as friendships that were 'simultaneously intimate and anonymous' (1992: 607). The English working-class social establishments, including the pub and the caff, have provided a base for informal meeting grounds, and a space for personal and political discussion. However, these social institutions are subject to economic and cultural change, just as the sense of what it means to be a 'local' is subject to transformation. Being a 'local' is diversely interpreted in Nick's Caff and shifts between understandings of *being locally born and bred* and practices of *being located*. Local qualifications range from a perceived commonality of origin (English) and culture (working class), to living life more or less within the confines of a local neighbourhood (territory). For others, being located referred to the ability to operationalise small networks across more than one local area, where regularity and face-to-face contact reinforced a local scale of interconnections between people.

Sub-cultures

In the Caff the collisions of quite different individuals within the same locale depended partially on sharing affinities, but also on sharing a particular organisation of time. *Shared time* allowed individuals and groups to congregate in Nick's Caff throughout the varied rhythms of the Walworth day, where many local uses and structures of time across the day were distinct from the regular working day of the formally employed. In Wallman's study, *Eight London Households* (1984) she observed and interviewed households with different demographic, ethnic and class profiles all living within the same area of the Louvaine Area Residents Association (LARA) housing project in south London. Wallman's empiric analysis points to how individuals orchestrate and rely on a variety of networks across the divisions of class, race and ethnicity, as an essential means of getting by in the city. But in refining an understanding of an 'urban resource network', Wallman defines resources as more 'to do with organisation', including the organisation of 'time, information and identity' (1984: 29), than to do with the bonds of ethnicity or kinship. Similarly, Armstrong's account (1998) of football hooligans points to the resource of time over class thereby challenging the stereotypical association of class with football hooliganism. Armstrong asserts that shared time provides a primary platform for belonging: 'In terms of participation, the most essential requirement for being a Blade was free time . . .' (1998: 169).

Many of the regulars who used Nick's Caff frequented the Caff during formal 'office hours'. The time that structured their routines, practices and everyday culture was quite different from the organisation of time by those who were clocking in for a nine-to-five working day. The Caff regulars largely consisted of people who no longer worked, including pensioners, as well as those who worked outside of regular, formal employment. In the Caff there were also individuals who worked within the realm of what Hobbs (1988) described as a particular 'entrepreneurial' urban culture that operates outside the structure of the law. One such entrepreneurial practice was referred to in the Caff as being 'on the fiddle'. Downes (1966: 204) offers a definition of fiddling as both sub-cultural practice and shared cultural understanding: '"Fiddling" is the adult practice of enlarging income tax-free by theft from one's work-place [. . .] the justification being that "Everybody does it".' Nick reported that participation in a combination of fairly minor illegal activities was common practice when he was growing up in Walworth: 'Tell you what, so many of the blokes were ducking and diving, doing a bit of time. But that's how it was done, wasn't nothing unusual or anything. Like Mike, he was a bit of a crook. But it's just how it was done.' Mike had mentioned to me months earlier that he had had high earnings when he was a dustman and Dan, sitting at the same table, replied, 'but you were on the fiddle'.

For those in the Caff engaged in these kinds of entrepreneurial activities there appeared to be a hierarchy. Gary was what Nick referred to with tongue in cheek as 'an innocent crook', and on the lower rungs of the local 'entrepreneurial' ranking system, or what Foster's (1990) interviewees described as 'sprats and mackerels' in her book *Villains*, based in inner-city south London. Gary did a bit of maintenance and repair work locally and popped in and out of the Caff throughout the day. He was initially reluctant to talk to me as he thought I might be a policewoman. But after my interview with his friends, Mike and Dan, he was always polite, and in occasional small talk asked what else I had found out about the street.

My minimal contact with the range of 'entrepreneurs' in the Caff remained at the lower level of the hierarchy with Gary. The middle section of rank was epitomised by Joe who, according to Nick, 'wasn't a criminal or anything' but who 'did some ducking and diving'. Joe watched me come in and out of the Caff with the faintest gesture of disapproval, and never acknowledged my presence. Then there was the upper rank. As a regular succinctly put it, 'See those two boys sitting over there? They are the "Xs". Have you heard of them? They're a well-known gangster family, notorious. But they won't speak to you, and you don't want to speak to them.' As a local resident, I was more than happy to leave it at that. The social and spatial organisation of the Caff allowed me to use the Caff regularly, to form relationships with some customers, and never to make eye contact with others. There was no obligation to participate and joining in simply meant sitting down.

Divisions

Social spaces inevitably reveal extents of allegiance and division. In Nick's Caff the notion of exclusion was not simply clarified by who socialised in the space; who was there and who was absent. Of far greater complexity was how individuals expressed on what basis 'others' should belong in the wider setting of the city. Amongst some of the regulars in Nick's Caff, these expressions straddled the contradictory terrain between generalisations around race, class and immigration, and the personal interactions in the Caff interior in which these categories appeared less overt. Although there was a core group of regulars who had frequented the Caff for years, it was difficult to describe the Caff clientele by way of any singular social group or designation. This may be related to the relatively undemanding nature of Nick's Caff, where there were few formal regulations beyond the rudimentary contract of paying for what you order. Mustafa, a pensioner who had grown up in Brixton, described the underlying informality of Nick's Caff: 'Cafes are better than restaurants. Restaurants are very formal. You can take time, eat, have a cigarette. Restaurants you got to eat your food and get out.'

Social regulations emerged from the ritualised practices of proprietor and customers – where regulars sat, where the loner sat, who talked to whom, and what people talked about at certain times of the day. However, the Caff was a place not without its tensions. These were often presented as perceptions about groups of people informed by generalisations of what differentiates one group from another. Various people in the Caff talked in broad terms about 'the Conservatives', 'the middle-class wankers' or 'the immigrants'. But daily interactions in Nick's Caff revealed forms of sustained interpersonal engagement that contradicted generalisations, and personal relationships evidently overlapped expressions of race, culture, age and personality.

Caff culture for the most part was convivial in its nature. Different people entered their local establishment to eat, talk or observe; there was very little conflict in its inherent sociability. Conviviality was at its peak when events or circumstances contrived to encourage different people to meet over common ground. One such event was the Football World Cup in 2006, which, as good fortune would have it, more or less coincided with the beginning of my fieldwork in the Caff. During this period individuals and groups talked over tables and counters and Nick and Dorah initiated a draw where various customers were allotted teams. Appropriate levels of jubilance or despondence were enacted when the name of a team was drawn out of a bag and assigned to a customer. This event seemed to bring people together effortlessly over a brief period. In general, being able to talk about football matches was a good way for people to make an easy social entry into the Caff.

But there were also counter events, or situations and occasions that brought out hostile or alienating experiences. Oddly enough, it was another large sporting event that effectively brought on one such adverse encounter for Nick. I popped into the Caff one afternoon to see how Dorah had done in the London Marathon. After Nick had sung her praises he said, 'Of course it didn't go so well for me, someone called me a "bloody foreigner"!' On the day that Dorah was running in the Marathon Nick had stood in the crowd trying to get a view of the race. At one point, as he told it, a young woman pushed him out of the way to get a better view of the race. Apparently her quick glance at Nick's skin and hair had induced her retort of 'bloody foreigner'. While Nick was offended by a racist dismissal essentially based on his appearance, a similar pattern of bigotry by way of stereotype played out in the Caff.

Race

One evening, early in my fieldwork, I was telephoned by Nick to come to the Caff to meet Mike, who reportedly had some 'strong views' about the immigrants to the area. When I got to the Caff, Mike was sitting at one of the family tables upfront. Mike was born in London and was in his seventies. His father had emigrated from southern Italy to London. Mike was white, and heavily set with an unruly beard. In contrast, Dan, who sat opposite Mike, was a thirty-something black man, immaculately dressed in a suit, with his hair styled in dreds. Dan first met Mike at the Caff, and this was where they continued to regularly meet up. It seemed an unlikely friendship, and Mike mentioned twice in our first conversation that the change in the area was down to 'the immigrants' and then later retorted 'the Blacks'. However, after seeing Mike and Dan on other occasions in the Caff, it appeared as if Mike saw Dan as he knew him – a friend. Mike's close relationship with Dan suggested that racism takes hold through publicly circulated forms of stereotype, where race and immigration are often conflated as 'the problem'. Public space, or spaces of exchange, allows for a collision between what one is familiar with or who one knows at a social level (in this case within the Caff) and the broad generalisations or 'public fictions' of groups of unknown people 'out there', as often informed by the conservative media. But in Mike's case his bigotry, or his perception of 'the Blacks', was not disrupted by his valued friendship with Dan.

Months later I mentioned Dan and Mike's friendship to Nick, raising the marked distinction between Mike's racist generalisations and his close friendship with Dan. Nick promptly replied, 'Dan's not that black.' He went off to serve a few customers and returning to my table stated, 'Mike says you should put all the blacks in a boat out to sea, and burn it. And yet he's so close to Dan.' I was taken aback by this comment, and the ease with which it was reported. It would have been easy to dismiss Mike as a racist, yet his friendship with Dan was more than simply contradictory: it revealed both the powerful role of racial stereotypes, and how through social interaction individuals unknowingly unsettle their prejudice.

Mike and Dan's friendship was based on a range of shared affinities like their mutual love of jazz and food. In *Slim's Table* Duneier (1992) describes relationships amongst the 'habitués' that developed across overt racial and stereotypical barriers at the Valois Cafeteria. But unlike Duneier's description of 'sitting buddies' (1992: 35), Mike and Dan's friendship was sustained beyond the confinement of the Caff. Although their friendship was formed in Nick's Caff and was sustained by regularly meeting there, they also met outside the Caff to do things together. Dan took Mike shopping in his car, and they would also go out to eat or have a drink. They shared important celebrations, and I was aware they had spent a Christmas Eve together. Mike and Dan had come to enjoy a genuine friendship, made all the more perplexing by Mike's verbal commitment to racism.

The way in which regulars in the Caff expressed their opinions about who belongs and under what conditions was often based on projected or externally formed portrayals of identity. However, daily relations in the Caff's diverse interior were generally convivial and events like the World Cup served to reinforce such conviviality. Sometimes events outside the Caff's intimacy served to denigrate identity, as was Nick's experience at the London Marathon. Stereotypes, particularly a combination of authorised caricatures around race and immigration, were exposed within the interior of the Caff in different ways. Sonja for instance made general reference to 'the ethnics' as an all-encompassing group of new migrants who represented for her one of the significant changes in the area. During my conversation with her, she mentioned that her daughter's mobile phone had been stolen that day. When her grandson asked who was responsible, Freddie looked up and said, 'one of those with a tan'.

Ironically, the job of the stereotype appears to assert a twofold constraint, denuding the individual 'object' of bigotry any personal value or stature, and denying the subscriber any critical judgement. Stereotypes encourage hierarchy and containment. Moreover it is a mechanism of constraint that cannot fail to replicate social ranking within a system of dominant values, and in participating in reducing 'the other' those within the ranks know too well that their status may well in turn be categorised or oversimplified. We move on now to the stereotype of the immigrant as circulated in the Nick's Caff, and the attempts to justify – within a system of ranking where worth is sometimes confused with race and ethnicity – why some immigrants are more deserving citizens than others.

Immigrants

Many of the regulars in the Caff who had negative views on more recent immigrants were themselves the citizens of paradox: second-generation immigrants. Their parents came to London from places like Cyprus, Greece, Italy and the Caribbean. Part of a generalised distinction they made, as justification of their resentment of the more recent generation of immigrants, was around the perceived ease of the routes taken from arriving in the country to receiving public resources, in particular social housing. Their resentments were primarily shaped around narratives of who should be entitled to public resources, and on what basis. The following conversation took place in Nick's Caff one morning:

> Nick: Late 40s, Greek Cypriots started coming over – economic reasons. Turks started coming in the 50s. You had to have a sponsor of a job and somewhere to stay.

> Nick asked Savvas when his dad came over. Savvas' dad was Greek Cypriot. Savvas was between forty and fifty, and raised his voice during the conversation, getting quite heated over his distinction between deserving and undeserving immigrants.

> Savvas: My old dad came over in '53. Nowadays people come fresh off the boat and want it all . . . That's why this country's on its knees.

> Nick: You had to have a job to come here. You had to have a guarantee of a job and accommodation. That meant you couldn't claim off the state. We were British citizens; Cyprus was a British colony until 1960.

Nick mentioned that his dad came over to London twice, once in 1950 and again in 1952:

You had to get permission from over there as well. You come through on a boat. 'Bout 5 pounds it was. My father was here for 'bout 6 years before my mum come over. There was no support, no interpreters, none of the support groups you have today.

Nick moved around the Caff while serving the mid-morning customers. A little later he came back to the table and talked about a different scale and rate of immigration, and his perceived difficulties with it:

We were assimilated into a system. Now there's so many. When they first come they have big families. They get the bigger accommodation and the places at the schools. The English resent that. That's how the English people see it, and I do too, to an extent.

(Fieldwork conversation 2007)

I was not entirely sure where Nick and Savvas' assumptions about the immigration process being easy and uncomplicated had come from. Certainly they were not informed by recent, stringent legal requirements of immigration into the UK. Since 2004, I had personally entered into a lengthy and costly process of immigration and my route into the UK, first on a limited four-year work visa, then as resident on a restricted spousal visa, and ultimately a dual nationality citizen, was an intimidating and expensive one. But within the narratives of deserving and undeserving immigrants lurks the question of ethnicity and race, and whether it is in fact the investments of time and work that are the basis of immigrant 'acceptability', or whether judgment is affected by racism.

Mike recalled the Walworth Road of the 1950s and 1960s: '[Walworth Road] was ordinary Cockney-type society. Most of 'em all in the graveyard now . . . There was big changes when the migrants came here, 50s onwards . . . There was small shops, no supermarkets . . . run by English people.' However, the information about the ownership and commercial activities along the Walworth Road accounted for in the *Post Office London Directories* challenges the accuracy of Mike's nostalgia, and the records of proprietors in the Walworth Road between 1841 and 1950 show that there was a mix of individuals working there who came from various places including Greece, Turkey, eastern Europe, Italy and Ireland.

Foreigners

In spite of Nick being an officially fully fledged citizen his own view of his status was complicated. One pronounced area in which Nick's perceived 'foreignness' came to the fore was in establishing the future prospects for his and Dorah's daughters. Nick had often talked to me about tertiary education and job prospects for his youngest daughter, who was an excellent student. Nick had mentioned that she wanted to study business at one of the 'top universities'. His concern for his daughter's progress was not about his daughter's ability, but rather her social standing: 'She's small, she's a woman, plus she's foreign. She got a foreign sur-name. She has to have more to get where she wants.' Nick and Dorah were both born in London and they had grown up in the same street as one another, only a few blocks from the Caff. Their daughters were also born in London. But Nick's vulnerability closely tied to a perception of being viewed as a foreigner suggests that while citizenship is granted by authority, it is ultimately validated by cultural perceptions.

Nick juggled being local and being foreign, a multiple identity that Bhabha describes as 'the migrant's double vision' (2004 [1994]: 5). Nick expressed a strong sense of his Turkish heritage but also of his local, working-class sensibilities. But both of these identities have increased his perceived vulnerability in relating to a London outside his local domains. His concern for his daughter's prospects is tied not only to her 'foreign' status, but also her 'local' status, alluding in passing to his family's working-class accents by saying, 'Our sorts give ourselves away with our mouths.' Hence Nick's absolute determination that his daughter, '*has to have more to get where she wants*'.

Both Nick and Dorah were brought up in Muslim households. Although Dorah had mentioned that they did not eat pork at home, pork was cooked and served to customers, always a hot favourite on the breakfast menu. I had known Nick for two years prior to my fieldwork, but only well into it did I feel able to broach issues of his identity more directly. One morning, after six months in the field, I asked Nick what it was like growing up in the area with his Northern Cypriot heritage:

Nick: I've never faced any racism on the whole, directly.
Suzi: Why do you say you're foreign?
Nick: Because of my colour. The English people are lovely, right. But the bottom line is I'm foreign. And what's worse, I'm a foreigner in my own country!
Suzi: Do your girls feel English?
Nick: I feel English in every way, except in some of our networks and family ways. We don't encourage our girls to go out like the English girls, you understand.
        (Nick got up to serve a customer and returned a little later.)
Suzi: Did you have to let being a Muslim go when you came here?
Nick: It was never an issue. It was more cultural. For instance I don't eat pork, don't let my children eat pork, because I've never had it cooked in the house. In many ways our culture is like the 1950s. We've still got the traditional ways, like being in a time warp. We're old-fashioned, even our language has stayed the same. They [Cypriots in Cyprus)] see you as English Turks!

                                                            (Fieldwork conversation 2007)

Nick partly managed his hybrid identity between place and time, between South London and Northern Cyprus, between urban practices and old-fashioned traditions.

Although Nick and Dorah had a second home in Cyprus, they had stated that Cyprus would not be their eventual retirement destination; London was not simply a means to an end, it was ultimately a home. But it was also a home in which Nick had two names: a Cypriot and English name, and where, during the Brixton riots, his father boarded up the Caff, and changed its name from *The Bosphorus* to *Nick's Caff*, in fear of ethnic reprisals. The outside face of the Caff, at least, was to merge with the street, and blending in was an adopted urban tactic.

Two proclaimed identities were used by Nick and Dorah to partially accommodate complex allegiances: being a Londoner and being working class seemed to accommodate living, or even being born in London, while having strong connections to another place. Perhaps as a 'Londoner' one could be tied to individual sensibilities, occupations or preferences that were not prescribed by nationality. Similarly, being working class tied people in the Caff to a cultural set of affinities, moreover one which was outside of the dominant value system, even if the material definition of labour and capital no longer directly applied. But being a local seemed a far more complex identity for many regulars in the Caff since local life incorporated both the embodiment of past memories, as well as the present experience of accelerated change.

This leads me to the question of how well the Caff, as a local space or cultural institution, is able to respond to change over time. In relating the demise of the London caff in general, and to the vitality of Nick's Caff in particular, it is valuable to consider the Caff's adaptability. In the first instance, the Caff has provided a work base within Nick's family for four decades and this is likely to continue at least until Nick and Dorah choose to retire. As Nick is approaching fifty, and Dorah is in her early forties, the longevity of Nick and Dorah's working lineage is likely to extend at least for a decade if not two. The familial line of parent to child succession in the Caff is likely to stop at Nick and Dorah's daughters, exemplifying a familiar pattern of immigrant shopkeeper to professional within three generations.

At some later date the Caff may well be run by other members of the extended family, but in other instances on the Walworth Road, as in the Walworth Café, which was run by an Italian family, the family business closed in 2007 after the second generation decided to retire. Social mobility and economic pressures partially account for these changes. Heathcote (2004) points to the rapid demise of the London caff, a factor he attributes, amongst other things, to the emergence of coffee franchises and chains across London. As an indication of the extent of this phenomenon, one only has to track the brief history of Starbucks in London; it started out in 1998, and rapidly expanded to 137 chains across London by 2007 (http://www.starbucks.co.uk 2007). Such coffee franchises or chains are now a notable feature on many London high streets, prominent for their ubiquitous prevalence and instantly recognisable by their global insignia.

Local caffs are also gradually being replaced by new forms of local eating establishments and meeting places that are not exemplified by global franchises. This is partly evidenced in the emergence of places such as the internet–coffee spaces, as well as the kebab shops on the Walworth Road. Although a 'traditional' caff opened in 2008 on the Walworth Road, new local eating and meeting places also include more culturally specific establishments such as the 'Somali Social Club' and the 'Sierra Hot Spot'. Nick's Caff itself has undergone its own trans-formations over time. Sonja remembered it in the 1950s, before it was owned by Nick's family, when it was open until late at night, frequented by youngsters who were out and about in the evening. It is this version of the London caff that Downes (1966) wrote about in the late 1960s, and from his research base in the East End, he described a congregation of teenagers, mostly male, who met in the local caff between eight and eleven in the evenings.

It is perhaps naive to romanticise the longevity of the Caff in the face of urban change, in spite of how local establishments like the Caff are able to adapt as cultural practices shift. The adaptability of places like Nick's Caff will be pitted against more stringent economic realities, as reflected by the high rental, high rates and steady increases in retail property prices in London. These economic trajectories will also make it increasingly difficult for the small business person and the entrepreneurial immigrant to access retail space. When Nick's father first bought the Caff and subsequently the home above it in the 1960s, property prices were still depressed from the economic aftermath of the Second World War. The ownership of their working premises in Nick's family has played a critical part in its economic stability.

However, for people to *be* local in changing local worlds, and to form ways of life and associations outside of or in addition to the remits of origin, community or territory, they require a range of spaces in which to meet, to encounter difference, and to engage in informal memberships. As a local meeting space, Nick's Caff reveals the social value of meeting places in which life and livelihoods are combined.

Conclusions

In Nick's Caff the contract of meeting is negotiated by the everyday rituals of sitting, and takes the social forms of active and passive participation. Amongst its occupants, the process of assigning who belongs in the context of a diverse and rapidly changing city may already be established by broader societal values and rules set outside the Caff. In the formal terrains of governance and the distributaries of the media, boundaries around the notions of who belongs are constructed, categorised, disseminated and publicly authorised. But the enactment of pragmatic rituals and spatial intimacy in the Caff's semi-public interior challenges some of the stereotypes of who belongs and on what basis. Having regular contact and a place to meet amongst others is critical to this challenge.

To pursue the question 'What kinds of space provide meeting points for a far more variegated, dislocated public?' this chapter has argued for a reconsideration of both 'migrant' and 'public' through the lens of repeated and face-to-face forms of contact in local spaces. Within the context of Nick's Caff, local forms of belonging exhibit multiple and inconsistent dimensions that reveal the variable ways of how individuals belong with respect to one another. Within their respective local domains of the city, individuals must grapple with change alongside their own shifts in status. The social formations between self and group and local processes of belonging are revealed in the small localities of the city, where informal memberships are claimed and granted through the rituals of gesture, timing and spatial organisation. In these social spaces or prosaic publics, the citizens of accelerated change engage with the familiar and the unsettling. Where their local worlds are substantially transforming, prosaic publics are one of the urban venues in which individuals confront their own social capacity to deal with change.

4   The art of attire

Reyd bustled down the Walworth Road towards me. He was set slightly apart in the crowd, a middle-aged man wearing a loose-fit, tailored suit and what I came to recognise as a pork pie hat, a Ben Sherman shirt and Bass Weejun shoes. Reyd wore the subtle signs of Mod culture, a deep affinity for music and style that travelled the distance of Black American jazz and soul from the 1940s and 1950s to the working-class housing estates in 1960s Britain. He reached me outside his shop-front, unlocked the grill, pushed open the glass door and flipped the sign around, establishing through an old-fashioned custom that his shop was 'open'. We stepped into the front room, a small space just large enough to accommodate the tailor and his customer. We had met a number of times in this small workspace over the course of two years, and each time Reyd had been both generous and measured in his expression. Between our conversations and his engagement with customers he revealed the connections between what he made, what he wore, and what he valued: between his observance of style as a bespoke tailor and Mod enthusiast, and his sense of society as a local, south London person.

This chapter explores style as a social form of participation, and unfolds from the perspective of the maker, specifically Reyd's practice of bespoke tailoring or what he defines as an art. Sociological perspectives that connect sartorial codes to subculture, specifically those of the 1960s Mod, are framed through lenses that include: *assertion* through cultural translation and relocation (Clarke 1976); *dialogue across race but within class* (Hebdige 1979); as well as the over-stated *portrayal* of seditious youth culture on the art of the media (Cohen 1972). What these lenses broadly share is the connection between affinity, resistance and public display, where the lived and symbolic dimensions of style depend on allegiance and distinction: the cultural effects of aligning an individual to a group, while simultaneously distinguishing one group from another.

Four decades on from its definitive historic moment, Mod style continues to be made, acquired and worn by aging and emerging mods, but this time within a different set of structures. While the histories of race and class are still present, the contemporary practices of tailors and stylists offer, I suggest, an additional lens to the frame – that of a sensibility – one neither confined to the specificities of epoch nor to a focus on youth culture. Mills (1959: 187) defined sensibility as the mutually refining process of learning skills and acquiring values. The sensibility of style on which sartorial allegiance is based, is explored from Reyd's Bespoke Tailor Shop as a time-protracted process of gaining cultural knowledge and emerges out of a continual renewal of shared cultural values or 'being in the know'.

Perhaps the best introduction to this account of style is articulated through Reyd's notes that he composed after listening to a recent *Radio 4* programme on bespoke tailoring:

The Bespoke Suit is Made –

– To the Specific Requirements – for the Client
– Using the Traditional Hand Cutting technique
– Along with the traditional hand craft tailoring methods
– Then fitted and honed to the mind and body of the client

Fashion Labels dictate the styles and do not embrace the client's personality.
(Reyd's notes, 8 January 2007)

Reyd's words reflect the precision customary of a good tailor, and distil the purpose of his art as he has come to know it. Much like our discussions, he selected his words carefully and left little room for superfluous expressions. His notes relate the making of a bespoke garment to the affinity between the tailor and customer, where traditional methods are merged with creative spirit. He positions his art between the process of making and imagining: between the conventions of tailoring and the inventions of personality. Averse to what he views as the limitations of fashion labels, Reyd distinguishes his art as a form of respect or reciprocal social exchange. Acquiring the skill to make, wear and recognise the bespoke garment is key to the circulation of its cultural value.

Through the process of attaining sensibility as suggested by Mills, one comes closer to a knowledge of self above that of the group, leading to the development of deep interests and the insights to participate in choice. The slow process of Reyd's acquisition of skill emerges out of the story of his apprenticeship, of how a black, working-class teenager from south London immersed himself in a well-established Jewish tailor shop in Fleet Street, north of the river in central London. After working his way up, Reyd ultimately elected to move out of the City and set up his own bespoke tailor shop on the Walworth Road. By following Reyd's formation of sensibility from home to street to work, we can explore how culture lives through its individual, groups and societal parts. Through following Reyd's transitions, this chapter opens out questions that connect sensibility to dialogue, choice and the influence of the city. Can cultural allegiances that are formed out of class and race within a particular epoch expand to include new forms of dialogue? In acquiring both the skills and values necessary to sustain sensibility, are individuals able to participate in choices about their futures, in the context of deep inequalities? Are the spaces of the city central to how style is made visible?

The cultural uses of work

The tailor's shop

Reyd's shop space off the Walworth Road was small but by no means insignificant. It served as a base to meet and make for his customers from all over London, who crossed the city in recognition of Reyd's skill as a bespoke Mod tailor. The shop appeared essentially as a workspace, a place in which things were made as opposed to a space in which things were sold. The surfaces of his workspace had emerged over time, and while there was little sense of a space contrived in the foreshortened process of professional interior design and decoration, the shop was not without a strong visual sensibility – a selection and layering of items and images to support Reyd's affinities as a Mod tailor. From the street the small shop-front was raised to form a seat, upon which a headless mannequin and one or two jackets at most were on display. This minimal enticement, a subtle and precise visual etiquette typical of small bespoke tailor shops across London, indicated a concern for the garment above all else (Figure 4.1). One could surmise that customers were more

Figure 4.1 The 'silent salesman'.

likely to be those 'in the know' than a casual passer-by. Stepping into the shop from the angled doorway, two rows of cloth flanked either side of the doorway area; mohair, wools, tweeds, two-tones and shiny inner linings were stacked in two seductive piles of cloth.

Reyd described the purposeful aesthetic of a traditional London tailor shop-front by ascribing to it the role of 'the silent salesman'. Although Reyd's front room was restricted by size, he had emulated the subtle principles of display to the street:

> The concept of the window to the street, that 'step-in-window' or inverted window space of the traditional tailor – let's call it 'the silent salesman' – was to draw the customer into the shop premises with virtually one foot in the door, without being approached by the salesman.
>
> There was also a 'foyer' window space. There was a small table with a number of cloth pattern bundles with various types of fabrics so that the potential customer could sieve through these patterns at their leisure. Prices for each fabric were individually priced so the customer could browse without being approached by the salesperson.
>
> Once the potential customer had decided they wanted to purchase the product, he'll then step into the shop. He is obviously now approached by a salesperson who would try and accommodate the client's request. Hence the silent salesman (the table and the window) have done half the job.
>
> (Fieldwork conversation 2006)

The front room of Reyd's shop was no more than 3.5 metres across by 4.5 metres deep, the two side walls pinching space for a measuring table on the one side and a row of suits in the making on the other. A collection of images were carefully displayed on these two walls, illustrating the specifics of the Mod suit – both how it is made and how it is worn. A picture that Reyd pointed out to me on more than one occasion as 'Bert, the old soldier', a tailor with whom Reyd did his apprenticeship in Fleet Street, had a prominent position. Bert's poise encapsulates the confidence in his skill as he stretched his hands between a pattern piece, dressed in the elegance of his formal work attire of tie and tailored jacket (Figure 4.2).

Below Bert were style icons of their time: slim-suited gents and dandies, including Wilson Pickett in a double-breasted jacket, and Cassius Clay in spats, bowler hat and umbrella. Reyd's selection of images revealed the circularity of style, from the adoption of formal English menswear from the nineteenth century by Black American jazz and soul musicians in the 1940s and 1950s to the subsequent reinterpretations encapsulated in the minimalist, three-buttoned, two-toned suits of Mod culture worn in 1960s Britain. The pictures convey the maintenance of a sartorial propriety across the centuries and the Atlantic. Bespoke Mod protocols are sustained both by the regard for the conventional cut of the cloth, and the cultural translations carried through the ritualised poise and parody of subsequent cultural adaptations.

Beyond the front room was the back room; heavy pairs of scissors, tape measures, reels of cotton, steam irons and an electric sewing machine were the paraphernalia of Reyd's domain where he cut and stitched the suits (Figure 4.3). At the back of

Figure 4.2 'Bert, the old soldier'.

the large work surface was a collection of CDs and tapes; amongst these my eye picked out James Brown's *Funky Good Time* and Stevie Wonder's *A Time to Love?* (Figure 4.4). For Reyd was not only a bespoke tailor, but a Mod tailor or a 'Soul Stylist', who nurtured an inextricable link between 'British working-class fashion' and 'contemporary American black music' (Hewitt 2000: 15). This back-room space, barely visible from the street, was essential for Reyd's creativity as a place of retreat. He talked about the value of working on his own, and described the solitary space and the time it offered him to think: 'Sitting and thinking on certain things, working on my own, most of the time, I'm constantly talking to myself. When you're talking to yourself, you're answering yourself. That's how you move from A to B. What am I looking for? A significance, a meaning.'

Skills and values

Reyd affirmed that 'Skill is learnt'. His own routes to learning his skill as a bespoke tailor were those accumulated over a lifetime, honed through his association with diverse social groups. Integral to his acquisition of skill are the local domains of south London street fashion, an apprenticeship in a tailor shop in Fleet Street, and an identification with soul music and Mod culture. Reyd's identity had developed through a sensibility for style, a deep affinity to a visual and auditory culture that combined his work and pleasure: 'I always wanted to be a tailor,' Reyd says, 'I grew up for the love of clothes.' Reyd expressed how his passion for his work was

Figure 4.3 The tailor's paraphernalia: working tools.

Figure 4.4 The tailor's paraphernalia: cultural tools.

sustained by his ambitions and his origins: both what he grew up with and what he dreamed of.

Gilroy's work (1987) on race and racism highlights the varied sources of cultural allegiance by questioning what brings individuals together in highly stratified and racialised societies. He differentiates between an individual's inheritance received or imposed by group status, like ethnicity or race, versus an individual's process of self-discovery that emerges out of affinities and ambitions. By privileging the importance of how individuals pursue their preferences and prospects, Gilroy emphasises the cultural significance of how individuals develop shared connections across the designated groupings of kin, nationality or class. The process by which Reyd's acquired skill – both a social and technical dexterity – indicates how cultural affinity emerges out of relationships to family, ethnicity and class, as well as the pursuits of pleasure, art and work. Reyd has had to navigate between the limited career trajectories for a black, working-class child growing up in Peckham in the 1960s and 1970s, and his passions for music and clothes that sustained his ambitions. His pursuit of his practice as a tailor has been a primary steer in this negotiation.

Reyd's story raises the question of what the social and cultural consequences are of becoming highly skilled. Do the practices of becoming skilled and maintaining skill support the possibility for any individual, irrespective of background, to access a fuller participation, albeit in a stratified society? These questions are pursued through two very different approaches to learning. The first, offered by Paul Willis (1977) in his seminal text, *Learning to Labour: How Working Class Kids Get Working Class Jobs*, is the persistence of a subculture imbued in lack of prospect. For Willis, what is effectively learnt in the curtailed transition from school to work is to be a labourer. The biased structure of opportunity ranked by class and driven by industrial capital provides the core for the cultural circulation of value. Sennett's focus in *The Corrosion of Capital* (1999) and *The Craftsman* (2008b) turns to the world of a service economy, in which the time-protracted accumulation of skill is undervalued in economic terms. However, in individual and cultural terms, Sennett argues that skill sustains a durable practice of refinement, one which affords a genuine form of participation.

If Reyd's skill emerged from the formal and informal learning processes exposed to him through interactions within diverse social groups, then his first lessons began at home. During our first meeting, Reyd told me that his father used to be a trouser-maker in Jamaica. When the family emigrated to London in the early 1960s, Reyd was almost five. The social and economic circumstances of post-war London in the 1950s forced Reyd's father into construction work. Glass's (1960) study of West Indian newcomers to London during the late 1950s by invitation of the British Government suggests that racism during this period effectively masked skill. Her study highlights not only the general change in the work practice of these immigrants compared with their positions in the West Indies, but also the unequivocal downgrading of their work status, irrespective of skill. Downgrading of expectations and prospects was apparently not something Reyd's father intended to pass on to his son. Reyd recalled a day when his father introduced him to manual labour, and made Reyd fetch and carry tiles to tile a roof. By the end of a day of manual labour Reyd's hands were raw, but the lesson was clear – there were preferable ways of making a living. On leaving school Reyd described his father's insistence, 'Boy, you better go out and get a trade, because I don't want no criminals in this house.'

Unlike his father, whose skill was not recognised in the climate of post-war Britain, Reyd was able to both pursue and sustain his ambition of being a tailor. He left school at sixteen to study tailoring at college and entered into the official apprenticeship system:

> When I left school I worked for Fleet Street tailors, Dombey & Son. They put a broom in one hand and a tea pot in the other. After two to three months they saw I was able to take instructions. Within this shop was a basement – I call it 'the dungeon' – with rows and rows of ready-made suits and I had to brush them. After a month or two I was asked to come up. I learned to work with clients, saw how to approach them. I worked with all their old soldiers, like cutters and fitters. I had experienced, senior people that I was able to work under. I was able to get the benefit of their experience. The apprenticeship was a three to five year course. By the time you passed that, there was an old soldier who was ready to move on, and you had a job. When the apprenticeships and industries were taken away, all that crashed with it.
>
> (Fieldwork conversation 2006)

The post-war apprenticeship mechanism offered Reyd not only direct exposure to a trade in which he started out with menial responsibilities, but also growth within the remit of the trade. After two months of sweeping and making the tea, Reyd was able 'to come up' and learn directly from skilled tailors. The apprenticeship had partly provided an avenue for Reyd, as a young black man from south London, to participate in a well-established tailor shop in central London, an opportunity that would neither have occurred without the official mechanism of the apprenticeship nor without the availability of work in manufacturing. Vickerstaff (2003) relates what is portrayed as the 'golden age' of apprenticeships in the UK, spanning the period from 1945 to 1975, to the structural trends of a positive labour market in the 1950s and 1960s. Apprenticeships were directly related to a strong manufacturing base to the urban and national economy.

Of pertinence to Reyd's story is that in the hundred years up to 1950, clothing was the largest manufacturing trade in London in terms of numbers of people employed (Hall 1960). But the apprenticeship system, while providing for the acquisition of skill through trade, was not without structural bias. Although Vickerstaff acknowledges the opportunities of mobility for working-class youth from school into workplaces within the 'golden age' of apprenticeships, she connects the apprenticeship system to a channelling of young people into labour niches, based on type of school attended as well as class background. Since the global economic crisis of 2008, both the Labour and subsequent Conservative–Liberal Democrat governments have voiced considerable support for the apprenticeship mechanism. On the one hand, the apprenticeship potentially offers access to a skill where work becomes a platform for learning, not simply for earning. However, in contemporary London and its economy defined by its service base economy and stratified job market, Reyd's story raises two crucial questions: without a manufacturing base to the economy what employment sectors would absorb the apprenticeships? and: how would apprenticeships address a lack of real work prospects, particularly for disempowered youth? In Reyd's words:

> The black youth in particular think, 'What is the use in studying, if when you do get the paper, you don't get the jobs anyway?' They are going to form their own ways, their own system, they've got brains. When I left school, apprenticeships were available because the industries were here. Within thirty odd years they have gone, and everything is made abroad. People are going to create a situation where they can earn, not just the black kids.
>
> (Fieldwork conversation 2007)

In subsequent conversations with Reyd, he referred to the growth of the drug trade, and the offer of group membership and lucrative prospects that might be attractive to what he referred to as boys who had 'gone feral'. He had been approached as part of a borough-based mentorship initiative to talk to disconnected youth, but was less than optimistic about the message he had to offer:

> So what I am telling is that I love my work. But when they ask about what I earn, it's going to be like, what I make in a month, they could pick up in a week on the streets.
>
> (Fieldwork conversation 2009)

Historically, individual mobility within the clothing industry at the turn of the twentieth century was partly assisted by the formal acquisition and recognition of a trade, which served both to skill the working class and also to contain their status within the stratified social ranks of the trade: 'Journeymen in Britain were craftsmen. Having served their apprenticeship they were highly skilled. Within the British working class to be called a journeyman was a sign of moderately high status, higher than the ordinary worker, but not as high as a master craftsman' (Godley 2000: 136). However, the development of a formal apprenticeship within the clothing trade had important consequences for the entry of immigrants into the UK job market. In particular, of the Eastern European Jewish emigrants to London between 1880 and 1914, two-thirds were employed in the clothing industry (Godley 2000).

Access to the clothing industry for immigrants in London during this industrial period was partly aided by the decentralisation of manufacturing, or 'piecework' – quite literally the small-scale, piece-by-piece organisation of work. Home industry was made possible by the ease of transportation of comparatively light-weight items of clothing and the mechanisation of the sewing machine, equally suited to factory or home. The exploitation within this fragmented structure of production, known as 'sweating', was also abetted by a large labour pool in general, and specifically the Jewish immigrant labour pool in Whitechapel, who lived in proximity to the concentration of wholesale clothing manufacturing in London's East End.

It was for a subsequent generation of Jewish immigrant tailors that Reyd undertook and completed his apprenticeship. Having acquired his City & Guilds certificate for craft tailoring, Reyd went on to work for Sidney Fox in Peckham, where he remained for twelve years. Before reaching thirty, Reyd had a repertoire of good tailoring skills, coupled with an ambition to go out and make it on his own terms. He had learnt both the propriety of how to deal with clients as well as how to cut a suit, allowing him to set up a partnership with two of his friends from college. Their theatrical tailoring company in Brixton Hill operated for eight years before Reyd left the partnership to set up his own shop on the Walworth Road. Here he formed a base through practising as a specialist on two fronts – a bespoke tailor in general, and the maker of Mod suits in particular. It is this absolute, stubborn regard for speciality, and for the time needed to attend to hand tailoring, that defines Reyd's work as an art. He made almost every aspect of the suit, including cloth buttons, not only designing but also cutting the suit to his standards. Through his particularity, he has developed and sustained a reputation:

> What am I doing to push it? I'm doing what I'm doing. Slow progression – is that what you'd call it? We've got this far because I didn't take the Savile Row route. I'm the salesman, the cutter, the fitter and the re-cutter. So I don't need three other people, to pay their salaries.
>
> (Fieldwork conversation 2007)

The 'cityness' of skill

Cultural associations between the city, its places of production and spaces of performance relate to the historically centralised locations of clothing manufacturing in London. Hall (1960) defined clothing manufacturing in the industrial period between 1861 and 1951 in England and Wales as essentially a metropolitan production, moreover one most prominent in London. Of the factors most significant to the location of clothing manufacturing in London, Hall emphasised the role of the metropolitan market, and the need for the makers of clothes to be closely associated with the lifestyles of a changing and unpredictable clientele. Hall's analysis of the *Post Office London Directories* confirmed that clothing manufacturing in London was explicitly localised and, significantly, concentration was most evident in two distinctly different agglomerations of a West End and an East End centre.

In distinguishing between the different tailoring practices in these West End and East End concentrations, Hall described the development of those in West End practice as increasingly in contact with and responding to the proximity of wealthy customers, where bespoke tailors sought to preserve the tradition and craft of tailoring through the Amalgamated Society of Tailors. In contrast, tailors in the East End concentration were represented by the Association of Master Tailors, and generally expanded through wholesale production, assisted by the proximity of the docks, wholesale houses and a large, low-wage labour pool.

Crucially in both distinctive concentrations, the scale of the organisation of work and a system of production meant that sub-contracting through divisions of tasks and specialisation persisted in the work of the bespoke tailor as well as the wholesale clothier. Indeed it is a practice and scale of production that persists today, one that provided Reyd with access to highly skilled finishers and jacket-makers who work off site, generally either in their homes or in small spaces in larger workrooms. It is equally crucial to note that in the face of global economic restructuring and clothing production, exclusivity has endured in place, while mass production of cheap items has tended to follow the cheapest places of production. In a BBC Four documentary on Savile Row (2008), Richard James, a bespoke tailor, asserts that exclusivity is an enduring asset in the circulation of contemporary value, 'The whole concept of luxury has moved on, everything is too available, we should go back to being less available.'

As the tailoring workforce fragmented across the city, the increasingly unusual practice of bespoke tailoring and its particular market has meant there is a contraction and concentration in the location of bespoke tailors. This tendency is evident in Hall's maps that span ninety years of tailoring in London and in my contemporary map of bespoke tailors in central London (Figure 4.5). This map shows the locations of 305 bespoke tailors in central London, accessed from a Google search (2009) by entering the search terms 'bespoke tailors London' and selecting 'local business results'. The map indicates two primary clusters of bespoke tailoring in central London, the largest in the W1 or West End postcode, including Savile Row, and the second around the vicinity of the City as the central business district.

Figure 4.5 The location of bespoke tailoring in central London in 2009.

The list of London's tailor shops included in another online local business survey, touchlocal.com (www.touchlocal.com), accessed in 2007 showed that the W1 postcode remains the area with the primary concentration of London bespoke tailoring in London: 53 per cent of tailors are located in the West End area of W1, including 15 per cent in Savile Row. Very few are located in south London, suggesting that tailors in Savile Row continue to offer prospective customers a reputation established on tradition, location and agglomeration, while the City's major advantage is its proximity to London's primary business centre. The question remains then of how Reyd has built and sustained a bespoke tailor service without having the assets of location and agglomeration. Reyd's reputation cannot rely on the iconic brand of a street or district, which his Walworth Road address fails to deliver. Equally, Reyd's local ties, according to a longstanding customer, 'are not enough to keep him making good money'.

At the same time that Savile Row was emerging as a tailoring street within an avant-garde district at the turn of the twentieth century, a tailor by the name of Norman Rose occupied the position of Reyd's current shop on the Walworth Road. The strong presence of *in situ* clothing manufacture and retail on the Walworth Road is recorded up to the 1950 *Post Office London Directory*, in which eight tailors are registered, as well as forty-six other clothing retailers including hatters, costumiers, bag and shoemakers and ladies outfitters. Also in this 1950 survey is the first record of a department store on the Walworth Road; Marks and Spencers Ltd is registered at numbers 311 to 315. Today, however, the tradition of tailoring is challenged by the availability of cheap clothes, and mass-produced, off-the-peg fashion is in abundance on the Walworth Road. In Reyd's terms, the culture of fashion has muscled in on the culture of bespoke style. 'Bespoke' and 'tailoring', once part of the working-class urban landscape in London, and historically evidenced in the number of tailors on the Walworth Road, have generally retreated from the experience of the urban high street.

However location has remained key for Reyd, as qualified by his references to his own roots and affinities as an 'everyday person, a south London person':

> The reason why I wanted to come into this area was because the owner of Sidney Fox's had lived in Peckham, but his heart's desire was to be in the City – Suit Land. I didn't want to be in the City, I didn't like the politics, the static. Areas like this, these are my people. I am a local, I grew up in Peckham. Working in the City, there's a snootiness. Sometimes I need to remind people that I'm not guessing at this. I know my art.
>
> (Fieldwork conversation 2006)

Respect

One-to-one respect

Critical to Reyd's work was his one-to-one relationship with his customers, and the requirement for a mutual understanding on both of their parts of the skill involved in making a bespoke garment. This was a two-way process of showing respect – a social pact between the maker and the wearer, chaperoned by social rules. On the few occasions that I had watched a prospective client come into Reyd's shop, I was surprised at how formal Reyd was in establishing a certain propriety and etiquette upfront. One morning a young man came in to have a formal coat altered so that he could wear it to a wedding. Reyd quoted £30 for the sleeves and £45 for the 'let'. The young man looked slightly taken aback at the cost, and this was how Reyd managed the situation:

Reyd:	That's what it's going to cost you. You know why? 'Cos I work on £600 to £700 suits. So if it's a problem, then we can't do it. (Pause)
Young man:	OK sir. No problem. I'll take it.
Reyd:	There's a drycleaner across the way. Go and ask him what he'll charge. I don't charge for pinning, so I don't mind.
Young man:	No boss, I'll do it. I don't want him to do it. I want you.
Reyd:	So, for my alterations, I'll charge you up front. (The young man takes out £70, instead of £75, hoping for a reduction.) You fell down at the last minute. I would have done it for £70, but you fell down. (The young man hands over the full £75.) So, it's two weeks.
Young man:	You take your time. Give me a call. That's OK. No worries boss.

(Fieldwork notes 2006)

Reyd clarified his worth to the uninitiated client in straight financial terms, but also provided an exit for the young man should he wish to save face. Not only did Reyd ask for the fee upfront, but he also ensured he was in charge of the bargaining process. Reyd took charge to assert the value of his skill as well as the value of the relationship between the maker and the customer. In describing the core relationship between the maker and customer Reyd stated, 'What we're doing is moulding the jacket. And we're moulding it not just to the body but to the mind.' This form of respect – the reciprocal recognition between maker and wearer – of the skill involved in making a bespoke garment is not a social relation that can exist in off-the-peg fashion stores, where the product on display is separated from its process of making. As the acquisition of the off-the-peg item takes less time, the social contract between customer and proprietor or customer and store manager is reduced.

Local codes of respect

So who were Reyd's clients, who were the people who participated on the other side of this social exchange, of this mutual establishment of respect? Part of the answer lay in Reyd's connection with his local clientele:

You get a different feeling from people in areas like this . . . they're my people, whatever colour they are. In the City I always felt like the boy. In an area like this you're allowed to grow, you can show what you can do.

Reyd suggested that local familiarities were key to his success, because of the ease of establishing connections through common social codes that chaperone the budding relationship. However, Reyd's customer base was varied and included celebrities, locals and people who traversed the city for specialist skills. In order to participate in the reciprocal act of respect, there needed to be a comfort level for both parties to engage with one another. Both parties needed to share common social codes, be they affinities with Mod culture that reach well beyond south London neighbourhoods, or local codes based on shared memories and language.

The associations with a local place were one aspect of a common social code, where social connections were established not only by a shared sense of the past, but also by day-to-day experiences of the present. 'Rags' was a friend and customer of Reyd's, a retired Bermondsey boxer and former world welterweight champion. He no longer lived in the area but affirmed, 'I'm always down in the area. I grew up in the area. I love this area.' I asked him what he thought about the Walworth Road and he replied: 'The Walworth Road has changed dramatically. It's a really multicultural society, a multinational society. Put it this way, I don't feel racism around here, I don't think colour matters so much around here . . . only with the police.' Racism mattered a great deal to Rags; as an emerging boxing talent, he had forfeited his welterweight title, rather than defend it in the then apartheid South Africa.

Appearance mattered to Rags, too, and when I first saw him make an entrance into Reyd's shop, he looked nothing short of what Robert Elms (2006) articulates as, 'sartorial brilliance'. Rags' bold street style merged with his easy-to-like, extrovert personality; when he stepped into Reyd's on a mild winter's day, he was wearing a full length fur coat, accompanied by a large, matching fur hat. His accessories included dark glasses, a shiny black walking stick topped with a gold skull, a diamond-studded ring and expensive black shoes gleaming beneath the precise fold of his grey trousers. He walked in and he had our attention. So did the current world cruiserweight champion who stared out at us from a poster on Reyd's wall – the raw and physical image of Nina Simone's soul song – *'Young, gifted and black'*. The champion had scrawled a message below his picture for Reyd: 'Fuck Savile Row. Reyd's is the only place to go.' In another picture, a photograph on the opposite wall, the young boxer was dressed in one of Reyd's suits – minimal, light grey – immaculate. Both boxers mentioned here were locals who came from the Bermondsey boxing gyms to the east of Walworth, and they came to Reyd's for bespoke garments. Undoubtedly part of the mutual respect between proprietor and customer was more easily forged because of their south London networks and shared local histories.

Stan, known simply as 'The Suit', was a local and a close friend of Reyd. I was greeted first by his laugh, an open hand, and a broad South London accent, 'Hallo! Pleased to meet you.' Stan liked to dress for an occasion every day, and at our first meeting he was wearing a three-quarter-length, navy, pin-striped Crombie coat. He was passionate about clothes, Mod culture and his local roots, and has written numerous books on these subjects. He described himself as 'a 1960s enthusiastic gentleman', and while patting his tummy he added, 'all right, an ageing Mod'. Although Stan described himself as 'comfortable in the West End and I'm open to ideas from over the river', he talked about his reluctance at getting a suit made in the West End. He emphasised this by saying, 'People don't realise how hard it is to walk into a place.' He went on to recall an uncomfortable experience he had walking in to a prestigious tailor shop in Jermyn Street, and contrasted this with the ease of walking into Reyd's shop for the first time: 'Reyd speaks the right language. We would be out of place in Savile Row. When I first came in here I thought, "I could talk to you, I could deal with you."' Entry points for talking to each other in this case included shared areas of affinity like football and clothes, while Reyd and Stan's more specific or more local affinity was their common language, shaped by accent, phrases and forms of delivery.

Language that has come from the urban working class in London and adapted through localised expressions is a mode of sociability still used on the Walworth Road today. Language shaped through what Stan described as 'banter' and what Reyd described as 'lyrics' is a linguistic performance, quite literally, a manner of speaking. Typically, banter allows for serious things to be said with humour, and obliges the response or retort to be equally quick-witted – sharp and funny. Stan described how as a teenager he worked in a factory with 'old geezers' who had been in the Second World War. They bantered with him mercilessly, but Stan could hold his own as he had the gift of the gab: 'You had to come back in cracks,' he said, 'then they would say, "You been brought up the right way mate."'

Self-respect

The music critic and radio broadcaster Robert Elms (2006) tells us that there is a moment in wearing a bespoke garment, when you first put it on, that the garment is all yours. You see yourself as if for the first time, transformed by the promise of the suit. That moment remains yours on each subsequent occasion you wear the garment before it is worn for a public audience. Reyd referred to this moment as 'preening': the sensuality of putting the clothes on and enjoying a sense of transformation in front of the mirror, either at the tailor for the first time, or subsequently at home. He said, 'I've seen people when they look in the mirror. I've seen city people drop expletives.'

In the case of a bespoke garment, the crafted item itself combined with the sense of wearing it potentially increases this personal sense of transformation. Stan commented that, unlike off-the-peg suits, the gratification from the bespoke suit is deferred until the end of the process, one in which 'you must invest two months of your life'. At some point the individual act of preening shifts past the process of self-recognition, and is taken to a broader audience. The audience, incorporating both a social group and a given situation, enhances the opportunity for the recognition of a mark of status, and a sense of self-respect. Such a social exchange depends on the recognition of value, and an appreciation of the craft and the identification with what the suit represents. As an immediate experience the bespoke garment is a sensory object, tangibly and visibly crafted for the pleasure of the individual. But the value of the bespoke garment is only partly in the pleasure of wearing it: it is also in the pleasure of appearing in it, an appreciation between the wearer and the observer, and for those who can read the nuances of the garment, there are the possibilities of connecting with the affinities of a refined group.

It is not only that the bespoke garment is worn for an occasion – typically weddings, funerals, rites of passage, celebrations – but also that wearing the suit helps assist in establishing a sense of occasion. An extract from Reyd's customer notebook described how a young recording producer felt when wearing his bespoke suit in recording sessions:

> I found out about 'Reyd' through the New Untouchables Mag. I desperately needed some new clothes – didn't like anything available on the High St. 'Reyd' has a great understanding of the look I want to achieve and I was very happy with the finished results and am now going to get lots more suits made. In my job as recording producer of 'TR Studios' the sessions I enjoy the most are the ones where I am wearing a fine suit, from now on these will be by 'Walworth Tailors'.
>
> (Copied from Reyd's customer notebook 2006)

In a 'thank you' letter to Reyd, another customer described his joy at wearing his suit to a wedding, and emphasised his thrill at people 'in the know' congratulating him on his suit. But perhaps more pertinent was his account of having to attend a funeral, and how wearing the suit helped him through this difficult occasion. The suit, once worn for special occasions, acquires associations with important events, increasing its personal significance and raising its aesthetic value. When Elms states that 'Clothes tell stories' (2006: 2), it is not only collective stories of status and affinity that are told, but also an accumulation of individual memories, associations and transformation.

The suit, not unlike the caff, was an integral part of the 'working-man's life' and both were part of the everyday life of working-class culture in South London. While the caff was the place working men went to during the working week, generally with work mates to consume a substantial, hot plate of high-carbohydrate food to meet the demands of physical labour, the working-man's suit was reserved for Sundays, to be worn down at the church or local pub. Stan recalled, with a measure of admiration, the stature of the suit in the 1960s:

> The working-man's suit is his Sunday best. Starting with the shoes, they had to be highly polished. For Christmas day you get a new shirt, a new pair of shoes and a suit. Up until twenty, twenty-five years ago, you left school, you had a suit made. It was all about suiting and booting. I found those guys really inspiring. They could be the roughest dustman in the world, and then on a Sunday they'd be like Beau Brummel.
>
> (Fieldwork conversation 2008)

Social style

Intermingling

The working-class ways of life were not altogether eradicated by fundamental changes to the structure and organisation of work, evidenced in London during the 1960s and 1970s as a deep economic shift from a manufacturing to a service economy (Fainstein, Gordon and Harloe 1992). The working-class 'suiting and booting' sartorial tradition was adopted and adapted by post-war working-class youth across Britain and, notably from the 1960s onwards, new style repertoires emerged. An intermingling of inspiration fostered by 'links between British working class fashion and contemporary American black music' (Hewitt 2000: 16) resonated in London in the housing estates, football grounds, Soho jazz clubs, Carnaby Street boutiques and south London dance clubs:

> As the soul man punched out his deep Memphis rhythms, so the boy in the suit did a slow-motion council-estate shuffle across the floral carpet we'd recently bought on HP from the Co-op. The music was his soundtrack; the dance was strictly for display. The shoes that shone out beneath this paragon of a two-piece were Royals [. . .] This was what you grew up for [. . .] Leave school at fifteen, save for a suit at sixteen. As I watched my eldest brother, ten years my senior, display the sweet fruits of the first year of his labours, with a shimmy and a show, parading his standing and his allegiance, his status and his taste, somehow I understood that this was a path, a lineage. My dad, a dapper man when he wasn't wearing overalls, nodded approval.
>
> (Elms 2006: 1–2)

The form and future of the working-man's suit, or the working-man's social style, has been altered by a number of changes, both structural and lived. The most obvious structural shift was the gradual decline of work in manufacturing and industries, accompanied by changes to livelihoods and lives. In addition, an increasing access to a far greater diversity of stylistic references was made available through an expanding media, as well as through new settings for sartorial display. The Sunday suit-and-pub routine shifted to new venues for entertainment – from localised pubs to less restricted clubs. Further, the bespoke suit simply became less available, limited by the mass production of suits and clothing more generally, as well as by changing patterns of culture and consumption. Stan commented that his dad and his mates 'would have had their own personal tailors. They've disappeared because of the expense and the waiting time.' When I questioned Reyd about the comparable expense and waiting time in today's terms, he answered, 'So in those days it was two to three weeks, four top wack.' Stan added, 'In those days a suit was equivalent to a week's wages, now it's half a month's at least. Now it's a lifestyle, it has to mean the world to you.'

The narratives about style and lifestyle described in this chapter include the cultural connections between varied working-class ways of life and the emergence of street fashion and Mod culture celebrated by Reyd and many of his customers.

But if the designation of class defined primarily in terms of work is no longer explicitly applicable, in what ways does 'lifestyle' accommodate an intermingling of working-class affinities with new ways of life? The way that Stan uses 'lifestyle' is not essentially aesthetic; it is about a process of associating with and relating to, in his narrative, a merging of past and present, expressed through shared sensibilities. Similarly, when I ask Reyd to explain Mod culture to me, before he described its aesthetic particularities, he offered a key description of interaction: 'How can I put this? Through the style or through the concept, it brings people together, who are not thinking on race, but on the concept of the dress and the music.'

Mod culture, although resonant with English working-class youth culture of the 1960s, is part of a wider spectrum of social, cultural and aesthetic affinities. Hewitt (2000) describes the range of what he terms 'Soul Stylists' rooted in Soho jazz clubs in the 1950s, through to the 'flash jewellery, white Bally shoes and Gabicci top' gear donned by the 'Casuals' in the 1980s and 1990s. Equally, the minimalist Mod look of the 1960s – two-tone suit, slim fitted with three buttons on the jacket, epitomised by Sting in the film *Quadrophenia* – is under constant re-interpretation by a contemporary audience. Reyd showed me pictures of a 1960s 'Traditional Mod', and then a 'Skin Mod' from the 1970s wearing a suit with a row of buttons down the arm, 'for fighting', and then a 'Mod Mod' with the 1960s suit, but this time accessorised with a gelled, spiky haircut. As Reyd commented, 'What I want to draw your attention to is how things move on.' Not only do things move on, but sources of inspiration and departure also vary. Mod looks have come from recording studios and LP covers, as well as the football terraces. Reyd's enduring source of inspiration has been from his neighbourhood experiences of socialising:

> These fashions actually came from the street. For example – my mother used to take me to a shop in Rye Lane, Peckham. I would ask my mum to get a blue blazer, no splits. Once I was home, I would make a split. Us boys in Peckham had the longest split, the largest vent. That was the trend for us Peckham boys. The Brixton boys had side vents. This is documented. It wasn't spoken of. It was just done.
>
> (Fieldwork conversation 2006)

Conventions and inventions

If style is the social translation of shared cultural affinities, the practice of tailoring is a technical and interpretive process, which is located between the conventions and inventions of tailoring. At one of our first meetings, I asked Reyd to describe the traditional process of making a suit. He spoke slowly, organising the sequence of his thoughts, and it was clear that he wanted the process to be documented exactly:

- The first person aside from the salesman would be the 'cutter-fitter', and would cut and fit the garment onto the client. Once the garment was fitted, any adjustments would be done by the cutter-fitter.

- You would then have a baste-maker who would make a baste or a fitting for the client.
- Once adjustments are made the garments would go into the various workrooms (trousers, jackets, etc). The jacket would always go to the jacket-maker who would then trim the jacket. He would cut the various parts for lining
- pocket bags, body lining, sleeve lining – for the pocket-maker to machine pockets and sleeves.
- Once the pockets are made and sleeve linings are made, the garment goes back to the jacket-maker for it to be assembled. Once the various parts are assembled into the jacket, the jacket is then given to the finisher.
- The finisher will make the necessary buttonholes on the front and the cuffs of the sleeve. The finisher will also hand sew the lining inside the jacket around the armhole of the sleeves (it's actually called the scye hole) and hand sew the cuffs of the sleeves, and the side seams of the lining inside the jacket.
- Once the finisher has done their job, the garment is given back to the jacket-maker who inspects the jacket. If the jacket-maker doesn't press the jacket himself, he will give it to a presser, who will then press the jacket.
- The jacket is then given back to the jacket-maker to button the jacket.

(Fieldwork conversation 2007)

What Reyd described as a traditional method and practice incorporates the piece-by-piece production of a tailored garment, at once fragmented and specialised. Each individual involved in this process is designated a specific role and position relative to the explicit nature of their task or craft. This mode of tailoring was inculcated in the apprenticeship process and, as previously mentioned, was highly suitable for piecework and sub-contract work that arose in clothing manufacturing in England over the industrial period. I asked Reyd whether within this ongoing stratification of the work process the different tasks are done by different people, and he replied:

> The finishers are usually women. I would say seven out of ten times; they would be middle-aged or senior. You won't find many young finishers today, 'cos they will be using machines. Jacket-makers, from what I've seen, I've seen very few women jacket-makers. Also middle-aged and senior – you won't find many young people in the bespoke end, maybe in theatre, but that's machining, it's a different trade.

(Fieldwork conversation 2007)

After about nine months of having had no contact with Reyd other than quick hellos, I returned to his shop with new questions. Reyd was excited about the prospects of designing and developing what he called his 'signature suit'. Although he had been adapting and creating suits for years, an inspirational moment came about when a customer of his brought a special cuff-link to Reyd, with a request to incorporate it into a suit. Working the suit out together to incorporate the 'zey link' (where a flared cuff is fastened by a link on a diagonal slit), Reyd and his customer formulated ideas for developing the suit as both an off-the-peg and a bespoke garment. Having operated as a sole proprietor Reyd was now entering into a venture where he had acquired new prospects, stating with unreserved ambition, 'I want to be the tailor that changes the face of the cuff on the high street.' Reyd described his 'signature suit'. It had diagonal button-holes, a slight flare on the sleeve, an open cuff, two high buttons on the jacket front, a fish-mouth lapel, cloth buttons and a frog-mouth pocket with a little split at the bottom. He concluded, 'It's all been done before, but not on one jacket.'

It was during this latter part of my fieldwork that I began to think of the issue of authorship, particularly with respect to Reyd's excitement over his signature suit. As mentioned, Reyd generally made every aspect of the garment, took responsibility for his shop display, and met with and worked with his customers. Yet Reyd made no sole claim to the conceptual aspect of this process. He defined it as collaboration across a number of levels, most notably for him a juxtaposition of his learned conventions of tailoring (technique), of the fashions he grew up with on the streets of Peckham (style) and of the contribution of the customer (personality):

> If for example you got a jigsaw, you got the person who paints the picture, the person who cuts the jigsaw to the shapes, the person who puts it in the box, the person who buys it and reveals the jigsaw, [and] the person who puts it back together.
>
> (Fieldwork conversation 2007)

Within Reyd's concept of creating, there was reference to both the solitary and collective processes of authorship, or what Becker (1982) defines as the 'co-operative joint activity' that serves to conceive, execute, manufacture, distribute, support and appreciate art. Becker's *Art Worlds* gives us an understanding of the organisation of networks spanning artists, mobilisers and distributors of art works, critics and audiences. But in describing culture primarily through the organisation of social relations, we are left with little sense of the sensualities, and indeed sensibilities that make up these social relations. Reyd's own conceptualisation of the art of attire as 'co-operative joint activity' is underpinned not only by economic organisation, but also an orchestration of sensibilities formed through deeply acquired appreciations. The shared affinity of sartorial style is explicitly social since it requires reciprocity, or mutual recognition between two or more persons. The physical quality of the suit – its cut, texture and tone – offers another kind of skin, one most readily recognised through shared sensibility.

Conclusions

Style, as expressed by Reyd, is a process of 'bringing people together'. His is an articulation of social affinities forged with individuals and groups, through a sharing of an aural and visual sensibility. Reyd's practice as a Mod tailor suggests that style is a consequence of multiple social relations and learning processes. In Reyd's case, home, street and shop, as well as the medium of music and clothes, are all different and integral sources for the constitution of his style. Because Reyd experiences style as a way of life, it is not only invigorated by moments of inspiration, but by a sociability that is located in two primary venues – his position and relationship with local customers on the Walworth Road, and his Mod affinities through which he has broadened his local horizons.

Further, it is this aspect of sociability, of diverse individuals relating to one another through music or through clothes, that contributes to the transformation and on-going interpretation of wearing style, of adapting culture. The working-man's suit is by no means dead, it has simply been recast in other urban performances, in south London nightclubs, or football terraces, or whichever stage it next finds for public display. In this sense Simmel's (1949) articulation of sociability as the combination of art and play, 'where society is played', serves the practice of style well; style is essentially social, and depends on the serious artifice of display and etiquette, where the visible signs of social status, be they born from class or race, are publicly parodied, circulated and reinvented. It is the nimble acts of translation that confer both distinction and allegiance.

Finally, in the process of making or crafting, the question of what it is that is ultimately made, or what the essential cultural artefact is, needs to be understood. In Reyd's practice as a bespoke tailor, the actual material garment is not the sole object or purpose of making. Bespoke garments are also the medium or practice through which Reyd has refined his way of life, from his apprenticeship to his set of social and business relationships with diverse customers. The measure of his success rests in both the skill honed in making a bespoke garment and the skill demanded in sustaining respect between himself and his customers. This is a specialisation of being 'in the know' on two fronts, social and technical, and the peculiarity and longevity of his small, independent shop depends on it. Important to this account is how the sociability of style is located in the everyday life and space of the city. For skill to be cultural – to be made visible – it requires an audience and a venue. In Reyd's journey it is through the street in its social, pedagogic and mercantile dimensions that he has acquired a sensibility.

5   The politics of nearness

Why is it crucial to recognise local forms of participation, allegiance and belonging? I turn now to the intimacy of local life on the street to explore a scale of contact from which to consider the urban effects of immigration, disparity and multiculture. I return to Williams' (1958) premise, that learning is a shared process and a form of contact that happens within everyday life. Against the fluidity of people, economies and objects in a global world together with the increasing networked memberships across space, the question remains as to whether local contact matters when learning to live with difference and change. Does physical proximity have any bearing on social propinquity? The question is as much social as it is political, and in focusing on the ordinary. I aim to deal in the untidy realities of life-worlds and life-chances. The probings of urban multicultures are invoked to distort the cohesive canons of community and multiculturalism that have permeated UK policy discourse and related local government programmes in London (Local Government Association 2002; Jones 2009). The paradox of officiated cohesion is twofold: the first assumption is that tolerance is the basis for experiencing racial, class or ethnic differences; the second is that instituted programmes are able to inculcate the contact that most readily emerges out of the spontaneity of everyday life.

One of Walworth's residents highlighted 'a lack of spaces where we can mix and learn from each other'. It is within the realm of local meeting spaces that this chapter focuses, and begins with situated social explorations and physical contact. 'Exploration' is, however, possibly an overly generous term for the full range of social interactions within the shared spaces of the Walworth Road. While exchange and testing certainly occurred within these local meeting points, so too were more closed forms of engagement. But this is precisely the point of focusing on ordinary space: that in the banal aspects of everyday life, shared local spaces are shaped by habitual associations rather than outright compatibilities. I suggest that it is through such local associations that face-to-face forms of cultural exchange and social retreat, and conviviality and complacency are brought to life.

Space itself is not typically the focus of recent thinking on ordinary or vernacular cosmopolitanisms where analytic efforts have oriented more towards the flows and transformations of ideas and affinities across time and space, as explored through the fluidity of music (Gilroy 1997), language (Pollock 2000) and literature (Bhabha 2004 [1994]: preface) for example. This diverse body of work challenges the ideals of cosmopolitanism as a common political project that spans national territories, or as shared moral ideology or cultural acquiescence. Rather, it refers to the dynamic social and cultural exchanges that emerge within an uneven and rapidly changing world.

The spatial departure pursued in this chapter, as situated firmly within the urban margin, is explored through two modes of being public: informal membership and everyday practice. The first point to highlight is that regular interactions in local worlds are ones in which the stakes are raised. For although everyday memberships in ordinary spaces are generally informal, they are often profoundly significant for how individuals access knowledge, grant and gain trust, and affirm their connections within a socially sustained familiarity. Of significance is that for many of those who occupy the urban margins, in particular the poor, the elderly, the young and the newcomer, local worlds are places in which they are not simply dependent, but also highly invested. Further, the full guise of social distance or anonymity is denied by regular forms of face-to-face contact, and in order to secure one's right to appear and not simply frequent, broad codes of sociability have to be respected. The implications of informal membership, given the variety of individuals who regularly use the street and its adjacent sub-worlds, are that while parochial and cosmopolitan expressions have a daily presence, the means of working out, ignoring, and/or asserting are part of what allows for any one individual's return the following day. De Certeau (1984: 29–42) referred to this as 'ways of operating' within a schema, in which he described the use of tactics as the nimble adjustments necessary for the everyday art of 'making do'.

In pursuing the social uses of local publics, this chapter develops three perspectives of local space. The first is *familiar space* and, while I explore how individuals use their coordinates of familiarity to navigate their everyday worlds, the point I aim to stress in a highly disparate urban context like London is that for the vulnerable, familiarity is not simply a tactic, it is, to use de Certeau's distinction, a strategy for living with inequality. Familiarity can therefore both orientate and limit social exploration. Second is the idea of *intimate space* that emerges out of face-to-face contact, but that also refers to a form of personal connection within a group setting that allows for communication beyond the perfunctory. Here the trust and confidence associated with social intimacy might support personal as well as political forms of allegiance. Finally, skilful space is the terrain in which imagination and acumen flourish, but unlike the factory, studio or academy, the street provides a public intersection of life and livelihoods where work and leisure are rendered visible. It is through these three tropes of familiarity, social intimacy and skill that I explore the extent to which regular contact within a local margin is a conduit for social adaptation, exploration and renewal.

Familiar space

> So when I joined the National Film Theatre, it was this middle-class place on the South Bank – Festival Hall, National Theatre and all that. And to me it was, like, not so much for my father, but for my mother, it's like she's going to

lose me. And metaphorically she did. Because, once I had joined that place
. . . I never forgot she stood at the window and watched me walk to the bus
stop. I think she was still probably standing there waiting for me to come home.
But I was only going up the road to the National Film Theatre . . . she had the
strange feeling that her son . . . It was a big thing for a kid from a working-
class family, from a council estate, to make that leap and it was a leap, a big
leap. But then I discovered it was a very middle-class place and I didn't really
feel comfortable, although I *loved* going to see the films. That was really my
only motivation for going. I didn't really feel at ease with middle-class people.
I never have, I still don't. I still don't. It's not a chip on my shoulder. Some
of my best friends are middle class – know what I'm saying (*grins*). But I
always seem to come back here, as long as I had here to come back to, I could
spend as long as I like in the West End, in the cinema bookshop at the National
Film Theatre.

(Fieldwork interview 2007)

John, whom I introduced in Chapter 2, was in his forties and lived to the south
of the Walworth Road when I met with him. He recalled the day when, at the age
of sixteen, he joined the National Film Theatre. Although the direct bus trip from
Peckham to Waterloo would have involved only forty minutes of travel, the journey
represented a far greater distance for John and his parents. For John it required a
cultural crossing from his working-class roots in Peckham into a world of
institutions, films and intellectualism, which he simultaneously felt an affinity for
and a separation from. His territorial narrative exemplifies the displacement associated with extending one's horizons. It captures the difficulty of accessing broader
opportunities, because of the confines of position inscribed in society and space
by both class and locality.

Space is a constitutive dimension of social exclusion, and ethnographies based
on socialisation within spatially confined neighbourhoods in the UK have tended
to reinforce not only the local nature of groupings but also their segregations on
the basis of race, ethnicity and class (see for example Parker 1974 and Alexander
2000). The reproduction of social enclaves within spatial enclaves, whether told
through stories of how white working-class children in Bermondsey fail to fit in
the educational structure (Evans 2006), or the collision of established and emergent
cultures in the London Docklands redevelopment process (Foster 1999), reinforces
how territorial communities are entrapped in place.

The diversity of local voices and interactions on the Walworth Road made it
apparent that the familiarity of the local was as much socially affirming as it was
at times socially constraining. Many of the narratives of belonging were firmly
rooted in a confined commitment to locality as expressed through a tiered sense of
local boundaries, including the perceived parameters of the River Thames, the
Borough of Southwark and the neighbourhood, as well as small territories within
the neighbourhood. In these narratives place was invoked to position a sense of self
with respect to locality, such as 'My grandfather was a Peckham person' or 'I was
born on this side. When we were kids we never went onto the other side. There

[the other side] was a different gang.' Place was also used to define the limits of personal exploration as described by one local who claimed, 'Everything is here. For the last ten years I haven't moved much beyond the borough.'

The comfort of local familiarity, however, also abetted a wide spectrum of social needs, which included convenience as sense of security and sameness. Individuals expressed an affinity for ways of life acquired at a local scale that were accessible, regular and repetitive. The pattern of small spatial distances between home and street supported the regular use of the Walworth Road by its surrounding local population, and the everyday use of the street contributed to the formation of local social connections. Regularity is therefore a component of public sociability reliant on the relative fixity of local places and on repeated participation; of knowing and being known through returning to the same spaces, engaging with familiar faces and, in the case of the Walworth Road, often buying more or less the same goods at the same shops. But what are the forms of social life that emerge out of local place that allow for social exploration, and does familiar space have a role to play in how people mix and learn on the Walworth Road?

The relationship between interaction and integration in local space is contested in the broad arena of urban studies and community studies. In his seminal study of the inner city slums of Chicago in the 1960s, Suttles (1968) defined locality as a proper element of social structure and focused on the effect of spatial boundaries or what he termed the 'ordered segmentation' of ethnicity and territory (1968: 23). For Suttles (1972) the interrelationship between local neighbourhoods and local groupings was primarily a constructed one, and his empirical work explored the idea of community as ascribed racial and ethnic groupings within defended neighbourhoods. Gans' research (1962) of Italian-Americans in New York's West End in the 1950s defined community as 'peer group society', or a process of social association that grows out of an economic and societal structure of which local place is a part. Gans emphasised the individual capacity to exercise choice within a limited range of available economic and social alternatives. He argued that class, as a lifestyle associated with occupational, educational and consumer distinctions, mattered more to the idea of a peer group society than ethnicity or territory.

In contrast, an area of urban studies that incorporates the impacts of capitalist globalisation has focused on questioning not only how fluid and mixed societies orientate in local space, but also whether local place is indeed fundamental to belonging. Massey's essay '*A Global Sense of Place*' (1994) is set against the backdrop of profound economic change in the re-organisation of the economy that occurred in the 1970s, and questions what effect the globalisation of finance and communication has for the lived resolutions of being local. In spite of the argued increase in a sense of placeless-ness or disorientation (Harvey 1989; Augé 1995), Massey emphasises the actual presence of local life, local relationships and local spaces, but rejects a conceptual definition of place that relies on drawing boundaries.

By taking us for a walk down Kilburn High Road in North London, Massey describes the very ordinary global–local connections between Kilburn High Road and the world, through the variegated sense of place carried in diverse bodies, spaces and objects. She calls for 'an extroverted sense of place' or, more explicitly, 'a global sense of the local, a global sense of place' (1994: 156). But in seeking to conflate the conceptual binary between global and local, Massey eliminates the analytic significance of local boundaries, and the real impact these have on how people participate in urban life. My fieldwork suggests that Massey's 'extroverted' or connected web of local places needs to be paralleled with familiar space as an aggregation of sub-worlds, many of which are introverted and bounded.

Individuals on the Walworth Road navigated their local worlds through coordinates of familiarity sustained by everyday practices in ordinary spaces – such as going to the caff, the internet café or the pub. Within these familiar spaces, social life tended to emerge from a combination of different forms of ease: the nearness of place, the routine of practice and the everyday or non-specific programmes within a space. Through the collective practices of acquiring familiarity, local social networks and local cultural institutions emerge. But significant changes in the economic structure alters the life and prevalence of these local institutions, and social institutions together with informal social memberships either adapt or disappear. There are far fewer pubs and caffs on the Walworth Road than there were in the 1950s when Walworth was largely a white working-class neighbour-hood (*Post Office London Directory* 1881–1950).

However, there are also new social proxies for the pub and the caff, as is evident in the growth of the independent kebab shops and internet cafés along the street. New technical advancements which sustain a networked sociability less dependent on place, such as Wi-Fi and computer stations, give customers access to e-mail and the internet while eating and meeting, and new ways of being social within a locale emerged from the invested presence of customers and proprietors within their local domain. Passing by Eroma – an internet café on the Walworth Road – one is aware of a different generation of street clientele using and shaping a different generation of everyday meeting establishments. There has been a rapid increase in the number of nail bars along the Walworth Road, and these are places for women to have their nails manicured, and spaces in which women and children socialise. While some spaces were gender specific, others were ethnically or culturally specific, such as the Somali Club, an eating establishment off the Walworth Road, frequented by individuals of Somali connection. User groups and realms of familiarity constantly transform the small spaces along the Walworth Road, and the street in turn congregates the collections of these cheek-by-jowl sub-worlds.

Place was also used as a coordinate for the familiarity of the past, a reference to how things used to be and a physical and perceptual barometer of the extent to which things have changed. Surfacing in many of the conversations that I had with locals who were born in the area was the sense that as their local worlds became increasingly unfamiliar, familiar remnants such as Nick's Caff became increasingly important. Locals who used the Caff regularly commented on how they valued Nick's Caff as a place in which 'little seemed to change'. The focus on familiarity in what was perceived as a rapidly changing world may seem fairly unremarkable – we all have places and spaces to which we wish to return, based on the comfort of knowing and being known. But there remains the important social question of the extent to which local people are captive to locality, and in particular the social consequences for those whose spatial and social confinement is exaggerated by vulnerability, such as the elderly or the poor. While ties to locality are reinforced by the daily use of local places, these same locality ties can also be asserted through urban economies, political systems and social structures that play a significant role in confining people to place on the basis of class, income and ethnicity.

Local place or locality is therefore also part of a system of power and control, where vulnerability or social exclusion is rendered more prominent by social and spatial stigmatisation. In Chapter 2, I explored how the spatial and social boundaries around Walworth had been historically authorised through official mechanisms such as the administration and allocation of public resources and the institutionalisation of welfare. These boundaries inscribed into the urban landscape through administrative divisions and corresponding physical forms had endured as socio-spatial stigma over time, long past the actual reconfiguration of territorial boundaries or the disappearance of physical structures. The double impetus of the stigma or the symbolic boundary is that it perceptually attaches to both place and people, not only relegating a negative value to a place, but also making it difficult for individuals to feel comfortable about leaving an area of familiarity to enter into new worlds.

In Chapter 4, although Stan, the 'ageing Mod', described himself as 'comfortable in the West End and I'm open to ideas from over the River', he also highlighted how excruciating he found it going into a shop in Jermyn Street in the West End to enquire about a suit: 'People don't realise how hard it is to walk into a place.' While it would probably be difficult for many people to walk confidently into a shop in Savile Row, Stan's point is explicitly one of disassociation on the basis of class synonymised as locality. Stan highlighted this by his contrasting experience of walking into Reyd's Bespoke Tailor Shop on the Walworth Road: 'Reyd speaks the right language. We would be out of place in Savile Row. When I first came in here I thought, "I could talk to you, I could deal with you."' Stigma serves as a parallel mechanism of attachment and detachment: it binds individuals to the familiarity of physical places and associated ways of life, and it detaches them from other places and other people.

However, familiarity is not necessarily only an introverted social form. Through a sense of comfort and everyday contact, familiarity can be used as an adaptive social form to combine different traditions, people and places. As is the case with the diversity of cultural life on Massey's Kilburn High Road (1994), my fieldwork data revealed that in many instances local people expressed more than one coordinate of orientation on their mental map of local place. Particularly for those locals who had more than one cultural inheritance, their local social worlds on the Walworth Road were navigated by combining it with other familiar worlds. Nick and Dorah's socialisation at their regular 'family' table at the front of the Caff was not only shaped by an entrepreneurial inclination, but by a Cypriot familial and cultural inheritance of meeting around a table, where eating and talking are core to everyday life. Around this table their local London world and Cypriot heritage effectively combined to make a social space for family, friends and locals.

Local places then, are about finding and fixing coordinates of familiarity to navigate everyday life. The individual use of local coordinates varies considerably with differing processes of finding and fixing: from regularity and convenience to the effects of stigma and territory, and to inter-cultural combinations of social life. In a place like the Walworth Road, the contemporary dilemma of what it means to be a local is therefore not resolved by separating fluidity from fixity, or cosmopolitanism from locality. Newcomers and established residents use local place to either narrow or expand their modes of belonging with respect to self and other. At times the sense of the local, or the everyday experience of belonging, constrains social and cultural exchange; at times it affords social connections within the apparently effortless acts of going about daily life. To reiterate, we need to understand the simultaneity of introverted and extroverted experiences of local place in the context of global change.

Intimate space

If familiar space is formed out of the orientating processes of daily convenience and regularity within a local area, intimate space forms out of the personal space that individuals carve from larger society or group space. Social intimacy develops through small-scale associations, galvanised by shared social understandings such as etiquette or discretion, or shared affinities as banal as meeting for a drink or as pointed as partaking in a political conversation. In his book *The Politics of Small Things* (2006), Goldfarb introduces the role of the kitchen table in the Eastern bloc during the Soviet period as a place to talk freely amongst equals without fear of recrimination. Goldfarb recalls from personal experience that it was within the collections of small, private spaces integral to daily life that people met to discuss the party, poetry and culture. But as Goldfarb's analysis spans other time periods and places, he shows that the need for small-scale meetings in which a public is constituted is not the preserve of repressive societies. In the context of the Walworth Road, I explore politics with a small 'p', to understand the significance of claiming intimate space within a group space, in which one can think and communicate at a personal level without being detached from the group.

The small table in Nick's Caff was an increment of space no more than 1 metre by 1.5 metres, which allowed for both personal and intimate occupation of shared space within the hub of the Caff (Figure 5.1). At my table in the Caff I read, wrote and observed, the table providing me with not only a personal domain, but also a spatial buffer from which I could elect to manage social distance without social exclusion from others in the Caff. I had explicitly selected a side table because I felt that it was a space from which I was less obtrusive and less likely to be required to join in with general conversations. Joining in could be negotiated by social nuances such as selecting a more central table, or making eye contact, or going up to the front counter, passing people at their tables on the way.

I noticed that the occupation of similar intimate territories within the Caff was undertaken with a level of precision, where social comfort was gained from the precise occupation of time and place. In the mornings Mark opened his office mail at his seat at a side table, and occasionally met his children at the same table in the evening. Hinga regularly occupied a table that was close to Nick's counter, returning

Figure 5.1 The intimate realm of table space in Nick's Caff, with a regular's reading
    material.

at the same time most mornings and always ordering the same items on the menu.
Our individual routines were central to our occupation of intimate space within
the Caff. I noticed that we returned not only to our same tables, but almost always
to the same seats at those respective tables. The occupation of personal spaces
within a larger social space, akin to individuals claiming a bench in a park, requires
a particular form of informal social membership. Informal social memberships
depend on learning and respecting the social codes common to the larger space
and group, as well as establishing the right to partially retreat or differentiate oneself
from the larger whole.

Joseph Rykwert (2000: 133) emphasised the necessary smallness of spatial
intimacy for 'semi-public, semi-private meeting', by referring to 'places of tryst'
where spatial intimacy is compatible with social discretion or secrecy within a group
space. The scale of inclusion works precisely because of its smallness, and therefore
while some are included on the basis of shared etiquette refined by regularity, others
are informally excluded on the same grounds. There are many individuals on the
Walworth Road who simply by-pass Nick's Caff, and others still who might feel
uncomfortable about entering and using the space. At different stages of their lives,
or from the base of different occupations or affinities, individuals select and occupy
their regular places, their 'local'. Laurier (2004) for example, has observed the
use of franchise coffee shops by London office workers, where the living-room
arrangements of the coffee shops are found to be conducive for business meetings.

However, what distinguished the informal memberships in the Caff was that the proprietor was long standing and had fostered enduring relationships with regulars, There was similarly a high correlation between regular customers and local residents. It is also noteworthy that that the entry level for membership was affordable – a mug of tea could be bought for 50p.

The idea of 'intimate anonymity' and the use of social etiquette to protect a personal preserve is key to small-scale sociability. Haine's (1992) historic exploration of the Parisian working-class cafés during the period from 1850 to 1914 offers two fascinating insights into the personal and political role of social intimacy within the Parisian cafés. He starts by tracing the historic location of cafés in working-class neighbourhoods, thereby emphasising their role as essentially local meeting places. He then scrutinised the archival records of marriage within these respective areas, revealing a fascinating social relationship: the marriage certificates lodged in Parisian working-class areas during the late nineteenth century show the café proprietor as the most prominent profession represented in the position of witness. The café proprietor, and his key position within a cultural institution, had acquired the cultural status of a public character. Because of the informal nature of membership in establishments like the café or caff, the role of the proprietor is pivotal to social interactions in these spaces. Nick's role as public character echoes the analogy of Haine's marriage witness, where Nick had taken on a caring role for his regulars, not only within the Caff but also in their lives outside it, as typified by his assistance in arranging Mike's access to sheltered housing for the elderly.

Haine also raised the issue of the organisational role of the café in worker politics, by asking how French workers could rapidly organise large-scale protests without, at that time, a strong union infrastructure. His works highlights the role of 'café friendships' across locally distributed cafés in Paris, in which workers regularly met, attending to their social and drinking pleasures, as well as their political ones. What is consequential about the personal occupation of this ordinary group/ institutional space is that individual lives are not necessarily separated from group or public life. Work, family relationships and political sentiments filter into public life through small-scale social practices, even if limited by the confines of small social groups. Because of the gradual process of becoming known in a local establishment, social intimacy may also allow for a decrease in social distance, or a shift from passive encounter to active forms of engagement. This means that congenial social spaces, as Haine's research suggests, can be experienced as places of personal and political contact, spaces to be known and looked out for, and spaces to express agreement and disagreement.

In general, conversations in Nick's Caff were convivial in nature, and often the social entrée was guided around football leagues and matches. There were also occasions in the Caff where conversations led to heated discussions. During the period of my observation, political conversations focused on the Iraq occupation and war and the perceived betrayal of working-class people by the Labour government in general and Tony Blair in particular. Immigrant rights were occasionally discussed, particularly the alleged discrepancies between those seen to be working or contributing to society and those claiming from it. When the subject of the Iraq war came up, Mike, who had himself spent time in prison, emphatically declared that 'Blair should be nicked for war crimes.' Nick endorsed this sentiment and on another occasion spoke of his disappointment in changes to the Labour Party. He drew a comparison between Tony Blair and Tony Benn to encapsulate the fundamental shift from Labour to New Labour: 'Tony Benn is by far the best leader for many, many years. He rips apart the Conservatives. He rips apart America. He tells it like it is, not as they want to see it.'

Local election results from the neighbourhood wards around the Walworth Road suggest that the area has been a Labour stronghold for a long time. The Labour Party headquarters was, until 1997, located at the northern end of the Walworth Road at John Smith House. Alan, the third of three generations of proprietors of the 'Walworth Health Store', talked about the symbolic relocation of Labour in 1997:

> The Old Labour headquarters was something that people knew about. But the only time you thought about it was when you saw people going in for general meetings. Of course New Labour didn't fit very well with its roots, and it changed to a council office.
>
> (Fieldwork conversation 2006)

The formal institutions of working-class life such as churches and working men's clubs have historically provided a larger social and political structure to everyday life, as well as broader organisational frameworks to belong in, such as the unions and Labour Party. As the impetus and functions of these larger structures have shifted alongside the reorganisation of work and the economy, the fora to collectively discuss and debate political, moral and ethical matters have altered if not altogether dismantled. Although spaces like the Caff allow for political discussion, there was a sense in the Caff that the ability to act on discussions through larger representative structures that are part of social and cultural life had been lost.

Skilful space

How do we frame a cultural and social politics of belonging and participation? In Calhoun's (2002) theoretical exploration of 'cosmopolitan democracy', he asks what the basis for collective membership is, and highlights the plural forms of allegiance. His is a political recognition of 'social solidarities' and thereby challenges the view that emerged out of the theory of cosmopolitanism in the 1990s, where the primacy of a global democracy was thought to be vested in international forms of governance and global capitalism. Calhoun refers to a sense of the lived obligations and commitments that tie individuals and groups where, for example, locality, tradition, community and ethnicity are essential to the cosmopolitan process. Participation and citizenship are therefore, ultimately layered practices emerging out of a range of small and large associations and interdependencies. Of significance to a contemporary understanding of the local is Calhoun's emphasis on the pragmatic resolutions of social, cultural and economic ties within everyday life, and hence the essential recognition of what he refers to as the 'life-world'.

I explicitly selected the 'life-world' of a city street because it represented not only the intersections of diverse individuals, but also the convergence of urban poverty, entrepreneurialism, banality and aspiration. The contrast between the Walworth Road and its adjacent social housing estates suggested very different possibilities for viewing, understanding and representing the social life of the area. My intuitive attraction to the Walworth Road was the cheek-by-jowl arrangement of the independent shops, and the potential roles that individual imagination, agility and acumen play in how the small spaces of the city are shaped.

I was also interested in whether individual occupational skills would result in different kinds of sociability, and whether the social life within the independent shops off the street that were partly public, but not institutional, would engender different forms of belonging. What emerged out of my observations of both Nick's Caff and Reyd's Bespoke Tailor Shop were the forms of social contact particular to the combination of workspace, social space and the street. Entrepreneurial agility and social skill on the part of proprietors was often central to initiating and sustaining social relationships over long time periods. In these shops a combination of social skills and work skills had increased Nick's and Reyd's capacities to participate in urban change. The forms of participation sustained through interactive work-social practices is not simply a form of exchange – it is ultimately a form of citizenship.

Here I refer back to the notion of sensibility developed in Chapter 4, to emphasise the kind of social solidarity that develops when there is a sharing of expertise and value. In Reyd's Bespoke Tailor Shop, tacit understanding was the basis of social interaction. In other words, shared affinity was more crucial to the social exchange than shared locale. Reyd's customers were located across London, and their association was formed by shared cultural affinities as symbolised in the choice of cloth, cut of suit, and image of the sartorial London Mod. Developing a sensibility requires skill, and Reyd's stories revealed the hours of investment in not only becoming a bespoke tailor, but also in learning about the lineage of American blues, jazz and soul in the evolution of Mod culture. This combination of learning skill and acquiring affinity had allowed for Reyd's life-world and his associated life-chances to expand beyond its local boundary. But there is a further dimension to sensibility revealed in the social exchanges within his shop: that of recognition. Central to the tacit engagement between proprietor and customer was the highly personalised exchange of respect, negotiated on the basis of the recognition of skill – not only a social acknowledgment of the technical skill of making the bespoke garment, but also for the social skill of wearing it.

Reyd's shop was therefore a cultural and social microcosm of shared sensibilities where Pickett and Davis commanded wall space together with Sting in the cult Mod film *Quadrophenia* (1979) together with the adolescent working-class lads captured in a photo of the east London English rock group the Small Faces (1960s). These affinities extended to local associations like Reyd's picture of the south London Millwall football team adjacent to Coltrane (Figure 5.2), and his photographs of customers including boxers, actors and musicians. The collage of local culture and Mod culture in his shop was not simply aesthetic – it was deeply cultural and social (Figure 5.3). Further, Reyd's combination of images suggests that however socially or economically 'local' the Walworth Road is, its colours, textures, shapes and influences are interdependent with the global.

Whether spatial intimacy or social affinities are formed through the mundane practice of occupying a table, or the more emblematic practice of commissioning and wearing a bespoke Mod suit, the small scale of these social interactions remains key to how differences are negotiated or shared. Both spaces are regulated by the social codes of informal membership, and both spaces will include some while excluding others. Simmel's (1949) idea of 'sociability' points to the social ability to share knowledge, where conversation, humour and gesture are part of face-to-face engagement. If Simmel's idea of social reciprocity is extended to include the aggregation of culturally diverse individuals, then the art of sociability can be explored as a multilingual form of communication.

In Reyd's shop, social understanding was essentially chaperoned by a shared regard for the art of attire, which was firmly founded in working-class cultural styles. Those with an established knowledge and respect of tailoring therefore had access to this sociability. In Nick's Caff, social etiquette was governed by how individuals occupy space, where regularity enhanced the capacity for sociability. Both forms of sociability required social skills that were acquired over time. The knowledge required to walk into Reyd's shop was not dependent on local know-

Figure 5.2 A convergence of local and translocal affinities: John Coltrane and Millwall Football Club in Reyd's back room.

ledge, and was inclusive of a wide array of individuals with a shared affinity. The knowledge required to use Nick's Caff regularly entailed local understandings of ways of life, but the form of inclusion was more wide ranging, allowing for secluded or central occupations of space.

The binary distinctions that are historically drawn between public and private domains as markedly different social, cultural and political realms support a

Figure 5.3 A collage of cultural and social solidarities: the changing room at Reyd's.

tendency to 'collectivise' public space, or to represent it as an ideological or spatial whole. Through my research process, directed in many ways by walking and stopping, I came to experience and understand the Walworth Road as a highly particular collection of parts. In hindsight, the emphasis on parts was crucial, not only because the social and spatial differentiations within the street have been so central to the research findings, but also because it allowed for the social value of smallness, or the role of cultural and social units of space within a wider public realm, to become apparent. Through this smallness within the larger domain of the street, individuals were able to participate in a collection of sub-worlds that together constitute the collective public life of this multi-ethnic street. Claiming personal space and developing shared expertise within a semi-public space were shown to be key social modes of allegiance, participation and belonging.

Conclusions

> [. . .] post-millennial Britain is inextricably and irrevocably multiracial, multi-cultural, multifaith; living with this reality remains, however, an enduring enigma. Living with difference (Hall 1993) or, indeed, with sameness (Nandy 2001) is the problem of the twenty-first century.
>
> (Alexander and Alleyne 2002)

Ordinary cosmopolitanism is, then, a living amongst and recognition of difference without a convergence to sameness – without an insistence on cohesions such as 'community' and 'ethnicity' as exclusive or even primary forms of belonging. Sociability, or more precisely the ability to socialise amongst others, is a skill that forms out of being exposed to a variety of social situations, and in the context of rapid urban change it is a skill that requires continual renewal. The social skills needed to engage with difference and change require more rather than less exposure and regular participation over fleeting encounter. The city and its varied locales and sub-worlds matter in accessing space in which to learn and exchange. The street offers one such global-local strip that 'works' in its side-by-side aggregation of parts.

I have argued that the local spaces of a city street and its dimensions of familiarity, intimacy and sensibility sustain social solidarities, since they offer the ease of access, comfort of contact and sharing of affinities, which underpin much of social life. The local is also the urban realm in which the vulnerable and the less mobile – the very young, the old, the poor, the newcomer – coexist in an overlap of structural circumstances. The importance of the local is therefore not as an exclusive form of territorial solidarity, but as a collection of spaces outside of the domestic sphere in which to engage in difference, particularly for those whose social mobility or global fluidity is less of a reality.

The analytic difficulty, as explored in this chapter, is that locality or territory is also a defensive strategy used to combat the effects of change or the perceived threats of difference. Place becomes a means for holding on to what is 'ours', an insistence on the endurance of boundaries despite, or because of, the persistence of change. I argue for the recognition of the ordinary combinations of life and livelihoods in mixed neighbourhoods as spaces of social value where individual imaginations and social skills shape, test and alter the routines of everyday urban life. Social interaction across the boundaries of class, race, ethnicity or territory requires active forms of engagement, and through the social processes of participation, the ordinary forms of belonging are constituted. Contact, I argue, refines our skills or capacities to socialise. The recognition of contact as a form of learning about difference requires a disaggregated view: a greater commitment to observing actual everyday life, and a willingness to acknowledge the variability and plurality of informal memberships engaged in the small meeting spaces of the city.

6 Street measures

Measuring, whether scientific or serendipitous, is an act of ascribing value. What values, then, are commonly assigned to the city street and do we have the tools to recognise its 'ordinary' uses? How, for example, are a street's requirements for efficiency and flow reconciled with its equally necessary inefficiencies of meandering and meeting? Does economic turnover count more to retail longevity than social exchange? Is mixed-use an (in)effectual proxy for mixed users? To tackle these questions I rely on contrast, and compare the life and livelihoods on the Walworth Road in its disparate, multi-ethnic and innovative setting, with notions of the 'village high street' that abound in much of the literature and policy around high streets in the UK. Indeed it is the underlying reference to the 'traditional high street' that encapsulates dominant cultural notations of high street vitality and viability (see for example *High Street London* (Gort Scott and UCL 2010) and *High Street Britain: 2015* (All Party Parliamentary Small Shops Group 2006)).

But the village and the traditional high streets are arguably symbols of local life that lie essentially outside of the contemporary challenge of how to conceive of local urban economies and cultures as mutually global. This in turn begs the question of how to recognise the city street as a pragmatic public terrain in which local adaptations to global change, such as immigration and difference, are advanced. The Walworth Road reveals the intersections of economic and social life on the street that tell us about the everyday experiences of contemporary dilemmas and forces through ordinary social and spatial organisational forms. The idea of the urban margin as developed in *City, Street and Citizen* incorporates cultures and economies outside of the dominant frame of values, and as such the assets, constraints and activities within it may well be invisible to the outsider, often escaping professional, political or official forms of recognition. This chapter explores ways of valuing the 'ordinary' economies and spaces of the city street. I focus on the independent shops along the Walworth Road to pursue connections between large-scale forces and small-scale, *in situ* resolutions: between global economic restructuring and migration, and adaptive retail practices on a high street in the urban margin.

A key question raised during my research was whether lessons from the Walworth Road would be useful in informing architects and planners how to design a street more appropriately. Would what I was learning through my process of social and spatial research have consequences for how I would conceive of a street as an architect? This is a crucial question, and I address it first by arguing that we need a different vocabulary to communicate the values of streets like the Walworth Road. An alternative notation is necessary, since the life and livelihoods on these global-local streets differ in important ways from those that we may associate with a comparatively 'upmarket' London street, like High Street Kensington for example, or a global retail high street like Oxford Street. The inadequacy of the generic term 'high street' to describe the vitalities of these diverse places is self-evident. Similarly, the aggregative term 'Main Street' as used in American towns and cities denotes a cultural ordinariness, but one which fails to capture the intensities of urban change in everyday life. Such transformations alter our sense of what is 'local', what is 'ordinary', as is made palpable on streets like Roosevelt Avenue in Queens New York, as evoked by Joseph Heathcott's (2008: 18) analysis of 'the immigrant city within its narrow corridor'.

To pursue the very ordinary values of the Walworth Road, I return to the larger analytic frame of adaptability, to expand on its social, spatial and economic aspects. In Chapter 1 I highlighted the practices of *improvisation and duration* as modes of adaptation played out in space and time. Improvisation refers to the quick-footed, agile tactic of 'making do and getting by', and duration to the gradual acquisition of skill and sensibility that allows for an investment, be it social or economic, to accrue. For the architect or planner the language of *flexibility* includes physical dimensions, such as the scale of land subdivision and ownership, as well as the transitions of territory from public frontages to private rears. Such explorations would incorporate what remains physically 'fixed' on the street as a spatial code of common agreement, and which of its parts alter with human appropriation. Finally, street-based retail, independent (or non-affiliated) retail and immigrant entrepreneurship on city streets are aspects of economic *diversity* that are significantly altering in response to large-scale economic restructuring. Observing the constraints on and capacities for adaptation on the part of small urban entrepreneurs and micro socio-economic networks allows for more culturally nuanced measures of viability and vitality.

Duration

The contestation that sits at the forefront of the future of high streets across the UK is one oriented around demise. In the public sphere, the fervent debate is captured by both the decline and homogenisation of high street retail. Organisations such as the New Economics Foundation (NEF), the Association of Convenience Stores (ACS) and the Save Our Small Shops Campaign assert the rapid disappearance of independent shops together with the dominance of developer-driven retail, visibly synonymous with what NEF articulates as *Clone Town Britain* (2004). NEF's reports on *Ghost Town Britain* (2002, 2003) focus on the impact of economic globalisation on small-scale retail livelihoods, suggesting that in the five-year period between 1995 and 2000, approximately one-fifth or 30,000 local shops and services were lost across Britain.

In contrast, the large retail chains are evidently immensely durable, and their spatial forms and economic formats regularly adapt to market and regulatory conditions. While the demise of the high street in the UK is closely associated with the staggering expansion of retail chains,1 it appears that the unintended consequences of planning legislation ushered their entry into high street locations. For example, *Planning Policy Statement 6* of 2005 established the guiding principle that the scale and form of any new development in a town centre area should respect the existing grain of urban fabric. The consequences of the protective form of planning legislation were broadly twofold: the approval numbers for out-of-town, big-box retail developments were significantly reduced; and the rapid adaptation of big-box retailers to smaller formats readily suited to high street locations resulted. Adaptation to legislation in this case directly correlates to access to power. The significant economic, legal and political apparatus of large retail firms, combined with their innovative and aggressive disposition, has meant that for the most part large retail firms in Britain have been highly adaptive to regulatory change, readily able to alter the scale, format, location and branding of their operations.

Small independent shops however, often operate with a far more localised knowledge base and their legal and political representation at national and urban scales is limited. However the paradigm of demise, too readily represented flatly across the national landscape, is not entirely applicable to London. In their University of Southampton study, Wrigley, Branson, Murdoch and Clarke (albeit in a study commissioned by Tesco, 2009) provide regional nuance to this hotly contested debate represented largely through the dichotomies of small and local versus large and global. They evidence for example that in London during the period from 2000 to 2006 there was a 78.5 per cent increase in non-affiliated independent convenience stores across the city.

The purpose here is neither to contradict the national decline of small independent retail across Britain, nor to reveal in any depth the debates that continue in the political, regulatory or civic arenas. Crucially, however, in each of these domains the values used to define high street 'success' are markedly different. For NEF the measure is articulated as 'vitality', a value to which they ascribe an interdependency of economic prosperity and social liveliness. In their terms, vitality is representative of, 'an economics of nearness and human-scale in which people have more control over their lives' (NEF 2002: 6). An alternative measure put forward in the national policy framework *Planning Policy Statement 4: Planning for Economic Growth* (2009) is 'turnover', vesting value in annual trade and yield.

Vitality and turnover are arguably measures of short-term success, and in contrast, an empirical exploration of duration broadens the scope to understand strategies adopted by independents proprietors to sustain longevity over the longer term. The excerpts from selected proprietors on the Walworth Road that follow emerge from interviews conducted with eight of the proprietors during 2006, seven of whom had at that stage been on the Walworth Road for more than ten years, and four of whom had had their shops in family ownership for forty years or more. These excerpts indicate not only how retail practices change over time, but how these proprietors establish entrepreneurial longevity that is closely connected to social relationships with their clientele over extensive time periods.

The website for the 'Walworth Health Store'2 claims that the shop, established in 1844, is 'London's oldest established herbalist' and 'the UK's leading herbalist and supplier of natural products and remedies'. The grandfather of the current proprietor, 'Alan', took over from the originator for whom he had worked, and the shop has remained a family business for three successive generations. Alan talked about the shop identity as strongly tied to the place and product: 'People associate us with the Walworth Road, or associate the Walworth Road with us. I think it's because we are a bit unusual. Unique.' I asked Alan what made his shop unique and he explained, 'These days it's the range of herbs, it's probably the biggest retail range of herbs in Europe.' The shop was also the original and once sole supplier of 'Sarsaparilla', a health drink made and sold from the shop premises. The drink is reputed to have permeated the smell of the shop, and the combined sensation of smell and taste featured prominently in interviews with local residents and their childhood memories of the Walworth Road. One adult reminisced, 'We used to go to Walworth Health Store every Saturday morning after the pictures. Used to come out of the Elephant cinema, go around and have our Sarsaparilla and then go home.'

Alan travelled into Walworth from the south London suburbs each weekday, parked his car at the Elephant and Castle Shopping Centre, and walked to his shop. He claimed to have little social connection to the street and drew strong contrasts with how he remembered the street as a child:

> I have clear memories of the street. My grandfather used to make me go off on errands. The whole street was shops, and you knew everybody. I really don't know many people here now. My grandfather knew everyone on the street. There was longevity. That's the difference now.
>
> (Fieldwork interview 2006)

Alan's measure of longevity combines the endurance of his family's business enterprise and well-established relationships with other longstanding proprietors on the Walworth Road. Although Alan claimed to make little use of the street for shopping or socialising nowadays, he was clear about his shop's enduring association with the Walworth Road locality: 'We've been here a long time. We don't envisage moving.' He also emphasised the importance of maintaining local, personal connections in the shop, 'We try to recruit local people and remain part of the community. This helps to give us a local identity.'

Alan differentiated his customer base as local versus mail order clientele. He described a strategy of running 'two businesses': the local shop trade; and the mail order trade that started in 1992 and now accounts for 60 per cent of turnover:

> I think it would be fair to say we have a mix of clientele. I dislike racial stereotyping but the West Indians could relate to what we sold, they were familiar with the herbs and roots we were selling. We've retained those people through the years. They're getting fairly old. Although we still get second and third generations, they're less – they're not quite so interested. The mail order customer base is far more diverse. But to develop the mail order we would need more space, and this location is too prime a location just for storage.
>
> (Fieldwork interview 2006)

Further along the street is 'Walworth Electrical Store' whose elderly proprietor, 'Mr Joffe' asked to be named formally by surname. He opened his electrical store in the 1950s on the site of the current Elephant and Castle shopping centre with his wife and one engineer, and moved to his current position on the Walworth Road in the 1980s. Although he still visited the shop a few days a week, the business was run by his sons. Mr Joffe had always lived in north London, but selected the Walworth Road as his preferred place of business, and confirmed that he expected the shop to remain in this location. He described how in the 1950s there were approximately twenty electrical stores between the Elephant and Castle and Camberwell, and he claimed his was the only independent electrical store left in the vicinity. He attributed the longevity of the store to relations with customers:

> Personal service, definitely. And it's nice that the customers know your first name, and they come in and ask for you by your first name . . . We have a large, local clientele and plenty of people from the outside who basically know our reputation. We're lucky enough to have grandchildren of original customers. It gives me great happiness that.
>
> (Fieldwork interview 2006)

Like Alan, Mr Joffe described the store's duration in terms of its uniqueness, but emphasised that the shop's distinction rested on service above product: 'We are unique, we offer the lowest prices by purchasing from the biggest retailers in Europe, we offer sales and repairs, and we offer speedy delivery and immediate fitting.'

Another important strategy for forging the proprietor–customer relationship was understanding the cultural aspirations of the local population. 'Kid's Brand' was an upmarket clothing store for children, which was opened by the proprietor 'Sayeed' in 1993. His family, who originated from Malawi, had three different clothing shops on the Walworth Road. Sayeed's family had been trading in clothing retail on the Walworth Road since the late 1980s, but 'Kid's Brand' specialised in what Sayeed referred to as 'aspirational products'. 'Kid's Brand' supplied the upper end of children's clothes and stocked *Armani Junior, DKNY kids* and *Baby Dior* labels. Many of the clothes had prominent external labels, thereby providing a clear indication of the related status and expense of the items.

Shahim who had worked in the store for nine years broadly described the shop clientele by coupling a particular type of income acquisition and consumption: 'It's high disposable income, no mortgage, no car payments, no private school fees. Sometimes it is black-market employment. We have high cash-to-credit ratios of around 65-to-35. In our other stores, this ratio is reversed.' He also mentioned that the 'lay-by' scheme whereby customers made monthly pay-offs was well used. He estimated that between 40 and 50 per cent of the shop's customers probably had a low income, but placed high value on status items. Amongst their other stores, located in what would be regarded as more affluent areas, Shahim confirmed that the Walworth Road store had the highest turnover. Although the shop did approximately 12 per cent of its trade from its website, Shahim stressed the local dimension of their customer base: 'We have a client database of around 4,000 customers, and I would say that 65 per cent are local', referring to their south-east London base.

Within these three proprietors' narratives, the common theme of the 'local client' is strongly associated with the 'service-oriented' proprietor. Beyond the encompassing identity of the local client, it was less easy to classify the Walworth Road customer or the Walworth Road product. High-end, luxury goods that one might have assumed to be out of place on the Walworth Road were apparent retail success stories. There were strong references to longevity primarily articulated as the relationships sustained between generations of proprietors and customers that cut across class, race and ethnicity, where a shared regard for service appeared to underpin the duration of these relationships.

For some of the proprietors interviewed, their duration on the street was challenged by large-scale economic forces and its social impacts on local retail and consumer practices. Pete, who grew up in the area and had run 'Walworth Uniforms' for over 40 years, recalled: 'There were lots of street like the Walworth Road, but they gradually disappeared, like the Old Kent Road. The Walworth Road and the Old Kent Road were places to shop within walking distance of where people lived.' Pete's comment captures the change of economic production and distribution of retail goods and the impact on the scale of shops and streets. Pete referred explicitly to the shift in the pattern of local, small-scale retail on the Walworth Road, to the economic dominance of large retail chains like Asda, Currys, B&Q and Tesco on the Old Kent Road. Pete's comment also points to the impacts of an increase in car ownership and the changes in the scale of production since the 1970s, from local patterns of urban manufacturing in London to mass-produced global brands:

> We've had a lot of changes recently. There were lots of individual shops, now they've become all-in-ones [convenience stores]. We had a lot of made-to-measure tailors. From the sixties onwards this was a street for fashion, now you have it in a different way with Nike sports fashion.
>
> (Fieldwork interview 2006)

The 1950 *Post Office London Directory* corroborates Pete's recollection: eight tailors were registered on the Walworth Road, together with forty-seven specialist clothing makers and distributors including hatters, costumiers, clothiers, corset makers, outfitters, hosiers and boot makers.

Many of the proprietors included in the Walworth Road survey raised the difficulties of paying high business rates and high rental costs. As one proprietor explained, rentals were not simply set by a factor of area profile, but by changing retail cultures:

> The rents are set by the fast-food shops and what they pay per square foot. They have quick turnover and are open until eleven at night. So it's difficult for the small guy to reign. Their review is always to do with rent . . . The new shops are up against it in the rent. Like in the barber shop, they rent the chairs out, that's how they make it.
>
> (Fieldwork interview 2006)

Within the dense accumulation of small, independent shops along the Walworth Road, individual stories range from adaptive strategies of duration to the precarious reality of change as associated with higher rents and rates and increasing competition from the large-scale retailers. As far as possible, the small independent retailers have adapted to large-scale economic change, and amongst the 44 per cent of the independent shops who had been on the Walworth Road for more than ten years, the proprietor-customer relationship or the notion of 'personal service' was emphasised.

Since the Walworth Road survey in 2006, small changes have occurred on the street. In January 2008, Holland and Barrett health store opened a branch, while a *Tesco* convenience store followed in December 2008, with an additional one in November 2010, readily adapting to the regulations set up by *Planning Policy Statement 6*. Also noticeable was the emergence of a number of independent beauty-related shops: a further five barbers, salons and hair and cosmetic shops emerged after the economic crisis in November 2008 adding to the twelve already in place, and appearing to be the most noticeable retail growth area on the street.

The relative longevity of the retail life of the Walworth Road has arguably been sustained in part by its economically marginal location. There has been very little competition for A-grade or chain-led retail space on the Walworth Road prior to 2008, and signs of gentrification, whether symbolised by the appearance of new local regeneration projects or high-street brand stores, have been largely absent. However, larger changes in the broader neighbourhood are imminent. A mixture of new private and social housing developments is being built in the area as part of the Elephant and Castle, Heygate Estate and Aylesbury Estate regeneration processes. Although the pace of regeneration has been held in check by the economic crisis, new, potentially more affluent residents, coupled with the dramatic growth in demand for retail space across London, is likely to challenge the Walworth Road's historic capacity for small-scale adaptation. Does this matter? Should high street adaptation respond in an unfettered manner, as it historically has, to the values set by market forces? Or is there room for global economic change to be regulated in ways that recognise less affluent, more diverse patterns of life and livelihoods on the street?

Diversity

In travelling past local high streets across London, it is not only small-scale entrepreneurial activity that is rendered visible by the varied shop-front displays, but also the prominence of ethnic minority proprietors. This is, in part, a factor of global migration, a convergence of flows that includes both an imperial history of colonisation and the contemporary movements of people and goods across the planet. But as Barrett, Jones and McEvoy (1996) show, it is also a factor of global economic restructuring, one aspect of which is the reorganisation of work labour in the UK and US since the 1980s. Economic restructuring correlates with the dramatic increase in self-employment rates amongst ethnic minorities in the UK and US: 'The overall impression is that ethnic minority capitalism is now virtually a standard feature of advanced urban economies and that, notwithstanding the recession and economic crisis, it is waxing rather than waning' (1996: 783).

Researchers on immigrant entrepreneurship expand on the structural relationships between limited opportunities and why ethnic minorities and migrants pursue self-employment. My question here is why ethnic minority retailers end up in certain locations in the city, in this case the Walworth Road in London's urban margin. To begin to address this question, I refer again to the *Post Office London Directory: Streets and Commercial* (Post Office 1881–1950), an annual survey of every proprietor and his/her respective trade on every street in London from the late industrial to the post-war period The Walworth Road records of proprietors and their respective trades on the street across the survey period from 1881 to 1950 provide a historic view of street-based, micro, urban economies as well as, in this case, its underpinning by waves of immigrant traders.

My own survey of independent proprietors on the Walworth Road conducted in 2006 corroborates that the street has effectively served as an entrepreneurial arrival point for generations of shopkeepers from within the UK and further afield. The origins of these immigrant entrepreneurs reflect connections to colonies of the former British Empire and territories historically under British occupation. As was previously assessed in Chapter 2, the countries of origin in the 2006 survey included Afghanistan, Cyprus and Northern Cyprus, Ghana, India, Ireland, Jamaica, Nigeria, Pakistan and Sierra Leone. This extends our understanding of the 'global' street as the contemporary convergence of a nation's historic claims to power, territory and people across the planet.

Further, the immense variegation of the range of these independent proprietors in terms of their respective ethnicities and countries of origin lends weight to the rejection by scholars of ethnic minority entrepreneurialism in advanced urban economies of the theory that entrepreneurial behaviour is endemic to particular ethnicities. Rather, it points to the interplay between pasts and presents, economic structures of opportunity and constraint, and their inevitable social and cultural resolutions in particular urban locales (see for example Kloosterman, van der Leun and Rath's crucial conceptualisation of '*mixed embeddedness*', 1999). High streets in London's urban margins might therefore provide a place for contemporary understandings of global economic forces in relation to diverse and emerging retail practices that are refined within, and duly transform their local contexts.

Reviews of ethnic minority business and emerging niche markets in Britain point to the emergence of the retail trade, specifically the restaurant and clothing trades (for example Barrett, Jones and McEvoy 1996). This is corroborated by my survey of the Walworth Road, where clothing (22 per cent), restaurants (17 per cent) and food retail (13 per cent) account for half of the retail activity on the street (Figure 6.1a). But in terms of high street retail in local areas it is questionable as to whether this is a new or ethnically specific phenomenon. Returning to the *Post Office London Directory* surveys, it is evident that food and clothing has, over extensive time periods, been the primary merchandise of this small-scale retail street. However, the mode and locus of material production has significantly altered, and historic references to hatters, clothiers, bootmakers and tailors as compared to contemporary clothing outlets on the street reflect the shift from London-based manufacturing in small-scale shops and sweat shops up until the 1950s to globally produced cheap clothes in sweat shops across the developing world. China now stocks the pound stores on the Walworth Road, and cheap goods ranging from household items to beauty products form a core part of the street's merchandise (Figure 6.1b).

22%

Clothing

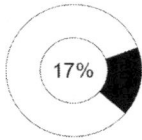

17%

Food Services

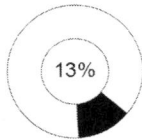

13%

Food Retail

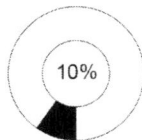

10%

Beauty

 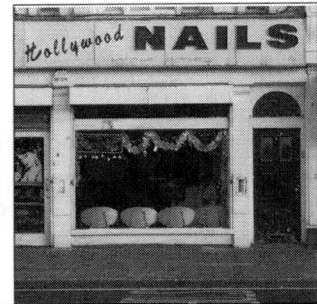

Figure 6.1a Retail diversity on the Walworth Road.

10%

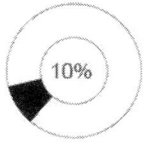

Furniture & Decor

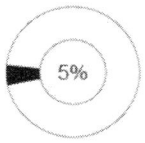

5%

Bargains

5%

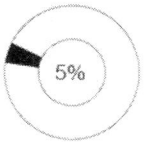

Jewellers &
Pawnbrokers

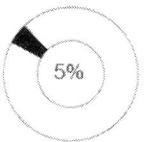

5%

Laundromats &
Drycleaners

Figure 6.1b Retail diversity on the Walworth Road.

A further important aspect to the range of retail activities on the Walworth Road is the spread between and reinterpretation of general convenience goods and highly specialised goods including ethnically oriented goods, in particular food. The survey suggests the prominence of specialised retail as part of a strategy to differentiate between shops on the street as well as to secure the support of a discerning clientele. Specific goods and services, including furniture stores, pharmacies, jewellers, barbers, salons, health food shops and herbalists, accounted for 68 per cent of the 93 independent shops. Ethnically oriented goods such as oriental 'supermarkets' and restaurants accounted for 16 per cent, echoing that the uneven and concentrated distribution of ethnic minorities across London, let alone Britain, 'are sufficiently large and dense to provide the market for a considerable number of ethnic minority businesses' (Barrett, Jones and McEvoy 2001: 245).

What is of real interest in the case of the Walworth Road, is the cheek-by-jowl diversity of ethnic concentration, and the effect this has had on the mixing of retail strategies, goods, spaces along this densely occupied street. In the 'Coskun Supermarket & Off Licence' store that sells 'Turkish, English, Caribbean, Mediterranean Food & Groceries' for example, the fine array of fresh fruits that forms the sumptuous daily street display attends to all of these clients, at prices that are still cheaper than those of the retail chains on the street. Inside, its aisles stock halal meat, South African Biltong, and an impressive range of olives, olive oils and cheeses. Its behind-counter shelves display the hard alcohol that tends to the needs of the late-night revellers around the Elephant and Castle. These tactics of combining a range of goods and services are a reinterpretation of the all-in-one convenience store, but one that is embedded in the particularities of place and its populace. Embedded innovations also extend to a recognition of the diverse array of individuals who lived in proximity to the street.

What we learn about urban multiculture from these street economies is that its modes of participation and expression have little to do with assimilation. It is not the subordination or conformity of one culture or practice to another, but rather a mercantile and human expression of how to combine things. Its vitality is procured by responsive and innovative, if ordinary, combinations, where the banality of everyday needs is met together with the requirements of its diverse urban cultures associated with age, income, gender, ethnicity and religious preference. The alignments of these shops or sub-worlds make the street at once global and local, a linear stretch that is neither economically nor culturally homogeneous, and an urban multiculture that redefines the processes of acculturation.

This begs the question of what kind of citizen the street makes of its proprietors. What kind of urbanite emerges out of the day-to-day participation in this tough, diverse, multilingual space? Portes, Haller and Guarnizo (2002) suggest that movement and exchange allow for more varied and multiple forms of allegiance and belonging amongst immigrants, where acculturation or assimilation is neither the logical consequence of spending time in a place, nor the undermining of full participation in more than place. Their cogent analysis of economic adaptation amongst Latin immigrant groups in the US explores how movement and exchange, in their case cross-border, and in mine cross-counter, builds economic and social networks that straddle boundaries.

> The notion that transnational activities are a transnational pursuit, to be abandoned as assimilation takes hold, is not supported by these data. Long periods of residence in the United States *increase* the probability of engaging in both domestic and transnational enterprise.
>
> (2002: 259)

In a fluid world, exchange across national and cultural borders offers new and emerging prospects for participation, allegiance and belonging. Such exchanges challenge the default position offered by assimilation that insists on a loss or subversion of one or more identities in favour of a curtailed idea of nationhood. The citizen that the street makes is therefore one immersed in the insistent pulse of change.

'Give'

A walk down the Walworth Road, any time from nine in the morning to six in the evening on most weekdays, is a walk on a busy street. Street life fluctuates from the early morning and afternoon activities of people going to school and to work, to elderly people and parents with babies and toddlers shopping around mid-morning, to pension and social benefits queues on pay-out days. Street activity appears to be most concentrated in the central vicinity of the street at the entrance to East Street Market, and is particularly pronounced on Saturdays. But just how busy is the Walworth Road, and how do the flows of people and their ease of access to the street translate into a viable strip for small shops? How does urban structure and urban form affect vitality? For a start, up to 80 buses an hour and over 20,000 vehicles a day move up and down the Walworth Road (www.southwark.gov.uk/walworthproject 2008). That's not all: approximately 12,000 people and 3,000 employees live and work within a ten-minute walk of the street (CABE 2007).

This very basic combination of density and connectivity means that although the Walworth Road has a low weekly expenditure per person within an 800-metre reach of the street, the total weekly expenditure on the street is comparably high in London terms.[3] The relationship of London's local area geographies to local high streets has been explored in the *High Street London* report (Gort Scott and UCL 2010) recently commissioned by Design for London on behalf of the Mayor's Office. The study reveals that two-thirds of Londoners live within 500 metres of a high street, and that two-thirds of the trips to the local street are made to access forms of exchange and interaction other than retail. This valuable report thereby provides us with a street-based image of London's local worlds: rather than a postcard map of prestigious spots, or a planner's map of strategic regeneration areas, the authors reveal to us a spider's web city of numerous radial and transverse threads activated by everyday life.

The urban patterns of convenience and connectivity that afford viability and vitality, and ultimately adaptability, are in many ways a planning vocabulary that we inherited from Jane Jacobs in her canonical work, *The Death and Life of Great American Cities* (1958). But how could we conceptualise, in design terms, ways in which the unpredictable becomes a primary consideration for urban design and architecture? To begin with, the emphasis vests more on the side of 'give' than determinate form or fixed programme. Spatial adaptability is based on the underlying principle that urban form absorbs a variety of appropriations over time. While the idea that urban space should be open to interpretation over time is not new, it is a concern that jars with the underlying professional cultures of both formal planning and developer-driven urbanism. While planning seeks to provide certainty and control, developers seek both certainty and brevity, limiting risks and minimising the turnover period of profit from built developments. How would one think, then, in practical terms, about the street as a system of common cultural and regulatory codes, in which certainty and control were to complement adaptability and interpretation?

For Habraken (1982) it is the lucid clarity and apparent simplicity of the spatial code of the street that enhances its capacity for individual adaptations. He argues that for individuals to appropriate a unit of collective space, such as a shop along a street, their efforts must be directed by the legibility of a spatial order. In other words, individual subjectivity and conviction responds to the limited collective regulation and repetitive arrangement of the street edge. In exploring individual investments in the street he comments:

> How to allow for a multitude of small territorial powers to exercise their right to build? The only way is to offer a clear context for action in such a way that the overall concept is understood by all concerned. Only when this understanding and acceptance is achieved can one expect people to invest in their life's saving and years of effort in a piece of common land. The street and the block are common knowledge.
>
> (Habraken 1982: 74)

A local librarian described the adaptability of the Walworth Road to me as reliant on its pattern of small-scale ownership along the stretch of the street: 'The whole of the Walworth Road was full of old Victorian property. While the damage wreaked by planning in the post-war period was colossal, Walworth Road was an exception, because it was not in the hands of the local authority.' The historical pattern of small-scale ownership along the street is corroborated in the *Post Office London Directory surveys*, and since the 1800s changes of use on the Walworth Road have been incremental, reflecting a plot-by-plot scale of flexibility (Figure 6.2).

The diverse retail strip grew out of a terraced residential urban form, which was inherently adaptable to small and medium-scale activities. The street was occupied largely by middle-class residents up to the late 1800s, and in response to the pressures of urbanisation and industrialisation, front gardens were gradually converted into shop extensions. The shops along the Walworth Road are simply extensions

ROQUE'S MAP

WALWORTH MANOR   1769

GREENWOOD'S MAP

WALWORTH NEW TOWN   1824

FIGURE GROUND (FROM ORDINANCE SURVEY DATA)

WALWORTH TODAY   2008

0 m   5 m   10 m   25 m

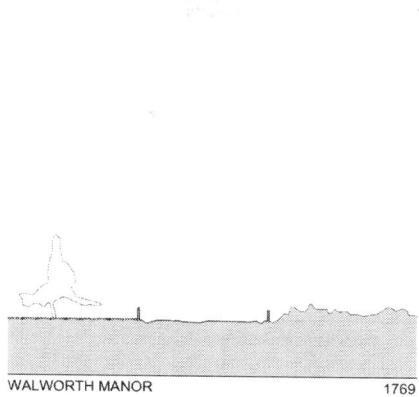

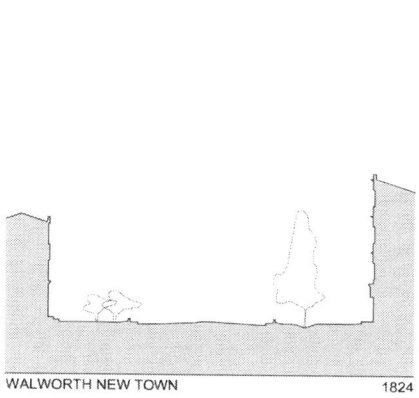

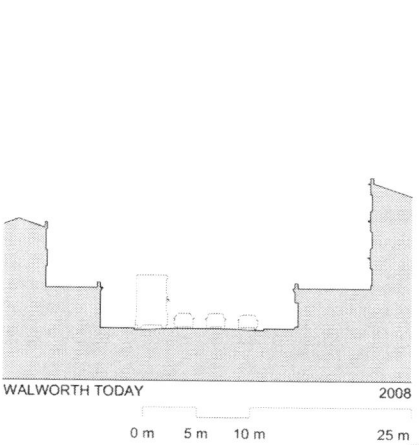

Figure 6.2 The incremental transformation of the Walworth Road over time.

to previous residential properties, where land subdivisions and small patterns of ownership have generated a street of front rooms. Many of these spaces are between 4.5 and 6 metres wide, and few are over 12 metres wide. The basic typology of individually owned and occupied narrow-fronted plots facing the high street remains more or less intact two centuries on, with three to four floors above the shops consisting of a mixture of office and residential space.

'Common knowledge' amongst the diverse shop proprietors along the Walworth Road has been readily acquired by the simple spatial logic of the street: minimal physical encroachment on to the busy pavement space; a selective display of signs and products within the shop-front area; and the intricate and specific transition of public to private space within the shop interiors. While the spatial order of the street is limited and rational it has allowed for infinite variations over time, provided that these basic codes of common agreement are respected. What has emerged is a 'thickness' – both a density and depth – of mercantile and cultural expressions in between the observation of the overarching rules. Think of the shop-front as a veritable room or even a website, generous enough or extensive enough to link the proprietor and prospective customers to a host of prosaic and poetic connections. Think of the shop interior as a public living room or a collection of secretive worlds for hanging out, making deals, getting information or at the very least, just shopping.

What the use and flexibility of streets directs us towards is a different kind of design language, where accretion and layering are key. In his book *Great Streets* (1995) Alan Jacobs acknowledges that 'the best streets encourage participation', and Jacobs places emphasis on the form of the street and whether the space 'will have been put together well, artfully' (1995: 9). The integral social and spatial life of the Walworth Road suggests that our understanding of artful space needs to expand to incorporate both the clarity of urban form and the mosaic of urban appropriations. If the street measures of duration, diversity and 'give' have value, then the imagination of the artful design of space needs to include this variety of participations, and to embrace an altogether more multiple and messier aesthetic.

The city street is also a shared space because it edges different areas and links one territory to another. The street, unlike the housing estate for example, lays claim to a wider range of citizens to whom the space 'belongs'. But the issue here of shared space is not simply about the street, but also how primary spatial assets and meeting places that have the potential to provide a platform for mixing, such as a market places, libraries and clinics, locate in relation to a public and prosaic space such as the street. It is therefore valuable when more particular public spaces, such as a school for example, touches the street to make a forecourt, interim space or social 'chaperone' to encourage a space between general and particular public life. Often it is in these rudimentary or very ordinary spaces that informal exchange can occur, precisely because such spaces don't explicitly belong to any one group or institution. One resident to the north of Walworth acutely described this kind of public space as necessary 'in-off-the-street', 'don't-book-in-advance' meeting places.

In more general terms, what we learn from the Walworth Road is a redefinition of one way of being public in everyday life within a series of ordinary, interconnected spaces. These street spaces are sufficiently small to allow for a level of self-determination and similarly aggregative to allow for a sense of a diverse city, and in this way, mixed-use extends its offer to mixed users. In contrast, conventional planning and design logic has tended to emphasise the role of urban centres that are generally embedded within specific areas as core to local life. The city street, however, spreads the centre out, often allowing for numerous smaller centres or pulses along the line. Because of the length and north–south reach of the Walworth Road, its upper and lower ends have a different status, as do its east and west sides, accommodating an association of different retail profiles, land ownership structures, patterns of use and user groups.

Local destination areas such as East Street Market locate midway in the length of the street, and the market's historic capacity to draw crowds results in rentals being at their highest on the east side of the street in proximity to the market. High-profile investment and prime retail opportunities tend to congregate at the northern ends of the street. This is where large-scale public investments such as the Elephant and Castle transport interchange, the London College of Communication and Southbank University are located, together with cultural resources such as the Metropolitan Tabernacle, the Coronet Cinema and the Ministry of Sound. In contrast, the retail life at southern end of the street is terminated by Burgess Park, and this tail-end profile therefore sustains smaller shops as well as the independents. The beads on a string model along the Walworth Road, unlike a focused town centre, has tended to support a less formally regulated, relative balance between old and new, high-profile and ordinary, big and small. Yet whether this model will be able to withstand the prospects of the redevelopment of the area together with an overwhelming national trend for brand-based retail remains uncertain, if not unlikely.

The opening of a branch of the Holland and Barrett health store in 2008, shortly followed by two Tesco convenience stores, while hardly representing 'premier' brands, possibly indicates a shift in investor confidence in the street. A Tesco convenience store followed in December 2008 with another following only months later. These incremental shifts in retail along the Walworth Road reflect more supportive legislation for the location of chain stores within high streets, as well as a mixture of new private and social housing developments that are occurring in the area as part of the Elephant and Castle, Heygate and Aylesbury regeneration processes. A period of increased change brought about by large-scale redevelopment is imminent in the Walworth area, challenging Walworth Road's existing capacities for the measures of adaptability explored in this chapter.

High streets are seldom static or singular in programme; they tend to be a linear collection of variegated spaces that are responsive to change. A casual conversation I had during my fieldwork with a woman who had lived for many years to the south of the Walworth Road emphasised just this quality: 'I tend to see the Walworth Road as a barometer of change.' She recalled her memories of the street during the 1980s as a mixture of pubs, caffs, independent shops, second-hand shops and charity shops, 'the kind of place you would go to if you needed something for an art project.' But this 'barometer' of adaptability is not simply the capacity for spaces along a street to absorb new uses. The measures of adaptability incorporate morphological, social and economic capacities to respond to change. With increasing pressure on city streets it is apparent that if adaptation is a measure of urban value, it will require a political dimension, one which acknowledges complex and intricate realities of urban change.

Conclusions

The city street is a spatial, economic and social configuration of global and local interplays, with forms and textures that are particular to place. The key question of how local streets like the Walworth Road 'fit' in a changing urban landscape and global economy remains one of how we come to see and measure value. Ordinary streets in the urban margin suggest alternative frameworks of accrued value, where high-profile spaces, high-profile customers and high property values are not the primary measures of 'urban success'. If the ordinariness of a street is to be understood through how social interaction is coupled with economic vitality in local areas, then the Walworth Road is a street we can learn from. The underlying narrative of adaptation has allowed me to explore the measures of duration, diversity and 'give', thereby revealing alternative measures of value. This social, economic and spatial process of analysis has brought me back to the start of this chapter and my underlying concern for the recognition of city streets in urban margins as dynamic, vital and viable worlds. However, the Walworth Road is neither compatible with the symbolic value of traditional or village streets nor comparable to upmarket city streets. Ordinariness ought therefore neither to be measured as an average condition, nor as an unaccomplished one.

I have argued generally for more interdisciplinary research and particularly for more fine-grained research in understanding the uses of ordinary city streets. And if policy and design are to be in sync with the life-worlds and life-chances of local places, a less normative, more contextual integration of spatial, social and economic values needs to be developed. My tools for measuring adaptability have depended on combinations of broad survey and detailed ethnographic data and show the flexibility of the Walworth Road as neither stable nor harmonious, but as continually shifting in response to change. However, if the scale and pace of change becomes more dramatic, driven by large-scale regeneration, and the dominance of corporate economies, the Walworth Road and its historically incremental, small-scale capacity for change may have reached the limits of its ability to adapt. Street measures of duration, diversity and 'give' require far more intricate forms of recognition by built environment professionals. They also require political support and policy articulation, not in terms of the high street as an average urban condition, nor as a nostalgic predilection for the past, but in terms of the ordinary street as a mercantile, civic and public space of exchange.

Notes

1   'By 2007 it [the UK food retail industry] had reached a position where eight large chains accounted for 85 per cent of grocery sales totalling £110 billion per annum, and where the four largest firms (Tesco, Asda/Wal-Mart, Sainsbury and Morrisons) alone accounted for just over 65 per cent' (Wrigley 2010: 182).

2   All shop names and proprietor names have been changed in keeping with an ethnographic practice of granting individual research participants anonymity.

3   The Walworth Road was the subject of one of the ten case studies included in the *Paved with Gold* report (CABE 2007) where a detailed shopper survey as well as land value analysis provided the basis for the comparative data across these London streets. From the perspective of the survey, the Walworth Road vicinity is shown as the most multicultural and most densely occupied of the ten high streets. But although there was great variance between the potential individual expenditure of a Walworth Road shopper and a Hampstead High Street shopper for example, there was far less variance in the estimated total weekly expenditure on these streets. In comparative terms, the Walworth Road is surrounded by a less affluent population, but because of the population density in proximity to it, the total weekly expenditure estimated for the street area was £4.3 million compared with £4.8 million on High Street Hampstead.

7 Conclusions

How can we learn from a multicultural society if we don't know how to recognise it? The contemporary city is more than ever a space for the intense convergence of diverse individuals who shift in and out of its urban terrains in daily, weekly and annual rhythms. As a variegated and fluctuating territory, the city foregrounds experiences of belonging, which in many ways are more to do with everyday experiences and pragmatic resolutions than to do with ideology. The city street is perhaps the most prosaic of the city's public parts, allowing us a view of the very ordinary practices of life and livelihoods, within which participations and allegiances emerge. In unpacking the imaginaries that shaped our modern notions of 'nation', Benedict Anderson (1983) asked what bound diverse groups in a common commitment to a territorial entity that was worth fighting and dying for. The question of creed or cohesive faith so essential to the idea of nation is not, I have argued, central to the contemporary reality of 'city'. In this way, London is not England, and its array of individuals, their aspirations and constraints are inadequately bundled up into a measurable and programmable 'ism' that 'fails' or 'succeeds' on the basis of individual, national or global temperaments. 'Multiculturalism' is a poor substitute for attempting to gauge the dynamic realities of living together in dense, intense and uneven urban landscapes.

City, Street and Citizen has focused rather, on the question of whether everyday life is significant for how individuals develop skills to live with urban change and cultural and ethnic diversity. To animate this question, I have turned to a city street and its dimensions of regularity and propinquity to explore interactions in the small shop spaces along the Walworth Road. The city street constitutes exchange, and as such it provides us with a useful space to consider the broader social and political significance of contact in the day-to-day life of multicultural cities. This book has claimed a primary standpoint: habitual practices, informal social memberships and ordinary spaces matter for social exploration in a context of profound change and urban inequality. Out of the stories and spaces expanded on in *City, Street and Citizen*, three core findings underpin my conclusions: 1. Local life is crucial to cosmopolitan formations. 2. Ordinary spaces outside of overtly public or private realms are core to social testing. 3. Historic and contemporary boundaries substantially incapacitate individual abilities to engage with difference and change.

In drawing out the essential lessons of this book, I structure the conclusions around two framings of everyday practices on a multi-ethnic street: the local and the ordinary. In *the layers of the local* I focus on the local as a social phenomenon, not so much as a singular or specific place, but more as a densely acquired network of familiarity that spans across people and places. Familiarity is a form of solidarity that can only emerge from being and doing, as it is a belonging that is associative – with people, with places and with senses. But while familiarity has much to do with how one becomes accustomed, it can both curtail and expand social curiosity. A core challenge, then, is how individuals become conversant in more than one familiarity, in more than one local world. In the recognition of the ordinary I emphasise the integral social and economic roles of the city street in the urban margins. The mercantile and cultural practices refined on the street make for forms of solidarity that attend to basic needs on the one hand, and to refined sensibilities on the other. These forms of solidarity are both accessed through exchange, as they are modes of belonging that are reciprocal: to recognise is to 'see' with skill, and to respond accordingly is to act with knowledge.

The layers of the local

The narratives and experiences of familiarity that feature so prominently in my fieldwork tell us about how local life on a city street is a primary platform through which people are known, and come to know others. These narratives also reveal that the need for familiarity is made more acute by the pace and scale of urban change. I have explored how diverse individuals orientate themselves in a context of rapid urban change, where both newcomers and established residents are all having to reconfigure their coordinates of familiarity. More specifically, I have focused on how individuals acquire spatial and social coordinates of orientation to locate themselves on a changing street such as the Walworth Road. Why do I emphasise the role of local life on a street that has historically mirrored much larger forces of changes, be it industrialisation or globalisation? My research suggests that one important way individuals understand who they are consists of maintaining connections with where they are from. But the understanding of where one is from was seldom narrated through a singular sense of a birthplace or origin, but rather through a sense of familiarity that combined cultural ways of life, forms of sociability and collections of spaces.

The practice of maintaining connections with a sense of where one is from was not only a retrospective or nostalgic act, but a way of being current. In the interiors of Nick's Caff and Reyd's Bespoke Tailor Shop, it was evident that 'being acquainted with' was one way that familiarity was sustained through day-to-day interactions; shared humour and shared colloquialisms, for instance, were key to maintaining *and updating* social etiquette and local culture. In the context of multicultural cities, where diverse individuals bring an array of cultural understandings and social modes to one place, how is local life practised as a platform for maintaining and acquiring familiarities? And in addressing this question, can we conceive of local vernaculars in fast cities, not simply as the maintenance of tradition but of socially sustained renewals that connect with the present? Ethnography has revealed two primary paths for addressing these questions. Suttles' research for example, (1968, 1972) suggests that the local is a physically bounded terrain, externally delimited by power and internally re-inscribed by the ways of life that emerge within regulated territories. And on the other hand, Wallman's (1984) and Back's (1996) research reveals to us a local that is a collection of familiar reference points and networks that individuals carry with them as they move about the city, adding to and editing their spheres of intimate knowledge of people and places.

Social interaction in local life can be addressed through a structural frame, which emphasises the experience of a local area or 'setting' as conditioned by an individual's position and place in society. This structural perspective highlights how individuals come to know and define their local worlds on the basis of the opportunities and constraints available to their group status. The frame of agency emphasises how individual pursuits of knowing and defining local worlds make active use of imagination and communication to express, meet, engage and shape local places. But while these distinctive frames are pertinent for understanding local places as a conditional setting and as situated forms of expression, neither is singularly sufficient. Further, whether the local and its uses in constituting cross-cultural meeting is analysed as a confined area and/or a collection of familiar reference points is, I argue, not simply a matter of contextual distinction.

What we may well need is a new ontology for understanding the local, one that refers far more to a myriad of layers, histories and networks. This would imply a re-examination of the job the local does in grounding individuals in a fluid and swift world. It would require ways of recognising the subtle differences between whether individuals and groups are grounded or entrenched, and whether they are able to navigate between and beyond local worlds, while maintaining solidarities and commitments to particular groups and places. There is no 'local', rather there is a layering and palimpsest of a multitude of 'locals'. I emphasise this point, as it is particularly crucial in the context of multicultural cities, to rethink the local from the variability of the aggregations of locals who inhabit any single urban area in any one moment. The local is a tangible place for the convergence of a multitude of histories, trajectories and expressions, made more dense and more layered in cities like London, by the historic processes of empire building and colonisation, and by the speed, scale and diversity of immigration since the 1980s.

Life within the interiors off the Walworth Road indicates that the local is primarily social, where mixing, touching base and updating emerges out of small-scale intimacies or relationships through which an individual comes to be known. By drawing on the rhythm of the street and small shop interiors, I argue that it is within local routines and ordinary spaces that our knowledge and understanding of different people is tested and negotiated. The idea of prosaic publics adds to Amin's idea of micro-publics in order to incorporate the more banal aspects of daily contact. The local can thereby be understood as small zones or spheres of familiarity and intimacy, starting with homes and connecting to streets, work places, schools, religious spaces and so on. However, propinquity is not necessarily only about a physical nearness, but expands to include a perceptual closeness. My interviews and conversations on the Walworth Road, as well as my visual analysis of the independent shop displays, show how the local is a personal and cultural collection of intimate relations and familiar places that spans neighbourhoods, cities and even countries.

In a layered framework of understanding the local, the space-time configurations expose us to different ways of exploring social interaction. In addition, near and far places are necessarily merged in the analysis of networks of familiarity, where minds, bodies and spaces respectively carry, enact and display references to many local places. The merging of more than one local world was repeatedly apparent in a variety of independent shops along the Walworth Road. Small shop interiors displayed an amalgamation of local references from more than one local world, as both a conscious effort to engage a diverse customer base, and as a subliminal combination of coordinates of familiarity that spanned any one location. The Walworth Road itself, as an aggregation of the small shop interiors, can be understood as a city street in which a multitude of local references from across the world abut, co-locate, mix and ultimately transform a sense of the local as being primarily embedded in any one location.

In defining the layers of the local as a palimpsest of pasts and presents and near and far places, I move away from the terminology of *local place* as a singular or even physical entity. I explore the capacity of *being local* as a way of becoming accustomed: accumulating networks of familiarity; and collecting a range of small worlds. However, this is not to say that my definition of local worlds is without geography, or without the particularity of forces of power and regulations of territory and boundary that exert influence in time and space. If the individual accumulates a local world by being social, rather than simply inheriting a local place by virtue of birthright or social position, the conditions and circumstances in which individuals are able to act, move and express are not insignificant. The related sociological question of how individuals and groups belong through their local world is then analysed through the extent to which it is possible to accumulate a broad, rather than a narrow collection of local worlds.

However, the apparent ease of contact and preservation of social etiquette in local life can also obscure prejudices that limit contact. If we are to understand cosmopolitan practices as lived processes in which exchange is primary, then we need to know about the causes and effects of containment: not only how boundaries are crossed but also how they are re-inscribed. In Chapter 2 I explored how deep divisions shaped by political, economic and administrative forces influence individual and collective perceptions of others, and profoundly affect individual capacities to participate in urban change and difference. I analysed two integral but distinct aspects of the boundary as both a frontier and a territory laden with the historic symbols of division and prejudice. This is to highlight that space convenes both the fluidity and fixity of our time: it interrelates global patterns of mobility, immigration and displacement together with what it means to settle or remain in a local place. The city street exemplifies this simultaneity: as a shared space it intersects those who would have travelled across origins and nations to arrive at the Walworth Road, with others already living in proximity to the street, who may seldom or never have travelled much beyond the boundaries of a local borough.

The presence of physical and perceptual boundaries means that learning to live with difference and change is as much a convivial process as it is a wrested-over one. Global–local frontiers like the street are crucial to understanding individual abilities and opportunities to breach social and spatial divisions, to cross boundaries, and to establish modes of belonging in a highly variegated, fluctuating landscape. But without an understanding of the accumulation of boundaries made manifest in bodies and spaces and how these affect contemporary social interaction, it would be all to easy to draw stereotypical conclusions about race, poverty and class in the urban margins.

The re-formation of local worlds in the here and now relates as much to individual practices of social intimacy and familiarity, as to collective practices of political, cultural or spiritual solidarity that are shared through local ways of life. Many social intimacies are formed and refined collectively on the basis of shared experiences of time and place. Nick's Caff for example, was not only a shared contemporary space in which individuals went to eat and relax on a regular basis. It was also a social institution of sorts that had emerged out of the everyday working-class rituals of meeting and eating in the city, combined with the culinary skills brought by immigrant communities to cities like London from the 1950s onwards. Shared histories and collective memories allow individuals and groups to attach cultural depth to their sense of their local worlds. The past was crucial to the layering of the local that individuals used to evoke an attachment to a collective and accrued sense of belonging. Traditions and customs (the working-man's suit worn on Sundays), sensory experiences (drinking a glass of Sarsaparilla) and particular spaces or informal institutions (the pub, the caff) had cultural resonance because they were experiences and memories that were socially shared.

Because the everyday life of local worlds is essentially constituted through small increments of individual practices – a daily routine, a conversation, a sign above a shop front, a space in a caff the size of a table – local worlds require larger frameworks of organisation in order to connect to systems of influence or power. The fragility or resilience of local worlds to adapt to change is dependent on a hierarchy of practices and institutions both inside and outside of local life. The local, as suggested by Haine's (1992) research of fraternity fostered in working-class cafés in Paris explored in Chapter 5, constitutes one significant tier in a hierarchy of collective memberships. The loss of collective assets, institutions and organisations from local places where individuals and groups can regularly assert opinion and register views therefore symbolises an erosion of the political significance of local life.

Individuals referred to the loss of collective places and practices from the local Walworth landscape as primary markers of change. The impacts of economic change on the local landscape were captured, for example, through descriptions of the loss of pubs and tailors along the Walworth Road, and the disappearance of the Surrey Canal to the south of the Walworth Road in the 1970s together with the building and timber yards that lined its edges. The disappearance of work associated with the canal and the docks from the 1970s, and the loss of local assets such as the 'Old' Labour Party headquarters that had sat at the northern end of the Walworth Road up until 1997, marked the gradual disjuncture from local life of a hierarchy of formal political institutions that were deeply connected to the organisation of work and labour.

Local institutions and workplaces symbolised political solidarity and actualised political influence, and their disappearance highlights the political fragility of life on the Walworth Road as increasingly separated from the tiers of collective political organisation and representation. While conversations about politics featured in both Nick's Caff and Reyd's Bespoke Tailor Shop, in both interiors there was a sense that there was limited opportunity to register these views more broadly; to be heard beyond the small circles of intimate social groups. However, other existing and emerging forms of civic and religious solidarity were visibly evident along the Walworth Road and its environs. Most notable perhaps is the increase in religious meeting spaces of various creeds and denominations to the south of the Walworth Road during the period of my research. Old bingo halls and vacant shops, pubs and banks have been filled with evangelic fervour.

Another emerging form of civic solidarity only just caught my eye by way of a small sticker in the window of some of the shops on the Walworth Road that read, 'Save Our Small Shops Campaign'. The emergence of the *Save Our Small Shops Campaign* launched by *the Evening Standard* in 2007 (http://www.esadvertising. co.uk/en/1/shop.html 2009) reveals the civic recognition of the economic and cultural consequences of the demise of small shops across the UK. In the context of raising the significance of and fighting for the political recognition of small-scale entrepreneurial endeavours that exist within local life, the individual or independent small operator is too small an entity to be heard on a political platform. As one shop owner pointed out to me, those who run businesses in local areas like Walworth are not entitled to vote in local elections, as residency not occupancy is the basis of local enfranchisement. The *Save Our Small Shops Campaign* represents another collective medium for local solidarity and civic protest, supported by a congregation of concerned individuals and groups widely disseminated across different places. As a national campaign or platform for diverse individuals to register opinion and to be heard, it is without the key aspects of social intimacy and face-to-face informal memberships apparent in Nick's Caff or Haine's Parisian café for example: it is a locally oriented solidarity shaped outside of local contact.

Within layers and networks of the local, individuals and groups adopt and refine their practices of orientation in the context of urban change. Everyday and face-to-face contact remains a primary mode through which individuals accumulate and edit their coordinates of familiarity. But a concern remains that the intimacy and smallness of the local, while crucial to social contact and exploration, also rely on and are subjected to larger forms of cultural, economic and political organisation. Without links to more than local world, or without collective membership or relationships with larger forms of organisation, the small forms of contact and informal memberships, together with the innovations and exchanges in the urban margins, remain invisible and unvalued to dominant orders. The local therefore needs to be understood as an essential space for interaction and exchange, and although a street like the Walworth Road has adapted to change, without recognition and representation its local worlds are increasingly fragile.

The recognition of the ordinary

The architect Louis Kahn referred to the places of meeting and exploration outside of the domestic realm as human institutions. He defined the street as one such foundation, qualifying the street as a place, 'where a child can discover what he wants to be when he grows up' (Kahn, in Giurgola 1996: 93). Kahn's definition of the street emphasises how the space of the street makes culture, and its components of work and life, visible. Without wanting to romanticise the banal aspects of shopping and consumerism more than evident on the Walworth Road, my fieldwork reveals ways that the street surfaces the commonplace aspects of skills, differences and common ground. This aggregation of prosaic publics, accessed through convenience and regularity, is particularly pertinent in the urban margins like Walworth. While the census data points to high indices of deprivation as well as an increasingly ethnically diverse populace, places in which to meet and exchange gossip, ideas, vulnerabilities and aspirations are apparent on the Walworth Road.

Contemporary city streets are complex spaces, integral to the social and cultural fabric of the surrounding locale, and simultaneously a litmus strip to larger, global impacts. Their values and uses are similarly complex, and thereby difficult to reduce to a set of norms without diminishing their contextual and particular substance. Research into small and medium retail on high streets across Britain points to the significant economic and social role of small shops on the one hand, and the need for more empirical research to bolster inadequate policy frameworks on the other. My comparisons of the contrasting measures of value applied by proprietors and customers who use the Walworth Road with those of planners and policy makers who tend to analyse and intervene from a relative distance yield stark differentiations in understanding or measuring the value of city streets in the urban margins. Just as crucial to contextually informed research, therefore, is the need to reconcile cultural value with economic and social practices: without contextually informed measures of value, 'ordinary' vitalities and viabilities remain camouflaged to the lens of power.

I have discussed the layering of the ordinary and the local as an essentially everyday practice sustained by remembering, exchanging, investing and adapting in local worlds, and as such the local is constantly being accumulated. Unlike authorised urban regeneration, which often seeks to make anew by dismantling or clearing local spaces and ways of life, layering is a process of renewal in which more layers are added. What the growth and change of the Walworth Road over time shows is that small increments of space, when set within a well-connected local street, are highly adaptable to change and are readily appropriated and renewed by diverse individuals over time. Because ordinary worlds such as the Walworth Road are the products of layering rather than the formal composition of architect or planner, they appear as messy and mixed aggregations of people, surfaces and spaces. But this should not equate to decline.

In Chapter 2 I explored the application of social ranking to areas across the city, where the use of cognitive maps (Suttles 1972) or signs of disorder (Sampson 2008) assign value to places on the basis of appearance. In Chapter 6 I went on to argue that formal design interventions or regeneration programmes in ordinary local areas are not necessarily a problem of design conception, but essentially one of cultural recognition: quite literally of being able (or not) to see the ordinary or everyday. If vibrant and animate local worlds are the products of layering, then we could by extension argue, as the Walworth Road shows us, that layering is an indication of vitality in the sense that space is being actively invested in, in all sorts of ways, by individuals and groups. We – our planners, architects, sociologists and local authorities for example – therefore need to become far more well-versed in the contemporary urban language of mélange.

Similarly, the political importance of recognising the complexity and intricacy of ordinary spaces leads me to suggest that many of the lenses and tools used to provide an understanding of local worlds are inadequate, since they are largely based on aggregates or generalisations rather than on particularities. The common use of census data as a representation of a local area for example, is based on an analytic framework of categorisation and separation where individuals are fitted to designated profiles such as ethnicity or work status. I have made use of census data and local indices of deprivation in my research to understand how people and places are officially represented. But the dilemma of these quantitative data sources derived from scientific survey is not necessarily what they render as visible, but what they omit – what human dimensions remain invisible.

A large part of *City, Street and Citizen* engages with the question of how we learn about complex objects of study, and how we capture complexity where existing notational systems are insufficient. By focusing on the smallest increment or unit of research – the individual, an experience, a conversation, the space the size of a table – ethnography learns from the variability of singular interactions and expressions. Through my ethnography I have developed an informed construction of the Walworth Road, one deeply influenced by the specifics and selective choices of the fieldwork process. The book you now have before you is one substantially influenced by the diversity of individual voices, and the means available to the writer to secure the richness and validity of the varied narratives and experiences.

A starting position I claim for the fine-grained research of urban multiculture is the inestimable value of placing the individual at the core of the unit of research, since the experience of difference and change is experienced in words, actions and spaces that constitute and reveal social meaning. It remains crucial to juxtapose individual expressions with the urban and global forces that impact on local worlds. To achieve an adequate understanding of everyday life, the notion of the ordinary and day-to-day needs far more temporal and geographic sedimentation: an intellectual commitment to the palimpsest of history and life, time and space. This has led me in part to the question of skill, or what C. Wright Mills articulated as sensibility, to ask whether researching skill – as opposed primarily to trajectory or disposition – allows for an alternative view of comparatively marginal or deprived urban areas and its urban citizens. My fieldwork exposed me to the important combination of workspaces and social spaces in which proprietors and customers were engaged in differing forms of contact and exploration. In Reyd's Bespoke Tailor Shop for example, a respect for skill formed the basis of the underlying social contract between Reyd and his diverse customers.

For Nick and Dorah, the connection of home and workspace was crucial to their work practices and to the way regulars occupied the Caff. Because Nick and Dorah's home was positioned above the Caff, their workspace and domestic space was connected, and allowed for a mix of family, regulars, Cypriot culture and local culture within the Caff. The quality of the home-cooked food in Nick's Caff was an important criterion for many of Nick and Dorah's customers, but as crucial was the underlying opportunity for social contact within the rhythm of the Caff. Nick's consummate work skill was his social role as public character and his capacity to make individuals feel at home by engaging them. The skill of the customer was a more watchful one, and generally required the assessment and acceptance of the social etiquette established as much by gestures, humour and points of entry to conversation, as by the layout and occupation of the small tables within the shop. But it is perhaps skill, more than habit, that allows each of us to recognise and respond to affinities, and in so doing challenge our own and our societal limitations.

In closing, I would like to restate that the street is a collection of social intimacies and spatial familiarities, in which individuals become known to themselves and others. Through face-to-face and regular contact newcomers and established residents engage in the everyday process of sharing and learning. In the urban context of rapid change where structural inequality manifests in local marginality, the process of learning is complicated by the convergence of lack of resources, limited mobility and the historic effects of physical and perceptual boundaries. However, ordinary spaces and informal memberships that are neither explicitly public nor private provide a place for interactions between diverse individuals. The skill of interaction is in part intuitive, in part acquired, and I highlight the local spaces along a street in which things are made and sold as significant venues for refining social skill. The city street – at once global and local – is an aggregation of small spaces and diverse groups in which boundaries are inscribed and transgressed, and through which work, skill and sociability are combined to provide space for belonging in our milieu of profound change.

Appendix

The survey of the independent shops, September 2006

Note: Every unit along the east and west sides of the Walworth Road was counted, starting with number 1 at the northern-most end of the street. In the table below, only the independent shops are listed. In the limited instances when the proprietor didn't want to be interviewed, NI is entered.

East side

Unit	Shop name	Proprietor's origin	Period of occupation	Tenancy
05	Baldwins Health Store	England	Since 1844	owned
06 NI	Castle Laundrette	–	–	–
09	Home Suite Home (furniture)	Pakistan	7 years	–
10	Choices (pizza and sandwiches)	Iran	1.5 years	leased
11	Bantwa News (convenience)	Pakistan	6 years	leased
12	Threadneedleman (tailor)	Jamaica	12 years	leased
17	London Bride and Groom	England	26 years	–
18	Aksu (clothing)	Turkey	3.5	leased
20	Lydo (footwear)	Vietnam	2	leased
22	W. Surplus Stores (army surplus)	–	–	–
23	Malata No. 2 Supermarket	Ghana	6 years	owned
24	Lilly's Nails	Vietnam	1 year	leased
25	A. H. Friends (travel, money transfers and internet)	Pakistan	1 year	leased
26	Shades of Fashion	'African'	6 years	–
27	£1 Store	Pakistan	4 years	owned
28	Hardy's Wine Store	Pakistan	11 years	leased
29 NI	Rejoice Ladies Wear	–	–	–
30	Brown's Clothing	–	3 years	–
32	The Works (hair salon)	Cyprus	6 years	leased
33	Hiep Phat (oriental supermarket)	Vietnam	7 years	leased
36	F. T. Gentleman's Jewellers and Pawnbrokers	–	–	–
37	Risky (women's clothing)	England	5 years	leased
41	Kander Chinese Herbal Medicine	China	1 year	–
44	Clothing Warehouse	'European'	2 years	leased
48 NI	Phoneshop	–	–	–
49	Clothing Club	Malawi	8 years	leased
50	A1 Stores (bric-a-brac)	England	94 years	owned

Unit	Shop name	Proprietor's origin	Period of occupation	Tenancy
51	Michael Leigh Beefy Boys (clothes)	England	10 years	–
55 NI	Risky (clothing)	–	–	–
59	Panache Kids (clothing)	England	10 years	–
61	Kennedy's (sausages and pies)	England	Since 1877	owned
63	Peppermint (children's clothing)	Malawi	10 years	–
64	Super Value Store (household goods)	Afghanistan	9 years	leased
67	The Original Pound Store	England	10 years	–
68	Sam's Butchery	Jamaica	4 years	–
69	Browns (men's clothing)	Malawi	16 years	leased
71	Art and Magic	India	2.5 years	leased
76	Fads (carpets and furniture)	–	2 years	–
77	Walworth Convenience Store	India	20 years	owned
80	Panache (footwear)	England	25 years	–
83	Linetech Computers	'African'	11 years	–
85	Hollywood Nails	Vietnam	8 years	leased
86	South London Press Newsagents	England	23 years	leased
87 NI	The Red Lion Pub	–	–	–
88 NI	Samico Discount Trading (electrical goods) (CLOSED)	–	–	–
95 NI	Base Bar	–	–	–
96 NI	T Bar	–	–	–
97	Absar Food Store	Sudan	1 year	–
98	Andy & Macs (Caribbean restaurant)	Caribbean	4 years	leased
99	Lemon Grass (Malaysian restaurant)	Malaysia	1.5 years	leased
101	Night Rider Bar (CLOSED)	–	–	–
102	Seville Furniture Ltd	Turkey	3 years	leased
104	Whitehall Clothiers (school uniforms)	England	40 years	owned
105	M. Bridal Fashion House	Nigeria	> 1 year	leased
107	Mary's Café	Cyprus	Since 1965	owned
109	Laundromat	Italy	+ 30 years	–
110	Genesis (barber and hair salon)	Nigeria	+10 years	–
111 NI	Emukay (restaurant)	Nigeria	–	–

West side

Unit	Shop name	Proprietor's origin	Period of occupation	Tenancy
03	Chatkhara (Indian restaurant)	India	1.5	owned
06	Communication and transport services	Nigeria	15	owned
08	Dragon Castle (Chinese restaurant)	China	>1 year	leased
09	T. Clarke (electrical contractors)	England	15	owned
15 NI	The Tankard pub & restaurant	–	–	–
18	Afroworld Superstore	Pakistan	4 years	–
20	Walworth Pharmacy	India	23 years	leased
21	Fanta's Beauty and Nails	Sierra Leone	4 years	leased
25	Omar Dry Cleaning	Cyprus	40 years	leased
26 NI	Café Time	–	–	–
27	Arif's Patisserie	Turkish Cyprus	21 years	–

Unit	Shop name	Proprietor's origin	Period of occupation	Tenancy
28	Vashti's Beauty Salon	Jamaica	20 years	–
29 NI	Hair Hunters (hair salon)	–	–	–
30	MCQ Entertainment	Trinidad	36 years	owned
32	Fads (decorating)	England	30 years	leased
35	Paul's Discount Store (household goods)	India	> 1 year	–
36	Champs Sports	England	15 years	–
38	Central Stationers	India	15 years	owned
39	Kodak Express	England	22 years	owned
41	Lynne's Electrical Store	England	+ 50 years	owned
42	Schwar & Co (jewellers)	England	Since 1838	–
43	Snappy Snaps	–	2 years	–
47	Chicken Cottage Fast Foods	Afghanistan	2 years	–
48	Bagel Store	Turkey	20 years	–
49	N.J. Newsagents	India	1 year	–
50	Temple Bar and Restaurant	Ireland	'a long time'	–
51	George's Barber Shop	'Multi-national'	–	–
53	The Best Kebabs	Turkey	45 years	–
54	Albone Jewellers	England	30 years	–
56 NI	Shoeholic	–	–	–
57 NI	Shoe repairs and key cutting	–	–	–
58	Eroma (internet café)	Turkey	2 years	–
59	Golden Palace Jewellery	Turkey	1 year	–
60	Baronjon (men's clothing)	England	20 years	leased
61	Dynamic Sounds (car and audio)	England	14 years	–
62	Pamukkale Restaurant	Turkey	3 years	–
64 NI	STAR video (CLOSED)	–	–	–
65 NI	Samra Convenience Store	–	–	–
68	Air Choice Travel	'West African'	10 years	–
69 NI	Shoeholic Kids	–	–	–
70	Hong Ha Fast Foods	Vietnam	5 years	leased
72	Oli Food Centre	Turkey	10 years	–
75	Beaumont Beds	–	8 years	–
77	Pan Afrique Travel and Tours	Ghana	–	–
78	Cascade Florists	England	–	–
79 NI	Beauty Terrace	–	–	–
80	Akdeniz Jewellers	Turkey	5 years	–
81	Walworth Kebab House	Turkey	22 years	–
83	Jackson's Furniture	'Jewish-British'	21 years	–
84	Liam Og's Pub	Irish	–	–
87	T. D. Sports	England	22 years	–
88	La Luna Pizzeria	Italy	10 years	–
89	Beds 4U	England	3 years	leased
92	African Prices (clothing, tailors)	Ghana	14 years	–
93 NI	Shades Hair Salon	–	–	–
94	Chinese Medicine	China	–	–
95 NI	Ruskin Private Car Hire	–	–	–
96 NI	Salon De Te	–	–	–
98	Mixed Blessings Bakery	Jamaica	14 years	–

Unit	Shop name	Proprietor's origin	Period of occupation	Tenancy
99	Rim World (barber and hats)	Nigeria	10 years	–
100 NI	Beauty Salon (CLOSED)	–	–	–
101 NI	Shoe Repairs (CLOSED)	–	–	–
102 NI	Ainra News	–	–	–
104	Sunlight Express Cleaners	Pakistan	20 years	–
105	Part 4U	Ghana	1 month	–
108	Autopoint Motor Spares (CLOSED)	–	–	–
109	Top Flooring	England	25 years	–
110 NI	Summy Fashions (children's clothes)	–	–	–
111 NI	The Clearance Shop (CLOSED)	–	–	–
116	Happy Bikes (motorcycles)	England	1 year	leased

Bibliography

Books and articles

Ackroyd, Peter (2001) *London: The Biography*, London: Vintage.

Al-Ali, Nadje and Koser, Khalid (eds) (2002) *New Approaches to Migration? Transnational Communities and the Transformation of Home*, London: Routledge.

Alexander, Claire (2000) *The Asian Gang: Ethnicity, Identity, Masculinity*, Oxford: Berg.

Alexander, Claire and Alleyne, Brian (2002) 'Framing Racial Difference: Racial and Ethnic Studies in Twenty-first Century Britain', *Ethnic and Racial Studies*, 25: 541–51.

All Party Parliamentary Small Shops Group (2006) *High Street Britain: 2015*, see: http://www.nfsp.org.uk

Amin, Ash (2002) 'Ethnicity and the Multicultural City: Living With Diversity', *Environment and Planning A*, 34: 959–80.

Amin, Ash and Graham, Stephen (1997) 'The Ordinary City', *Transactions of the Institute of British Geographers*, 22: 411–22.

Anderson, Benedict (1983; revised edn 2006) *Imagined Communities: Reflections on the Origin and Spread of Nationalism*, London: Verso.

Anderson, Elijah (1999) *Code of the Street: Decency, Violence, and the Moral Life of the Inner City*, New York: W. W. Norton.

Anderson, Stanford (1978) *On Streets*, Cambridge, MA: MIT Press.

Armstrong, Gary (1998) *Football Hooligans: Knowing the Score*, Oxford: Berg.

Augé, Marc (1995) *Non-Places: Introduction to an Anthropology of Hypermodernity*, trans. John Howe, London: Verso.

Back, Les (2009a) *The Art of Listening*, London: Berg.

Back, Les (2009b) 'Researching Community and its Moral Projects', *Journal of the Academy of Social Sciences*, 4: 201–14.

Back, Les (1996) *New Ethnicities and Urban Culture: Racisms and Multiculture in Young Lives*, London: UCL Press.

Back, Les and Solomos, John (2rd edn 2009) *Theories of Race and Racism*, London: Routledge.

Barnes, Julian (2011) *Pulse*, London: Jonathan Cape.

Barrett Giles, Trevor Jones and McEvoy, David (2001) 'Socio-economic and Policy Dimensions of the Mixed Embeddedness of Ethnic Minority Business in Britain', *Journal of Ethnic and Migration Studies* 27: 241–58.

Barrett Giles, Trevor Jones and McEvoy, David (1996) 'Ethnic Minority Business: Theoretical Discourse in Britain and North America', *Urban Studies* 33: 783–809.

BBC Four (2008) *Savile Row*, documentary, broadcast on 4 and 18 February.

Beaverstock, Jon, Richard Smith and Taylor, Peter (1999) 'A Roster of World Cities', *Cities*, 16: 445–58.

Beck, Ulrich (2007) 'Beyond Class and Nation: Reframing Social Inequalities in a Globalising World', *British Journal of Sociology*, 58: 679–705.

Beck, Ulrich and Sznaider, Natan (2006) 'Unpacking Cosmopolitanism for the Social Sciences: A Research Agenda', *British Journal of Sociology*, 57: 1–23.

Becker, Howard (2007) *Telling about Society*, Chicago: University of Chicago Press.

Becker, Howard (1982) *Art Worlds*, Berkeley: University of California Press.

Becker, Howard (1963) *Outsiders: Studies in the Sociology of Deviance*, New York: Free Press of Glencoe.

Bhabha, Homi K. (1994; 2nd edn 2004) *The Location of Culture*, London: Routledge.

Boast, Mary (2005) *The Story of Walworth*, London: London Borough of Southwark.

Booth, Charles (1902) *Life and Labour of the People in London*, London: Macmillan.

Bourne, Stephen (2005) *Speak of Me as I Am: The Black Presence in Southwark since 1600*, London: Council of the London Borough of Southwark.

Brah, Avtar (1996) *Cartographies of Diaspora: Contesting Identities*, London: Routledge.

Breckenridge, Carol, Sheldon Pollock, Homi K. Bhabha, and Chakrabarty, Dipesh (2002) *Cosmopolitanism*, Durham, NC: Duke University Press.

Breward, Christopher (2002) 'Style and Subversion: Postwar Poses and the Neo-Edwardian Suit in Mid-Twentieth-Century Britain', *Gender and History*, 14: 560–83.

Burawoy, Michael, Joseph Blum, Sheba George, Zsuzsa Gille, Theresa Gowan, Lynne Haney, Maren Klawiter, Steven Lopes, Séan O'Riain and Thayer, Millie (2000) *Global Ethnography: Forces, Connections, and Imaginations in a Postmodern World*, Berkeley: University of California Press.

Burdett, Ricky and Sudjic, Deyan (2011) *Living in the Endless City*, London: Phaidon.

Burdett, Ricky and Sudjic, Deyan (2008) *The Endless City*, London: Phaidon.

CABE (2007) *Paved with Gold: The Real Value of Good Street Design*, see: http://www.cabe. org.uk/files/paved-with-gold.pdf

CABE and DETR (2000) *By Design: Urban Design in the Planning System Towards Better Practice*, London: Thomas Telford.

Calhoun, Craig (2003) '"Belonging" in the Cosmopolitan Imaginary', *Ethnicities*, 3: 531–68.

Calhoun, Craig (2002) 'The Class Consciousness of Frequent Travellers: Towards a Critique of Actually Existing Cosmopolitanism', *South Atlantic Quarterly*, 101: 870–97.

Calhoun, Craig and Sennett, Richard (eds) (2007) *Practicing Culture*, London: Routledge.

Carter, Leonard J. (1985) *Walworth 1929–1939*, Surrey: L. J. Carter Services.

Cavan, Sherri (1966) *Liquor License: An Ethnography of Bar Behavior*, Chicago: Aldine Publishing Company.

Certeau, Michel de (1984) *The Practice of Everyday Life*, Vol. 1, trans. Steven Rendall, Berkeley: University of California Press.

Chase, John, Margaret Crawford and Kaliski, John (eds) (1999) *Everyday Urbanism*, New York: Monacelli Press.

Clarke, John (1976; Routledge edn 2006) 'Style', in Stuart Hall and Tony Jefferson, *Resistance through Rituals: Youth Subcultures in Post-War Britain*, London: Routledge, 147–61.

Coca-Stefanial, J. Andres, Alan Hallsworth, Cathy Parker, Stephen Bainbridge and Yuste, R. (2005) 'Decline in the British Small Shop Independent Retail Sector: Exploring European Parallels', *Journal of Retailing and Consumer Services*, 12: 357–71.

Cohen, Stan (1972; Routledge edn 2002) *Folk Devils and Moral Panics*, London: Routledge.

Collins, Michael (2004) *The Likes of Us: A Biography of the White Working Class*, London: Granta.

Dench, Geoff, Kate Gavron and Young, Michael (2006) *The New East End: Kinship, Race and Conflict*, London: Profile.

Department of the Environment (1996) *Planning Policy Guidance 6: Town Centres and Retail Developments*, London, June 1996.

Downes, David (1966) *The Delinquent Solution: A Study in Subcultural Theory*, London: Routledge.

Duneier, Mitchell (2002) 'What Kind of Combat Sport Is Sociology?', *American Journal of Sociology*, 107: 1551–76.

Duneier, Mitchell (1999) *Sidewalk*, New York: Farrar, Straus and Giroux.

Duneier, Mitchell (1992) *Slim's Table: Race, Respectability, and Masculinity*, Chicago: University of Chicago Press.

Duneier, Mitchell and Back, Les (2006) 'Voices from the Sidewalk: Ethnography and Writing Race', *Ethnic and Racial Studies*, 29: 543–65.

Durkheim, Émile (1893; Free Press edn 1964) *The Division of Labour in Society*, London: Macmillan Free Press.

Elephant and Castle Regeneration Partnership (2005) *Elephant and Castle Regeneration Newsletter*, issue 7.

Elms, Robert (2006) *The Way We Wore: A Life in Threads*, London: Picador.

Evans, Gillian (2006) *Educational Failure and Working Class White Children in Britain*, London: Palgrave Macmillan.

Fabian, Johannes (1983; reprint 2002) *Time and the Other: How Anthropology Makes Its Objects*, New York: Columbia University Press.

Fainstein, Susan, Ian Gordon and Harloe, Michael (eds) (1992) *Divided Cities: New York and London in the Contemporary World*, Oxford: Blackwell.

Foster, Janet (1999) *Docklands: Cultures in Conflict, Worlds in Collision*, London: UCL Press.

Foster, Janet (1995) 'Informal Social Control and Community Crime Prevention', *British Journal of Criminology*, 35: 563–83.

Foster, Janet (1990) *Villains: Crime and Community in the Inner City*, London: Routledge.

Foucault, Michel (1977) *Discipline and Punish*, London: Penguin.

Frisby, David (2001) *Cityscapes of Modernity: Critical Explorations*, Cambridge: Polity.

Frisby, David (1981) 'Snapshots Sub Specie Aeternitatis?', in David Frisby, *Sociological Impressions: A Reassessment of Georg Simmel's Social Theory*, London: Heinemann, 102–31.

Gans, Herbert (1962) *The Urban Villagers: Group and Class Life in the Life of Italian-Americans*, New York: Free Press of Glencoe.

Gilroy, Paul (2006) 'Multiculture in Times of War', *Critical Quarterly*, 48: 27–43.

Gilroy, Paul (2004) *After Empire: Melancholia or Convivial Culture*, London: Routledge.

Gilroy, Paul (1987; Routledge Classics edn 2002) *There Ain't No Black in the Union Jack: The Cultural Politics of Race and Nation*, London: Routledge.

Giurgola, Romaldo (1996) *Louis I. Kahn: Works and Projects*, Barcelona: Editorial Gustavo Gili.

Glass, Ruth (1960) *Newcomers: The West Indians in London*, London: Allen and Unwin.

Glennie, Paul and Thrift, Nigel (1996) 'Consumption, Shopping and Gender', in Neil Wrigley and Michelle Lowe (eds), *Retailing, Consumption and Capital: Towards the New Retail Geography*, Harlow: Longman. 221–37.

Godley, Andrew (2000) 'Cultural Determinants of Jewish Immigrant Entrepreneurship in the UK and USA and British and American Culture', in Mark Casson and Andrew Godley, *Cultural Factors in Economic Growth*, Berlin: Springer-Verlag, 125–36.

Goffman, Erving (1967) *Interaction Rituals: Essays in Face-to-face Behaviour*, London: Transaction Publishers.

Goldfarb, Jeffrey (2006) *The Politics of Small Things: The Power of the Powerless in Dark Times*, Chicago: University of Chicago Press.

Gort Scott and UCL (2010) *High Street London*, June, London: Greater London Authority.

Gospodini, Aspa (2002) 'European Cities in Competition and the New "Uses" of Urban Design', *Journal of Urban Design*, 7: 59–73.

Greater London Authority (GLA) (2008a) *Indices of Deprivation 2007: A London Perspective*, London: Data Management and Analysis Group.

Greater London Authority (GLA) (2008b) *A Profile of Londoners by Country of Birth: Estimates from the 2006 Annual Population Survey*, DMAG Briefing 2008-05, February, London: Data Management and Analysis Group.

Habraken, John (1982) 'Signs of Structures', *Space and Society*, September, 64–83.

Haine, W. Scott (1992) 'Café Friend: Friendship and Fraternity in Parisian Working-Class Cafés, 1850–1914', *Journal of Contemporary History*, 27: 607–26.

Hall, Peter (1960) 'The Location of the Clothing Trades in London, 1861–1951', *Transactions and Papers*, 28: 155–78.

Hall, Suzanne M. (2012) 'High Street Adaptations: Ethnicity, Independent Retail Practices and Localism in London's Urban Margins', in *Environment and Planning A* (in press).

Hall, Suzanne M. (2011) 'Being at Home: Space for Belonging in a London Caff', reprint from *Open House International* 34: 81–7, in Dick Hobbs (ed.), *Ethnography in Context: The Urban Condition*, Vol. 1, London: Sage.

Hall, Suzanne M. (2009) 'A Mile of Mixed Blessings: An Ethnography of Boundaries and Belonging on a South London Street', unpublished thesis, London School of Economics and Political Science.

Hall, Suzanne M. and Datta, Ayona (2010) 'The Translocal Street: Shop Signs and Local Multiculture along the Walworth Road, South London', in Robert Tavernor (guest editor), Theme Issue on 'London 2000–2010', in *City, Culture and Society*, 1: 69–77.

Hall, Stuart (1997) *Representation: Cultural Representations and Signifying Practices*, London: Sage.

Hall, Stuart (1993) 'Culture, Community, Nation', *Cultural Studies*, 7: 349–63.

Hall, Stuart and Jefferson, Tony (1993; Routledge edn 2006) *Resistance through Rituals: Youth Subcultures in Post-War Britain*, London: Routledge.

Hammersley, Martyn (1991) *What's Wrong with Ethnography?*, London: Routledge.

Hamnett, Chris (2003) *Unequal City: London in the Global Arena*, London: Routledge.

Hannerz, Ulf (1997) 'Flows, Boundaries and Hybrids: Keywords in Transnational Anthropology', *Mana*, 3: 7–39 (first published in Portuguese as 'Fluxos, fronteiras, hibridos: palavras-chave da antropologia transnacional').

Harvey, David (1989) *The Conditions of Postmodernity: An Enquiry into the Conditions of Cultural Change*, Oxford: Blackwell.

Haylett, Chris (2001) 'Illegitimate Subjects?: Abject Whites, Neoliberal Modernisation, and Middle-class Multiculturalism', *Environment and Planning D: Society and Space*, 19: 351–70.

Heathcote, Edwin (2004) *London Caffs*, Chichester: Wiley Academy.

Heathcott, Joseph (2008) 'The Street as a Transnational Space', *On Site: Journal of Architecture and Culture*, 19: 14–18.

Hebdige, Dick (1979) *Subculture: The Meaning of Style*, London: Methuen.

Hewitt, Paul (2000) *The Soul Stylists: Six Decades of Modernism – From Mods to Casuals*, London: Mainstream Publishing.

Hills, John, Tom Sefton and Stewart, Kitty (2009) *Towards a More Equal Society? Poverty, Inequality and Policy since 1997*, Bristol: Policy Press.

Himmelfarb, Gertrude (1984) *The Idea of Poverty: England in the Early Industrial Age*, London: Knopf.

Hobbs, Dick (1988) *Doing the Business: Entrepreneurship, the Working Class, and Detectives in the East End of London*, Oxford: Clarendon Press.

Home Office (2001) *The Cantle Report – Community Cohesion: A Report of the Independent Review Team*, January.

Isin, Engin F. (2002) 'City as a Difference Machine', in Engin F. Isin, *Being Political: Genealogies of Citizenship*, Minneapolis: University of Minnesota Press, 28–51.

Jacobs, Alan (1995) *Great Streets*, Cambridge, MA: MIT Press.

Jacobs, Jane (1961) *The Death and Life of Great American Cities*, New York: Vintage Books.

Jacobs, Jane M. and Fincher, Ruth (1998) *Cities of Difference*, New York: Guilford Press.

Jenks, Charles and Neves, Tiago (2000) 'A Walk on the Wild Side: Urban Ethnography Meets the Flâneur', *Cultural Values*, 4: 1–17.

Jones, Hannah (2009) 'The Exception that Provides the Rule? Policy Makers Negotiating Multiplicity and Seeking Authenticity', paper presented at NYLON conference, Cambridge, UK, Spring 2009.

Kahan, Arcadius (1978) 'Economic Opportunities and Some Pilgrims' Progress: Jewish Immigrants from Eastern Europe in the US, 1890–1914', *Journal of Economic History*, 38: 235–51.

Keith, Michael (2005) *After the Cosmopolitan? Multicultural Cities and the Future of Racism*, Oxford: Routledge.

Kloosterman, Robert, Joanne van der Leun, and Rath, Jan (1999) 'Mixed Embeddedness: (In)formal Economic Activities and Immigrant Business in the Netherlands', *International Journal of Urban and Regional Research*, 23: 253–67.

Lamont, Michèle and Aksartova, Sada (2002) 'Ordinary Cosmopolitanisms: Strategies for Bridging Racial Boundaries among Working-Class Men', *Theory, Culture & Society*, 19: 1–25.

Lamont, Michèle and Molnar, Virag (2002) 'The Study of Boundaries in the Social Sciences', *Annual Review of Sociology*, 28: 167–95.

Laurier, Eric (2004) 'Busy Meeting Grounds: The Café, the Scene and the Business', paper presented at ICT Conference or Everyday Life and Urban Change, Utrecht, November 2004.

Lawler, Stephanie (2005) 'Disgusted Subjects: The Making of Middle-class Identities', *Sociological Review*, 429–46.

Lefebvre, Henri (1974) *La production de l'espace*, trans. Donald Nicholson-Smith (1991) *The Production of Space*, Oxford: Blackwell.

Liebow, Elliot (1967) *Tally's Corner: A Study of Negro Streetcorner Men*, Boston MA: Little, Brown.

Local Government Association (2002) *Guidance on Community Cohesion*, London: LGA, January 2002.

Marcus, George (1995) 'Ethnography in/of the World Systems: The Emergence of Multi-Sited Ethnography', *Annual Review of Anthropology*, 24: 95–117.

Massey, Doreen (1994) *Space, Place and Gender*, Cambridge: Polity.

Mayhew, Henry (1851 and 1861) *London Labour and the London Poor*.

Megicks, Phil (2001) 'Competitive Strategy Types in the UK Independent Retail Sector', *Journal of Strategic Marketing*, 9: 315–28.

Mehta, Suketu (2004) *Maximum City: Bombay Lost and Found*, New York: Alfred A. Knopf.

Mills, C. Wright (1959) *The Sociological Imagination*, London: Oxford University Press.

New Economics Foundation (2004) *Clone Town Britain: The Loss of Local Identity on the Nation's High Streets*, London: NEF.

New Economics Foundation (2003) *Ghost Town Britain II: Death in the High Street*, London: NEF.

New Economics Foundation (2002) *Ghost Town Britain: The Threat from Economic Globalisation to Livelihoods, Liberty and Local Economic Freedom*, London: NEF.

Newman, David and Paasi, Anssi (1998) 'Fences and Neighbours in the Postmodern World: Boundary Narratives in Political Geography', *Human Geography*, 22: 186–207.

Newman, Katherine (2006) *Chutes and Ladders: Navigating the Low-Wage Labour Market*, Cambridge, MA: Harvard University Press.

Norman, Matthew (2008) Restaurant review of Dragon Castle on the Walworth Road, *Guardian Weekend*, 8 November.

Nuttall, Sarah (2009) *Entanglement: Literary and Cultural Reflections on Post-apartheid*, Johannesburg: Wits University Press.

O'Neill, Alistair (2007) *London after a Fashion*, London: Reaktion Books.

Parker, Howard (1974) *View from the Boys*, London: David & Charles.

Parker, Tony (1983) *The People of Providence: A Housing Estate and Some of Its Inhabitants*, London: Hutchinson.

Pearson, Geoffrey (1993) 'Talking a Good Fight: Authenticity and Distance in the Ethnographer's Craft', in Dick Hobbs and Tim May (eds), *Interpreting the Field: Accounts of Ethnography*, Oxford: Clarendon Press, vii–xviii.

Pollock, Sheldon (2000) 'Cosmopolitan and Vernacular in History', *Public Culture*, 12: 591–625.

Portes, Alejandro, William J. Haller and Guarnizo, Luis Eduardo (2002) 'Transnational Entrepreneurs: An Alternative Form of Immigrant Economic Adadptation', *American Sociological Review*, 67: 278–98.

Post Office (1881–1950) *Post Office London Directory – Streets and Commercial Directory*, London: Post Office.

Power, Anne (1996) 'Area-based Poverty and Residential Empowerment', *Urban Studies*, 33: 1535–64.

Power, Anne (1987) *Property before People: The Management of Twentieth-century Council Housing*, London: Unwin.

Power, Anne and Tunstall, Rebecca (1991) 'Swimming against the Tide: Polarisation or Progress on 20 Unpopular Council Estates, 1980–1995', York: Joseph Rowntree Foundation.

Power, Anne and Wilson, William Julius (2000) 'Social Exclusion and the Future of Cities', CASE paper, 35, London: Centre for Analysis of Social Exclusion, London School of Economics and Political Science.

Raban, Jonathan (1974) *Soft City*, London: Harvill Press.

Ricoeur, Paul (1981) 'Narrative Time', in William J. T. Mitchell (ed.), *On Narrative*, Chicago: University of Chicago Press, 165–86.

Robinson, Jennifer (2006) *Ordinary Cities: Between Modernity and Development*, London: Routledge.

Robson, Gary (2000) *'No One Likes Us, We Don't Care': The Myth and Reality of Millwall Fandom*, Oxford: Berg.

Roy, Ananya (2011) 'Cities at the Speed of Light: Asian Experiments of the Urban Century', public lecture, London School of Economics and Political Science, May 2011.

Rykwert, Joseph (2000) *The Seduction of Place: The History and Future of the City*, Oxford: Oxford University Press.

Sampson, Robert (2009) 'Disparity and Diversity in the City: Social (Dis)order Revisited', *British Journal of Sociology*, 60: 1–31.

Sandercock, Leonie (2003) 'Mongrel Cities: How Can We Live Together?', in Leonie Sandercock, *Cosmopolis II. Mongrel Cities of the 21st Century*, London: Continuum, 85–96.

Sandhu, Sukhdev (2004) *London Calling: How Black and Asian Writers Imagined a City*, London: Harper Perennial.

Sassen, Saskia (2001) 'The Global City: Strategic Site/New Frontier', *American Studies*, 41: 79–95.

Sennett, Richard (2008a) 'The Public Realm', unpublished paper for QUANT, see: http://www.richardsennett.com/

Sennett, Richard (2008b) *The Craftsman*, London: Allen Lane, Penguin Books.

Sennett, Richard (1999) *The Corrosion of Character: The Personal Consequences of Work in the New Capitalism*, New York: W. W. Norton.

Sennett, Richard (1996) *Flesh and Stone: The Body and the City in Western Civilization*, London and New York: W. W. Norton.

Sennett, Richard (1977; 1992) *The Fall of Public Man*, New York: W. W. Norton.

Simmel, Georg (1949) 'The Sociology of Sociability', trans. Everett Hughes, *American Journal of Sociology*, 55, 3: 254–61.

Simmel, Georg (1957; 1904) 'Fashion', *American Journal of Sociology*, 62, 6: 541–58 (first published in *International Quarterly*).

Simmel, Georg (1903) 'The Metropolis and Mental Life', in David Frisby and Mike Featherstone (eds) (1997) *Simmel on Culture*, London: Sage, 174–85.

Sklair, Leslie (2006) 'Iconic Architecture and Capitalist Globalisation', *City*, 10: 21–4.

Soja, Ed (1989) *Postmodern Geographies: The Reassertion of Space in Critical Social Theory*, London: Verso Press.

Somers, Margaret and Gibson, Gloria (1994) 'Reclaiming the Epistemological "Other": Narrative and the Social Construction of Identity', in Craig Calhoun (ed.), *Social Theory and the Politics of Identity*, Oxford: Blackwell, 37–99.

Spence-Smith, Thomas (1974) 'Aestheticism and Social Structure: Style and Social Network in the Dandy Life', *American Sociological Review*, 39: 725–43.

Suttles, Gerard (1972) *The Social Construction of Communities*, Chicago: University of Chicago Press.

Suttles, Gerard (1968) *The Social Order of the Slum: Ethnicity and Territory in the Inner City*, Chicago: University of Chicago Press.

Taylor, Charles (2009) 'The Future of the Secular', public lecture at The New School, March 2009, see: http://fora.tv/2009/03/05/Charles_Taylor

Thompson E. and Abery K. (2006) 'Home Sweet Home', *Southwark Life*, November issue.

Tonkiss, Fran (2005) *Space, the City and Social Theory*, Cambridge: Polity.

Turner, Victor (1981) 'Social Dramas and Stories about Them', in William J. T. Mitchell (ed.) *On Narrative*, Chicago: University of Chicago Press, 137–64.

Velleman, J. David (2003) 'Narrative Explanation', *Philosophical Review*, 112: 1–25.

Venturi, Robert, Denise Scott Brown, and Izenour, Steven (1972; 2nd edn 1991) *Learning from Las Vegas: The Forgotton Symbolism of Architectural Form*, Cambridge, MA: MIT Press.

Vickerstaff, Sarah (2003) 'Apprenticeship in the "Golden Age": Were Youth Transitions Really Smooth and Unproblematic Back Then?', *Work, Employment and Society*, 17: 269–87.

Wacquant, Löic (2007) *Urban Outcasts: A Comparative Sociology of Advanced Marginality*, Cambridge: Polity.

Wacquant, Löic (2002) 'Scrutinising the Street: Poverty, Morality and the Pitfalls of Urban Ethnography', *American Journal of Sociology*, 107: 1468–532.

Wacquant, Löic (1993) 'Urban Outcasts: Stigma and Division in the Black American Ghetto and French Urban Periphery, *International Journal of Urban and Regional Research*, 365–83.

Wallman, Sandra (1984) *Eight London Households*, London: Tavistock.

Wallman, Sandra (1982) *Living in South London: Perspectives on Battersea 1871–1981*, Aldershot: Gower.

Whyte, Wiliam F. (1943) *Street Corner Society: The Social Structure of an Italian Slum*, Chicago: University of Chicago Press.

Williams, Raymond (1958; 2001) 'Culture Is Ordinary', in J. Higgins (ed.), *The Raymond Williams Reader*, Oxford: Blackwell.

Willis, Paul (1977) *Learning to Labour: How Working Class Kids Get Working Class Jobs*, Aldershot: Gower.

Wilmott, Peter and Young, Michael (1957; 2007) *Family and Kinship in East London*, London: Routledge.

Wirth, Louis (1938) 'Urbanism as a Way of Life', *American Journal of Sociology*, 44: 1–24.

Wright, Patrick (1991) *A Journey through the Ruins: The Last Days of London*, London: Radius.

Wrigley, Neil (2010) 'The Shifting Geographies of UK Retailing', in Neil Coe and Andrew Jones (eds) *The Economic Geography of the UK*, London: Sage, Chapter 13: 181–95.

Wrigley Neil, Julia Branson, Andrew Murdoch and Clarke, Graham (2009) 'Extending the Competition Commission's Findings on Entry and Exit of Small Stores in Britain's High Streets: Implications for Competition and Planning Policy', *Environment and Planning A*, 41: 2063–85.

Young, Giles (1930) 'Dickens's Southwark Revisited', from *St. Saviour with St. Peter, Southwark, The Parish Paper and the Diocesan Gazette*, Jan.–Dec. 1930.

Zukin, Sharon (2010) *Naked City: The Death and Life of Authentic Urban Places*, New York: Oxford University Press.

Websites

English Indices of Deprivation 2007: http://www.communities.gov.uk (accessed 2008)

Home Office: http://www.homeoffice.gov.uk (accessed 2006 and 2007)

Office for National Statistics: http://www.statistics.gov.uk (accessed 2007); http://www.neighbourhood.statistics.gov.uk (accessed 2007)

Save Our Small Shops Campaign: http://www.esadvertising.co.uk/en/1/shop.html (accessed 2007)

Savile Row Bespoke: http://www.savilerowbespoke.com (accessed 2008)

Southwark Analytic Hub: http://www.southwarkalliance.org.uk (accessed 2008)

Southwark Business Centre: http://www.southwark.gov.uk/businesscenter (accessed 2007)

Southwark Walworth Project: http://www.southwark.gov.uk/walworthproject (accessed 2008)

Starbucks: http://www.starbucks.co.uk (accessed 2007)

Touch Local Business Survey: http://www.touchlocal.com (accessed 2007)

Statistics and surveys

1861 Census: Census of England and Wales (1863) HMSO, Division 1.

General Register Office (1966) *Census 1961, England and Wales: Greater London Tables*, HMSO.

Morrey, C. R. (1976) *1971 Census: Demographic, Social, and Economic Indices for Wards in Greater London*, Greater London Council Research Report 20, Vol. 1.

Office of Population Censuses and Surveys (1983) *Small Area Statistics, 1981 Census*, London: OPCS, 1983.

Southwark Council (1993) *Information from the 1991 Census of Population: Ward Profiles*, Southwark Council.

Index

Taylor & Francis

eBooks
FOR LIBRARIES

ORDER YOUR FREE 30 DAY INSTITUTIONAL TRIAL TODAY!

Over 23,000 eBook titles in the Humanities, Social Sciences, STM and Law from some of the world's leading imprints.

Choose from a range of subject packages or create your own!

Benefits for you

▶ Free MARC records
▶ COUNTER-compliant usage statistics
▶ Flexible purchase and pricing options

Benefits for your user

▶ Off-site, anytime access via Athens or referring URL
▶ Print or copy pages or chapters
▶ Full content search
▶ Bookmark, highlight and annotate text
▶ Access to thousands of pages of quality research at the click of a button

For more information, pricing enquiries or to order a free trial, contact your local online sales team.

UK and Rest of World: **online.sales@tandf.co.uk**
US, Canada and Latin America:
e-reference@taylorandfrancis.com

www.ebooksubscriptions.com

ALPSP Award for BEST eBOOK PUBLISHER 2009 Finalist

Taylor & Francis eBooks
Taylor & Francis Group

A flexible and dynamic resource for teaching, learning and research.

eupdates

Taylor & Francis Group

Want to stay one step ahead of your colleagues?

Sign up today to receive free up-to-date information on books, journals, conferences and other news within your chosen subject areas.

Visit
www.tandf.co.uk/eupdates
and register your email address, indicating your subject areas of interest.

You will be able to amend your details or unsubscribe at any time. We respect your privacy and will not disclose, sell or rent your email address to any outside company. If you have questions or concerns with any aspect of the eUpdates service, please email eupdates@tandf.co.uk or write to: eUpdates, Routledge, 2/4 Park Square, Milton Park, Abingdon, Oxfordshire OX14 4RN, UK.

Mail

Routledge
Paperbacks Direct

Bringing you the cream of our hardback publishing at paperback prices

This exciting new initiative makes the best of our hardback publishing available in paperback format for authors and individual customers.

Routledge Paperbacks Direct is an ever-evolving programme with new titles being added regularly.

To take a look at the titles available, visit our website.

www.routledgepaperbacksdirect.com

Routledge
Taylor & Francis Group

ROUTLEDGE PAPERBACKS DIRECT

ROUTLEDGE
Revivals

Are there some elusive titles you've been searching for but thought you'd never be able to find?

Well this may be the end of your quest. We now offer a fantastic opportunity to discover past brilliance and purchase previously out of print and unavailable titles by some of the greatest academic scholars of the last 120 years.

Routledge Revivals is an exciting new programme whereby key titles from the distinguished and extensive backlists of the many acclaimed imprints associated with Routledge are re-issued.

The programme draws upon the backlists of Kegan Paul, Trench & Trubner, Routledge & Kegan Paul, Methuen, Allen & Unwin and Routledge itself.

Routledge Revivals spans the whole of the Humanities and Social Sciences, and includes works by scholars such as Emile Durkheim, Max Weber, Simone Weil and Martin Buber.

FOR MORE INFORMATION

Please email us at **reference@routledge.com** or visit:
www.routledge.com/books/series/Routledge_Revivals

www.routledge.com

Routledge
Taylor & Francis Group

21805476R00099

Printed in Great Britain
by Amazon